LOGO DESIGN WORKBOOK

ROCKPORT

LOGO DESIGN WORKBOOK

A HANDS-ON GUIDE TO CREATING LOGOS

Sean Adams & Noreen Morioka with Terry Stone
Designed by Sean Adams & Jennifer Hopkins

GLOUCESTER MASSACHUSETTS

ROCKPORT PUBLISHERS

© 2004 by Rockport Publishers, Inc.

First published in the United States of America by
Rockport Publishers, Inc.
33 Commercial Street
Gloucester, Massachusetts 01930-5089
Telephone: (978) 282-9590
Fax: (978) 283-2742
www.rockpub.com

Library of Congress Cataloging-in-Publication Data
Adams, Sean.
    Logo design workbook : a hands-on guide to creating logos / Sean Adams & Noreen Morioka
        p.   cm.
    ISBN 1-59253-032-X (hardcover)
    1. Logography. I. Morioka, Noreen. II. Title
NC1002.L63A3 2004
741.6—dc22   2003022913
                                                                          CIP

ISBN: 1-59253-032-X

10 9 8 7 6 5 4 3 2 1

Design: Sean Adams, Jennifer Hopkins
Cover image: Terri Weber

Printed in China

Thinking isn't agreeing or disagreeing. That's voting.

—Robert Frost

contents

Introduction

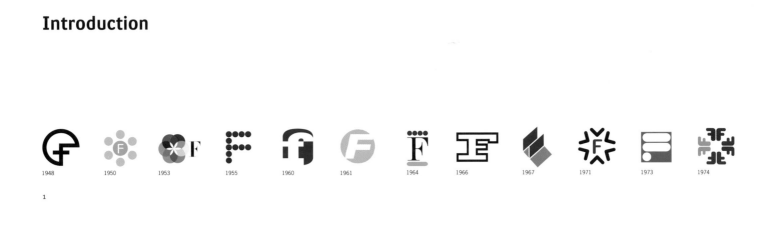

1948   1950   1953   1955   1960   1961   1964   1966   1967   1971   1973   1974

1

Ten years ago, AdamsMorioka was asked to produce a logo for a major Los Angeles institution. We began the project sketching on a pad and playing with type on the computer. The more time we spent designing logo options, however, the more questions we asked. If the client were to change his business in a year, would the logo need to change? If the logo promised community involvement, would the client deliver? Very quickly we began to understand that making a formally successful logo was important, but making something that communicated as a base for all the client's endeavors was critical.

1
A fictional history of logos used in a promotion postcard series for Frederator, a multifaceted communications company. AdamsMorioka, Inc.

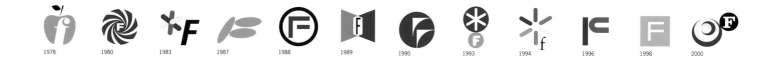

A strong logo and subsequent visual system is one of a corporation's greatest assets. As the international corporate structure has expanded in the past fifty years, so has the need for distinct corporate identification. The world is now filled with every imaginable icon and monogram, as well as all forms of logos. Our task, as designers, is to take the commonplace—letterforms, geometric shapes, and images—and make them distinctive and meaningful. This is a unique time, however, and we are now able to design in ways unimaginable in the past. The breadth of opportunity and the possibilities for the designer's involvement in multiple media, combined with the strategies of our clients' business, make the logo more than a nice decoration; it becomes a vital component in a company's success.

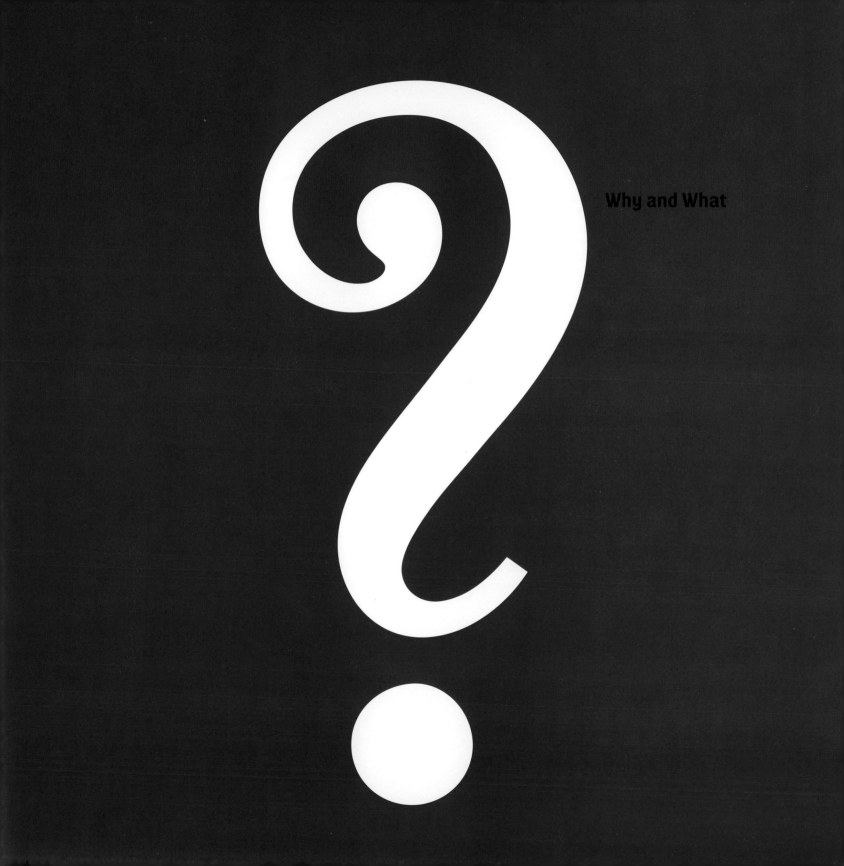

Why and What

Why a Logo?

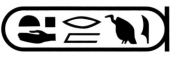

hieroglyphs/petroglyphs

historical context

3oo AD

8oo AD

Let us begin with motive. Man's desire to claim ownership is inherent. Whether this is a result of pride, greed, or hope of immortality is personal. We mark our names on childhood drawings. We develop a signature, unique to each of us, to protect our identity. We carve initials into tree trunks with a heart, hoping to make a union permanent. The logo is an extension of these acts. It redefines these motives from the individual to the collective.

The idea of using marks to claim ownership is not a modern invention. Mesopotamian and Egyptian bricks were marked with stamps indicating their intended construction site. Roman bricks were stamped with the mark of the manufacturer, place of origin, and final destination. The practice of using marks to identify objects continued with housewares, decorative items, and weapons. These marks were typically a single straight line of letters or letters set on a circle or crescent. In time, figurative icons such as a palm leaf or wreath were incorporated into the symbol. Accompanying slogans were absent, although items stamped with the phrase *Felix Roma* (Happy Rome) are often seen, similar to current slogans such as "The Sunshine State."

The population of medieval Europe was, largely, illiterate; thus the mark served the purpose of a signature. Illiterate societies tend toward secret practices and knowledge. The medieval stone-masons, for example, developed a complex set of rituals using specialized speech and behavior. They recognized each other by standing with their feet at right angles, by their greetings, and by following certain dress codes. Their desire to maintaina secret society led to their system of marks. Based on the cross, these marks were more like symbols than letters.

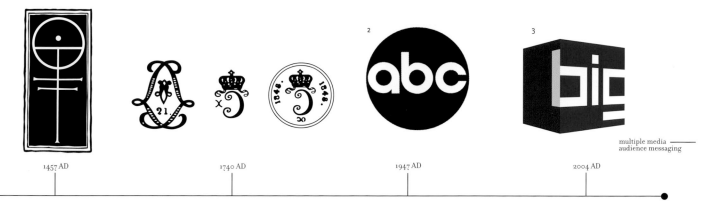

multiple media ———
audience messaging

1457 AD   1740 AD   1947 AD   2004 AD

The invention of the printing press created the craft of the printer. Early printed books were considered inferior to written manuscripts, however, and there was no desire to claim ownership for the product. As the need and appreciation for printed books grew, printers began to mark their work. In 1480, Nicola Jenson and Giovanni da Colonia in Venice introduced the prototype of the orb and cross mark. The symbolic design, earth plus faith, became one of the most typical forms used in early printer's marks.

In 1740, the first factory to produce Sèvres porcelain was founded in Vincennes, France. Twenty years later, a decree was issued assuring the King of France a monopoly on porcelain production. Every piece of porcelain was carefully marked with the symbol of the factory. The succession of regimes caused the continuous redesigning of the mark. This parallels the redesign of corporate marks with the appointment of a new CEO.

The Industrial Revolution increased the value of identification, and trademarks were critical for visual recognition. After 1950, the usage of trademarks changed radically. Multinational corporations with a wide range of products began to utilize the logo as a tool to maintain a cohesive message. Broader usage of the logo by a more diverse group of designers and advertising agencies provided the need for a comprehensive visual system to accompany the logo. The ABC mark was the foundation for the network's clear and cohesive advertising and communications. The use of negative space, and simplicity, combined in a circle, provided a clear and consistent message to the audience.

The needs we now face are a direct result of two thousand years of identity evolution. In the same way that management and business practices have changed, so has the role of the logo. We now place a strong emphasis on teamwork and the creative process for everyone involved in a project. The logo and supportive visual system must not only talk to the external audience, but must also provide a clear intent to the internal audience. The logo will be handled and mishandled by in-house departments, outside consultants, advertising agencies, and web designers. A simple mark for identification is not enough. A clear message conveyed to a wide and diverse audience over an extended amount of time is paramount. Ownership is needed, not only by the creative maker and client, but by the audience as well.

2
ABC
Paul Rand

3
Brand Integration Group
Ogilvy & Mather

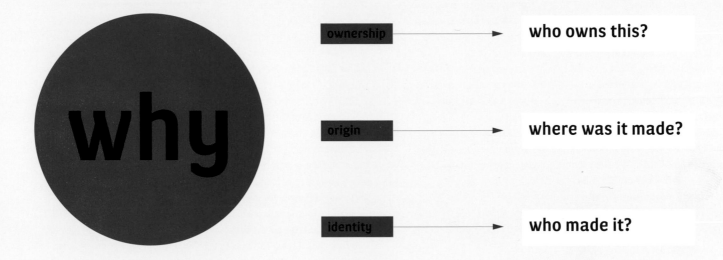

ownership → who owns this?

origin → where was it made?

identity → who made it?

object
idea
company
person

place
time
culture

company
individual
group
community

differentiate from competition

create a focus internally

provide clear identification

enable the audience to form a personal relationship

create merchandising opportunities

create credibility

bring order to chaos

communicate the message

Logo:
a distinctive symbol of a company, object, publication, person service, or idea.

What Is a Logo?

This seems like an easy question. A logo is a mark on the bottom of the television screen, the top of a cereal box, or the side of a letterhead. Unfortunately, it's not that simple. The word "logo" has multiple meanings, and to make the issue more complex, different words are used to describe this thing we call a logo.

Mark

A recognizable symbol used to indicate ownership or origin of goods.

Trademark

A name or symbol used to show that a product is made by a particular company and legally registered.

Signature

A distinctive mark, or combination of visual forms. A graphics standards manual may call for the "signature" to be applied to all brochures. This is simply a synonym for "logo."

Wordmark

A wordmark uses the company name with proprietary letterforms.

Advantages

The proliferation of logos in the world has made recognition of symbols very difficult. Using the entire name sidesteps the problem of recognition. When asked if the Mobil logo belongs to Mobil, most people would agree that it does. When asked who owned the Pegasus logo, many people would name other oil companies such as Chevron or Texaco. Mobil uses the Pegasus in addition to the wordmark.

Disadvantages

If not handled skillfully, a wordmark alone may be generic and lack mnemonic value.

Symbol

The symbol is the iconic portion of a logo: The Chase Manhattan Bank symbol, the Cingular man, the Time Warner Cable eye/ear. At times the logomark may exist without the wordmark, examples being the Nike swoosh, Apple's apple, and the CBS eye.

Advantages

The benefit of utilizing a symbol alone follows the idea that "a picture is worth a thousand words." The eye/ear symbol is easier to read on an object such as a computer or hat, than the name Time Warner Cable.

Disadvantages

If the symbol is separated from the wordmark and the mark does not have equity it may be difficult to recognize.

Monogram

A design of one or more letters, usually the initials of a name, used to identify a company, publication, person, object, or idea.

Advantages

The monogram solves mnemonic and legibility issues. Fitting Wisconsin Energies on a one-quarter page newspaper ad is much harder than using the WE monogram.

Disadvantages

Monograms are often masquerading as logos. Generic initials, treated in clever ways may look better on towels or glasses than on a corporate business card. Initials woven together have very little meaning. Most monogramatic logos depend on large-scale audience contact and repeated viewing for recognition.

4
Halfords
Lippa Pierce

5
Mobil
Chermayeff & Geismar

6
Time Warner Cable
Chermayeff & Geismar

7
Chase Manhattan Bank
Chermayeff & Geismar

8
Wisconsin Energies
SamataMason

9
Evans Foden
Ph.D

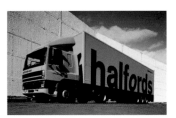

4

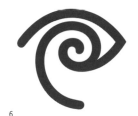

6

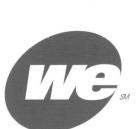

8

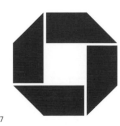

5

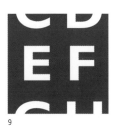

7

9

rococo™

rococo™

rococo™

Rococo is a software developer specializing in blue-tooth enabling technology.

According to Damian Cranney, of Dynamo, "We adopted a very light friendly approach more akin to a retail brand than a technology company. Basically, the market was flooded with very similar looking technology brands—making it harder for new organizations to distinguish themselves. These companies also seemed to present themselves in a very similar fashion—masculine, pumped-up, and aggressive with verbose promises and tired visual themes.

"We decided to design a brand that was friendly, that made people smile, and crucially, that presented a very complex offer in a way that wasn't scary, overly complex or patronizing."

Identity

The combination of the logo, visual system (typeface, colors, imagery), and editorial tone work together to form a unique and cohesive message for a company, person, object, or idea.

Brand

The identity is not a brand. The brand is the perception formed by the audience about a company, person, or idea. This perception is the culmination of logo, visuals, identity program, messages, products, and actions. A designer cannot "make" a brand. Only the audience can do this. The designer forms the foundation of the message with the logo and identity system.

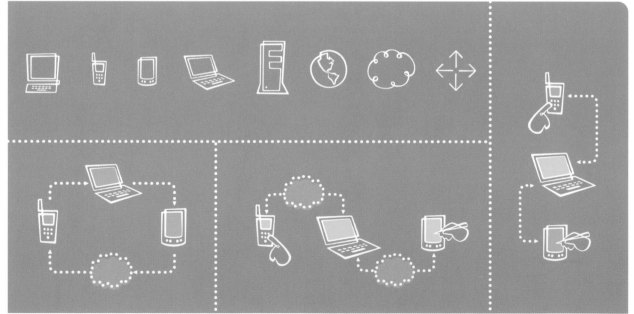

10

A logo is not a brand, unless it's on a cow.

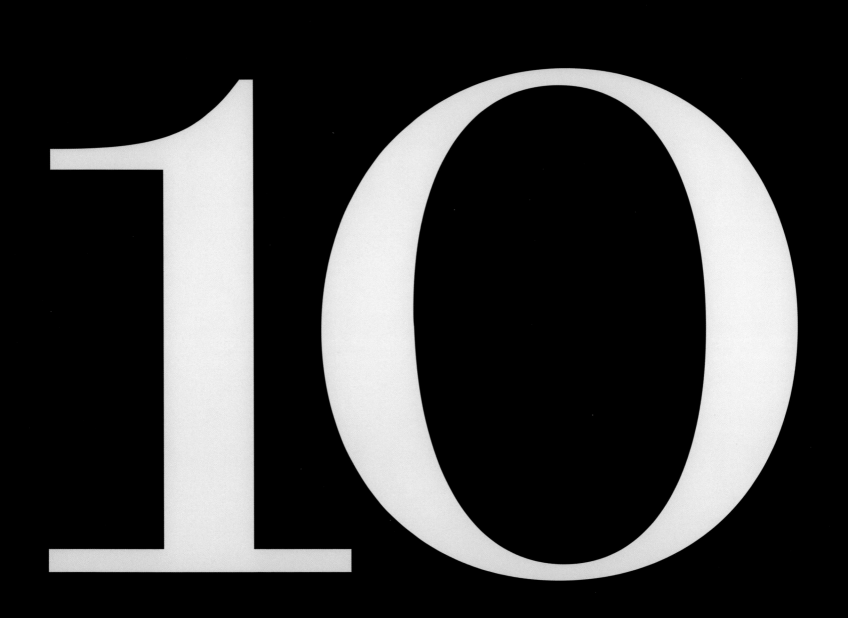

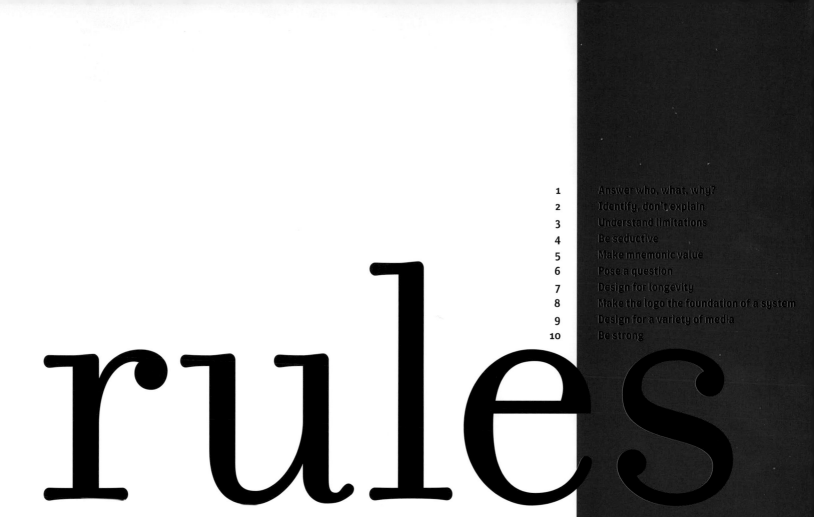

1	Answer who, what, why?
2	Identify, don't explain
3	Understand limitations
4	Be seductive
5	Make mnemonic value
6	Pose a question
7	Design for longevity
8	Make the logo the foundation of a system
9	Design for a variety of media
10	Be strong

rules

1

Answer who, what, why?

Before anything begins, the most basic questions that must be asked and answered are "Who is the client?" "Who is the audience?" "What is needed?" A logo should grow organically from the answers to these questions. Rather than imposing an idea onto the problem, the problem should dictate the solution. This is a statement repeated by every design teacher. Unfortunately, it is often ignored or misunderstood. It does not mean that the whims of the client should be obediently followed. It does not mean that the designer's vision should be sublimated. It does mean that as much information as possible should be gathered, criteria developed, and creative work created, through the filter of the designer.

Who is the client? In the simplest terms, this addresses the company's values, attitudes, and goals. Who is the audience? This may be answered demographically—women eighteen through thirty-four, or psychographically—athletic men who love adventure. And, more specifically, who makes the final decision on this logo? Is it the marketing manager who hired the designer, or the CEO, whom the designer never met? Finally, what is needed? Is a logo the answer? Or is the problem larger—a bad product, staff, or message? Will a good logo be lost in a quagmire of a creative department that is understaffed or poorly managed?

Answering these questions may solve the current problems. The wrench in this plan, however, is that a client's current business may be radically different from his long-term goals. What does the client want to be in the next year, five years, and ten years? Every company will evolve and change. The size of the company, product, and needs are in constant flux. While the client may currently have a small, regional company with one product, the goal might be to eventually expand and produce a greater diversity of goods. It is human nature to focus on our current needs; it is the designer's job to presuppose future needs.

Goals and promises
It is important to look at the client's business and communication goals. Identifying the promises the client makes to its audiences synthesizes what the client stands for because it states what their audience is assured that they can expect.

Briefing questions

1. Positioning
Compared with other companies, what is the client's current positioning?

2. Purpose
What is the client's business? What is the client's purpose?

3. Mission
Beyond the economics, why is it worth doing? What is the client's mission?

4. Composition
What is the client's current internal structure?

5. Culture
What are the client's distinctive shared behaviors that best support the purpose and mission?

6. Personality
What is the client's chosen style and manner?

7. Client goals
What are five key goals over the next year/five years?

8. Growth
What are the greatest opportunities for the growth of the client and its image?

9. Promises
What promises does the client make?

10. Current audience
Who is the client's current audience? Who, where, when, why?

11. Audience goal
Does the client want another type of audience? What is the desired demographic?

12. Perception
How does the client's target audience currently view the brand?

13. Desired perception
How does the client want the audience to view the brand?

14. Competition
How is the client different from its competition?

15. Response
What response does the client want the target audience to take away with them?

16. Objective
What is the marketing objective?

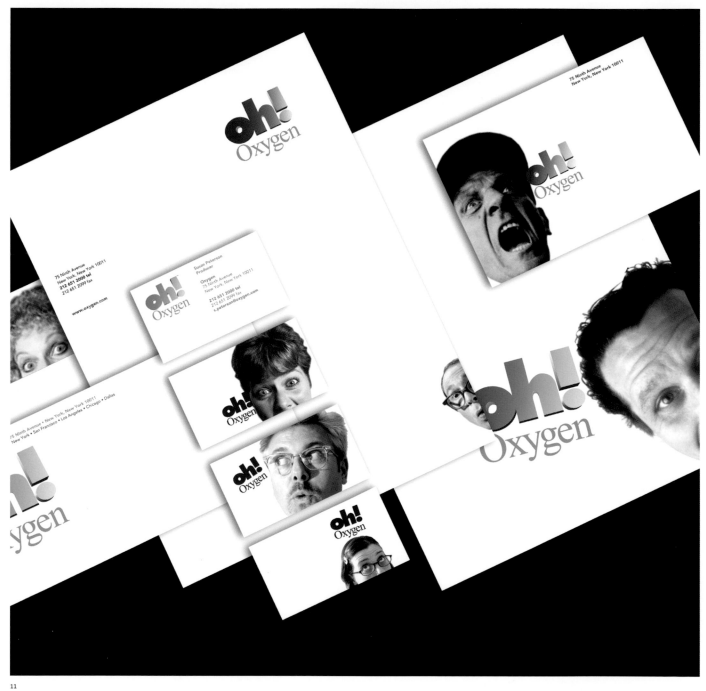

11

2

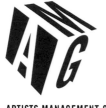

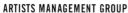
ARTISTS MANAGEMENT GROUP

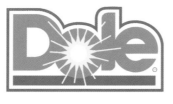

12   13   14   15

We are identified, in good company, with names like John, Maria, or Frank. We prefer to not to be called "the guy who lives on Maple Street and works at the pharmacy" or "the woman who has a beehive hairstyle and runs a trucking company." This is long-winded, confusing, and forgettable. In the same way, a logo should not literally describe the client's business; a logo is an identifier. Many clients would like their logo to describe every aspect of their company. This is natural, they're proud of their achievement. It is problematic, however, and may lead to a restraining identity. The logo is a signpost that identifies the company and reflects its attitudes and values.

There are many companies who use illustrations, but have been convinced by well-meaning, but underequipped designers that these are logos. A logo is a shortcut, a visual language that is quickly recognizable and memorable. An illustration is a drawing or photograph that helps to explain text. Speaking with the most straightforward and clear voice is always more successful than the convoluted or overwrought.

11 (opposite)
The Oxygen Channel's logo does not describe every aspect of the company or specify television as its primary product. Rather than illustrating the physical element of "oxygen," or explaining the network's demographic, it uses the reaction "oh!" to communicate the attitude and surprise of the product. AdamsMorioka, Inc.

12
The logo for Artists Management Group is a tumbling cube made up of the companies' initials—AMG—that expresses the ever-changing nature of the entertainment industry they serve. AdamsMorioka, Inc.

13
The current Dole logo positions Dole with the ability to expand into other businesses. Landor and Associates

14
The logo for the graphic design company Pato Macedo does not illustrate the tools of the graphic design industry. It identifies the company as fresh, clear, and credible with its elegant, no-nonsense approach. Pato Macedo

15
Stealing Time is a full service video editing company serving the advertising and broadcast industries. The "running man" logo represents a clever visual pun of the company name.
Concrete Communications

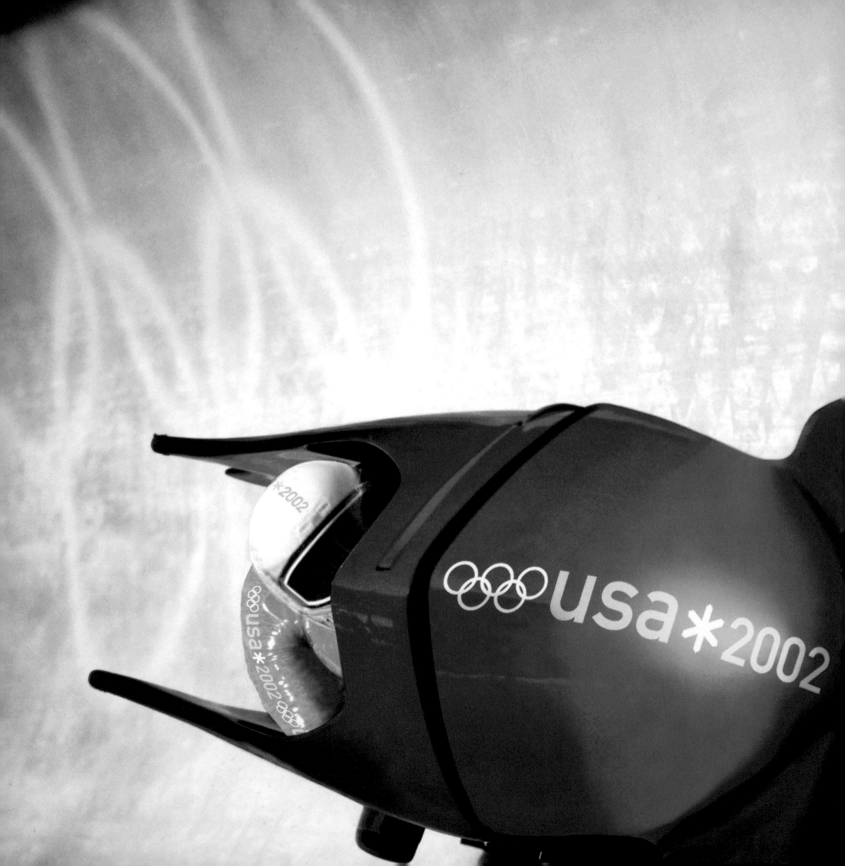

3

Understand limitations

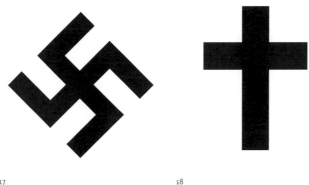

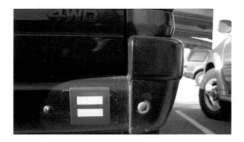

17   18   19

Here is the bad news: A logo is not a magic lantern. It can't make a bad product successful or save a poorly managed corporation. This is the good news: A well-designed logo will always help a good product realize its full potential. Smart design, along with the power of repetition, can make an enormous impact. The logo gives direction and attitude, while the product informs the meaning.

16 (opposite)
The story of the 2002 Salt Lake City Winter Games emblem represents the four components of the theme: (1) the graphic elements feature the contrast of the mountain snow and the desert sun of Utah's landscape; (2) the symbol is suggestive of the unique culture of ancient marks that are woven into our heritage, thus emphasizing the history of the Olympic games; (3) the emblem is also a snowflake, symbolic of the winter games; and (4) the bold, bright , vivid colors further suggest the true essence of the games—a celebration of Olympic ideals and the courage present in the spirit of the athlete. Landor Associates

17
Until the Nazis co-opted the symbol, the swastika was used by many cultures throughout the past 3,000 years to represent life, sun, power, strength, and good luck. In 1920, Adolf Hitler adopted the swastika for the Nazi insignia and flag. The swastika, a primitive and simple geometric form, became a symbol of hate, anti-Semitism, violence, death, and murder.

18
Various peoples from Asia, Egypt, the Americas, and Africa have used multiple forms of the cross in early history. The cross typically signified the contrast of heaven and earth or space and time. When Christianity adopted the symbol in the fourth century, the mark came to represent man's redemption. Inherently this symbol has no meaning, but when combined with the ideas it represents it becomes an extremely powerful message.

19
As America's largest gay and lesbian organization, the Human Rights Campaign provides a national voice on gay and lesbian issues. It increases public understanding through innovative education and communication strategies, with a focus on equality. The logo, an equal sign, has taken on the attributes of HRC through widespread dissemination.
Stone Yamashita Partners

4

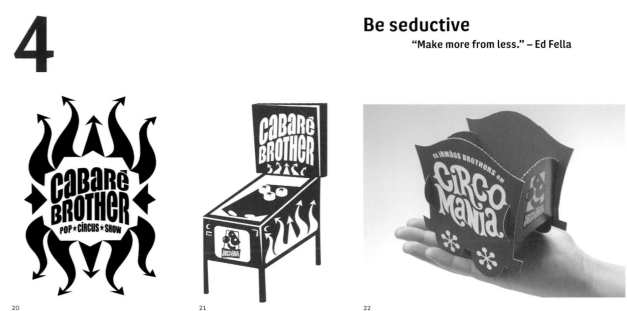

20

21

22

Be seductive

"Make more from less." – Ed Fella

There is an enormous amount of dialog in design education and design-oriented critical thinking about the irrelevance of pleasurable aesthetics. Over the past fifty years, the idea of logos as visually satisfying forms has been minimized. While this may play into fashionable cynicism, most people would prefer to be seduced by a mark than repulsed by one. The message must be the most important part of the identity's design, but the form must draw the viewer into it. Making visuals aesthetically seductive is another book, but logos are most successful when they are simple and dynamic.

Unfortunately, there has never been a client who considered their company simple. Products, services, and companies are inherently complex. Multiple personalities interact, natural evolution changes the internal culture, and society at large is constantly shifting. The logo, however, must remain a clear expression of the client. Because the logo will be seen only for a moment the use of forms that are easily recognizable is important. The logo will also be subjected to abuse, either by production processes or designer creativity. A simple form will survive these violations, while a more complex form may not. Being direct is powerful. Many logos fail from their own cleverness or overproduction. Let something be what it is.

20-21
"Cabaré Brother" is a modern variety show that presents a different selection of clown acts, musical guests, poets, magicians, and a sensual stripper. Two different logos were developed for collateral material (T-shirts, banners, tickets, newspaper ads) that did not feature the poster's four-color illustration. Porto+Martinez designStudio

22
Circomania is a children's theater production presented by the Irmãos Brothers, a clown group. Due to its low production budget, Circomania called for a logo that could entice its audience with thematic applications. A pop-out, build-it-yourself invitation, ticket, and poster set was created that when assembled, and displayed side by side, would form a long line of circus wagons. Porto+Martinez designStudio

23 (opposite)
The poster for "Cabaré Brother" presents the logo as the centerpoint of a noisy vernacular pinball machine. The irreverent and exuberant attitude of the mark is exaggerated by the illustration and vibrant color palette. Porto+Martinez designStudio

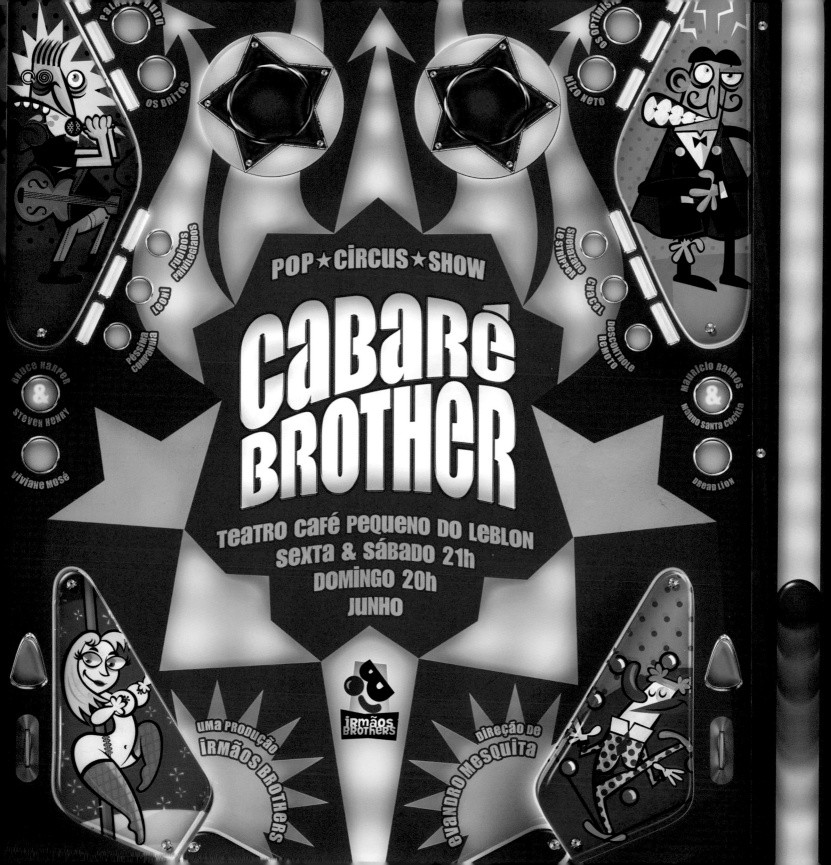

5 Make mnemonic value

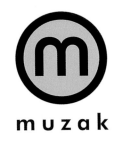

muzak

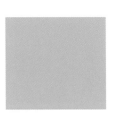

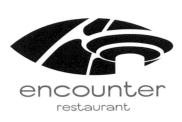

encounter
restaurant

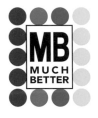

24   25   26   27

When we deconstruct how memory is made, we find there are four critical attributes of the process: (1) We see shape and color. All our visual recognitions are based on this. Is something square and red, or round and yellow? From the way we read letterforms, to the way we identify faces, shape and color form the basis of this skill. Once the shape and color of a form have been determined, we (2) position it within our understanding of historical continuity. We ask ourselves, "Does this look contemporary, Victorian, or Medieval?" "Does this have relevance to me at this time?"

(3) We then use the information we have from learned responses to form meaning. We are taught very specific ideas: blue is masculine and pink is feminine, a red light means "stop," a green light means "go." (4) Mnemonic value is linked seamlessly with emotional association. This is the "wild card." It is personal and difficult to predetermine. If a green car hit you when you were a child, you may have an aversion to green. If your mother wears Chanel No. 5, you may feel warm (or other more complicated emotions) when seeing the Chanel logo. Being aware of and utilizing these four attributes provides the tools to produce mnemonic value.

24
Shape
The muzak logo uses circular shapes referencing record albums and CDs. Even the negative shapes inside the counter of the letterforms are circular, echoing the containing form. Consistency of shape contributes to the power of this logo. Pentagram SF

25
Color
Tiffany blue is unique and is used consistently on advertising, packaging, and bags. While this shade of blue is not copyright protected, the association with the logo and brand is critical.

26
Historical Continuity
The logo for Encounter Restaurant at the Los Angeles International Airport alludes to 1960s jet-set culture. The interior of the restaurant (designed by Walt Disney Imagineering) and the graphics were derived from forms in Tomorrowland (1967). These signifiers give us insight into the attitude of the restaurant experience.
AdamsMorioka, Inc.

27
Emotional Resonance
The set of logos designed for Much Better relies on the positive associations we have with games like Twister and the Milton Bradley Toy Company.
Carlos Segura

28 (opposite)
Learned Response
The logo for Newton Learning uses our knowledge of the story about Isaac Newton's discovery of gravity when the apple fell on his head. Doyle Partners

Newton
Learning

S1-60-LW.LIVE

28

curious?ictures

29

6

Pose a question

"If you can't explain the idea in one sentence over the telephone, it won't work." – Lou Danziger

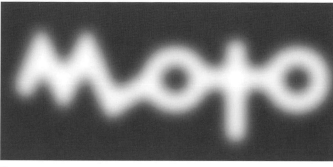

30

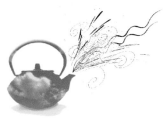

The REPUBLIC of TEA

31

32

When we receive input from our senses, there is a question, "What is this taste?" and a response, "This is chocolate." We also do this when we watch television, listen to music, or read a book. This is part of our thinking process. The books and television programs we find the most unsatisfying are often the most predictable. If the viewer is given all the facts there is little reason for him to process the information. Alternatively, if the question is presented, and the viewer must provide an answer in his head, he will be forced to spend more time with the message and therefore become more intimate with it. There is a fine line, however, between posing a question that invites a response and asking an unsolvable one. A visual solution that takes hours to interpret, or needs accompanying text will not succeed, and will soon be resigned from usage.

29 (opposite)
Curious Pictures is a production company for television programs and commercials. The use of wit and humor in the unexpected letterform usage seduces the viewer into the logo. Pentagram NY

30
Moto is a consulting firm specializing in technology design strategy. The company delivers high-tech solutions to complex problems in a smart, energetic manner, which the logo reflects. Tenazas Design

31–32
The Republic of Tea logo utilizes a teapot icon because it is an easily recognizable symbol, which also alludes to the mystical power of the company's various brews. The icon, used with and without a steam graphic, is based on a traditional Japanese teapot recalling a certain set of ceremonial and cultural associations. The Zen-like "magic teapot" can take a person to places real or imaginary. Clement Mok

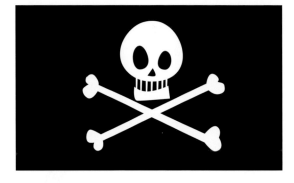

7

33

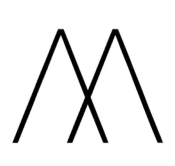

34

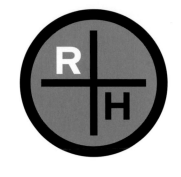

35

Every hour we are barraged with an endless array of images and ideas. Our visual landscape is composed of billboards and signs, television commercials, magazine advertisements, messages on packaging, and other forms of visual communication. Almost every one of these messages is combined with a logo, but many of these have little impact and are quickly forgotten. The ideas that connect are the ideas that resonate with us emotionally. Style and trends may be enticing, but they rarely have lasting emotional resonance. Marks that date quickly result from a concentration on "formal," rather than "conceptual" ideas. The logo must be able to convey its message over a long period of time and it must be able to adapt to cultural changes. It might be exciting to design a logo that is influenced by the typeface du jour, but it will quickly become embarrassing and will need to be redesigned in later years. Marks designed with a focus on current style and trends are often outdated in a short amount of time and soon become "quaint." There are very few clients who would like to be perceived as either outdated or quaint.

33
The Jolly Roger or *Joulie Rouge*, the fierce flag of pirate ships first seen in the mid-1600s, was a symbol of death. It continues to symbolize pirates, and their exploits, 400 years later.

34
The R+H logo is made with extreme simplicity. The weights of the letter-forms and cross are refined. The relationship of the outer ring to the negative space is considered. The minimal forms and skilled craft provide the tools to give this logo a long life. Ph.D

35
Pentagram took the "M" for Marcus and created a simple but stylish branding device, inspired by the hallmarks used to identify and authenticate precious metals.
Pentagram UK

36 (opposite)
The ABC logo, developed by Paul Rand, has been in continual use since 1962 and has never been modified. Rand said that he designed it for durability, function, usefulness, rightness, and beauty. Paul Rand

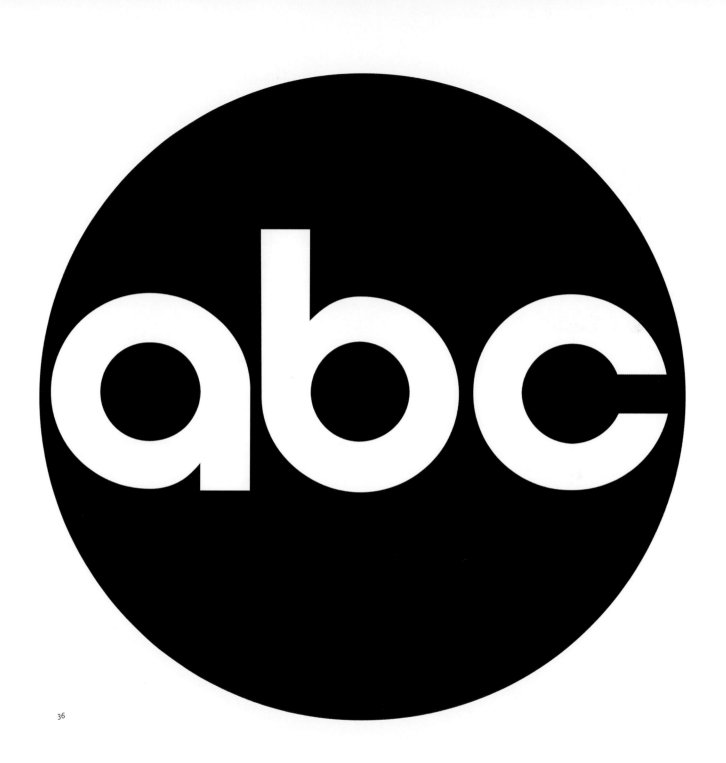

36

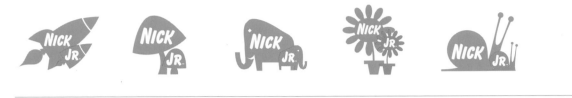

Primary color

PMS 116

PMS Warm Red

PMS Purple

PMS Rhodamine Red

PMS Orange 021

PMS 306

White

Black

Secondary color

PMS 117 · PMS 1375 · PMS 145 · PMS 1615 · PMS 179 · PMS 231 · PMS 239 · PMS 2985 · PMS 3125

PMS 3262 · PMS 3272 · PMS 375 · PMS 376 · PMS 382 · PMS 384 · PMS 804 · PMS 805 · PMS 806

PMS Blue 072 · PMS Process Blue · PMS 2726 · PMS 100 · PMS 1485 · PMS 2365 · PMS 2975 · PMS 331 · PMS 380

Info Display Bold

ABCDEFGHIJKLMNOPQRSTUVWXYZ
abcdefghijklmnopqrstuvwxyz
1234567890

Info Display Semi-bold

ABCDEFGHIJKLMNOPQRSTUVWXYZ
abcdefghijklmnopqrstuvwxyz
1234567890

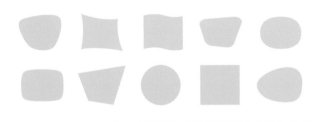

Primary background palette

Secondary background palette

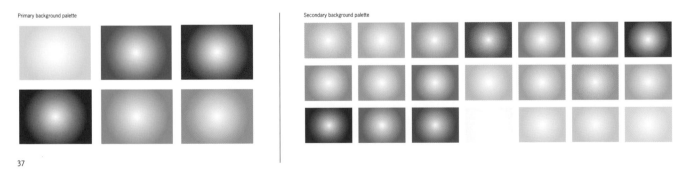

37

Make the logo the foundation of a system

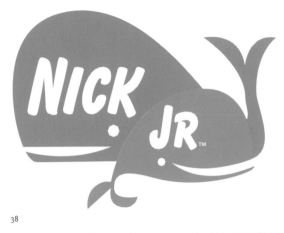

38

Like the foundation of a building, the logo is the base for all other messages. When the designer is in the process of designing a logo, it will be the only item on his computer screen. Often, when presented to a client, it will be the only item on the page. This is a mistake. The audience will never see the logo in a void. It will always be in context, accompanied by other visuals and ideas. It may be seen on business cards, on vans, and on top of buildings. If the logo is the foundation, the visual system is, to keep the construction metaphor alive, the framing of the structure. A visual system is derived from the logo. It does not copy the mark's form, but complements it. The visual system will include guidelines for usage of color, typography, imagery, copy style, and product usage. Without these guidelines, very bad things can happen to the logo. Party hats could be put on it for Christmas cards, its color could be changed to something inappropriate, or it might be used as signage on the lobby floor, stepped on daily. The guidelines protect the mark and clarify the environment it occupies. This, consequently, protects the integrity of its message and the company it represents.

37 (opposite)
The color palette complemented, but did not replicate, the mark. The typeface, Info Display, designed by MetaDesign, was chosen as a counterpoint to the Nick Jr. letterforms. A freeform shape library was created for use as enclosing or background shapes with typography or television characters. These were deliberately different from the "caregiver" mark. A palette of gradations was created as backgrounds for the logo, allowing the environment to change without overpowering the Nick Jr. logo. The Nick Jr. mark dictates the elements of the visual system. Maintaining the original criteria and message is the foremost goal, and understanding who will design with the visual system is paramount to achieving that goal.
AdamsMorioka, Inc.

38
The Nick Jr. logo's relationship to the visual system is critical. The logo is a changeable set of icons. The letterforms and colors are always consistent. The "caregiver" shape changes on each application. The attitude of play and levity is built into the logo, and the visual system reinforces these ideas.
AdamsMorioka, Inc.

9

Design for a variety of media

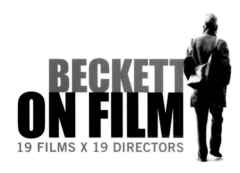

39

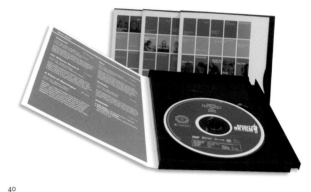

40

Until the 1950s most logos needed to work technically in only one medium, print. The expansion of digital, broadcast, and interactive media over the last fifty years has changed this. The logo should now be legible and clear on a one-color newspaper ad, a website, three-dimensional signage, and on television. Most clients will have a predisposed idea of the logo's usage. At the time of its inception they may only intend to use the mark in print. Given the constant evolution of media and information delivery systems, it would be very unique for the mark to exist only in one medium over its lifespan. Once again, it is the designer's responsibility to plan for the unplanned.

39
The logo developed for the Beckett on Film Festival concentrates on the artistry, genius, and introspection of Samuel Beckett, the man. This open-ended approach is not only personal and resonant, but also allows the logo to be incorporated successfully on a variety of applications, each with different needs. Dynamo

40-42
The communications program for the Beckett on Film Festival has a distinctly Irish image, making it worthy of global publicity and marketing to international visitors. The logo is utilized on applications as varied as DVD packaging, promotional box sets, the website, tickets, and posters. The logo succeeds in maintaining a clear vision across platforms while allowing each item to communicate a specific message. This cohesive quality across the programs is possible because of the consistent use of the logo. Dynamo

43 (opposite)
Nineteen different film directors with varying viewpoints are represented on the poster. The connection of portraits of these film directors to the image-based logo maintains a clear and direct spirit. Dynamo

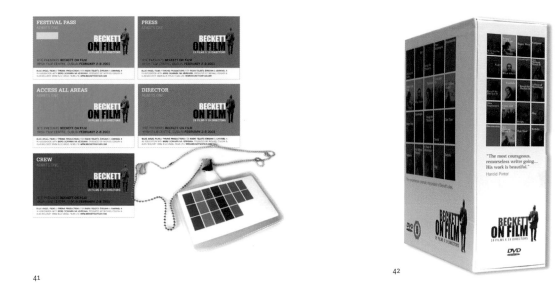

41

42

43

10

Be strong

**"Design depends largely
on constraints."**
–Charles Eames

**" The businessman will never
respect the professional who
does not believe in what he does."**
–Paul Rand

**" God helps them that
help themselves."**
–Benjamin Franklin

There is an often-told story about a well-known designer throwing a leather office chair across the room when a client rejected his design. Being strong is not about throwing chairs. That's a temper tantrum. Being strong is understanding your role, the client's role, and maintaining a clear vision.

There is a fine line between intransigence and confidence, or between uncertainty and collaboration. The design process is often subjective, with logos and identity at the core of a sense of self. A client's love of red, for example, may be irrelevant to the strategy, but rejection of that idea may become a deeply personal issue. On the other hand, the designer may fall in love with the style of a logo that is not conceptually relevant. In order to reach a solution that solves the problems with sustainability, the final logo must address the client's goals and messages. Sidestepping the emotional landmines and personal politics is one of the most challenging aspects of the design process. While every situation is different, the best solution is to maintain a clear vision and connection to the primary goal. The designer, as an outside consultant, will be able to see the larger picture without being distracted by day-to-day operations. Frequently reminding the client of the desired outcome and central message is critical.

As the design of a logo is burdened with emotional and political issues, the designer may find himself in the role of "the bad guy" to others in the company not involved in the design process. This is not a negative. No one likes change and the designer is the catalyst for change. Achieving "buy-in" from these other voices is important and can be done with updated information and patient listening to internal issues. Making people feel good, however, is not the designer's job; producing a viable and effective logo is.

"Good designers make trouble."

—Tibor Kalman

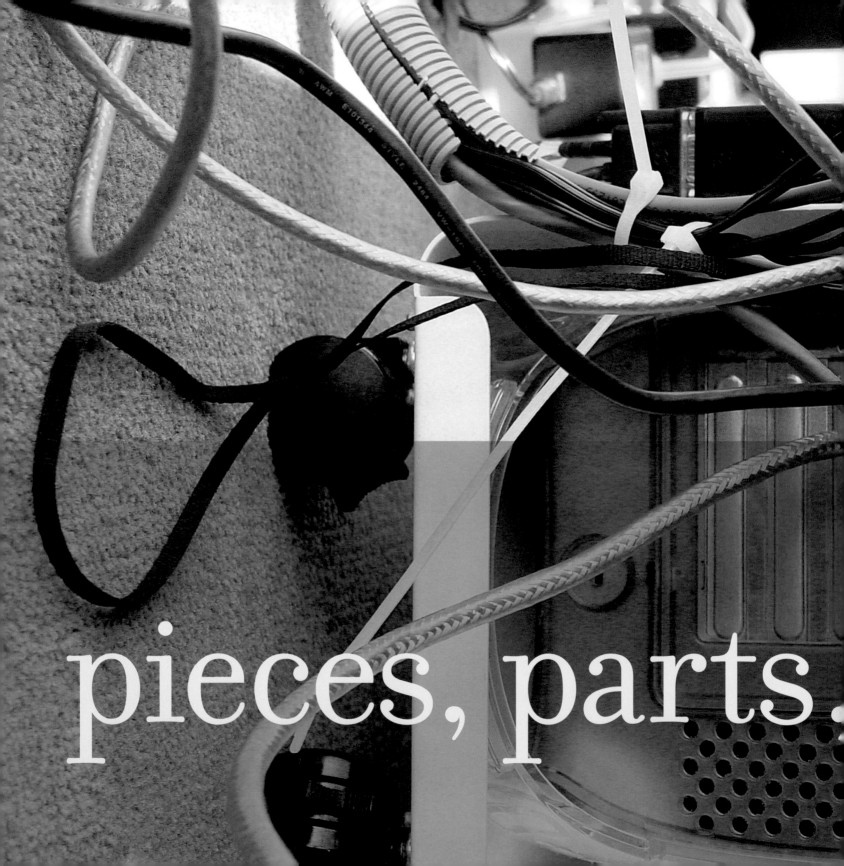

pieces, parts.

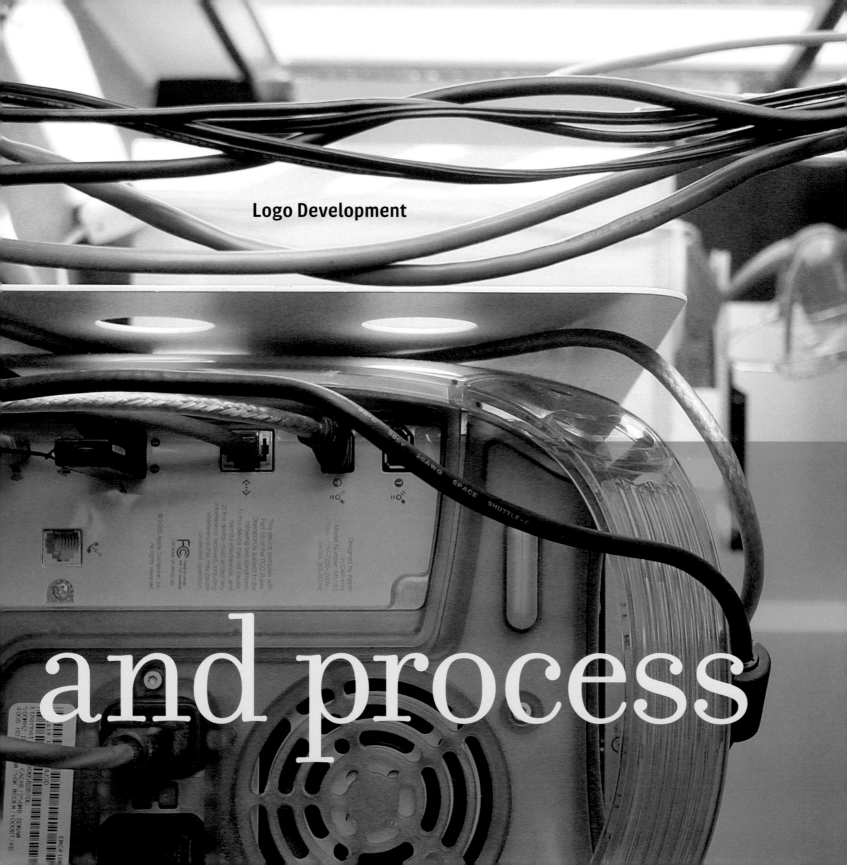

Logo Development

and process

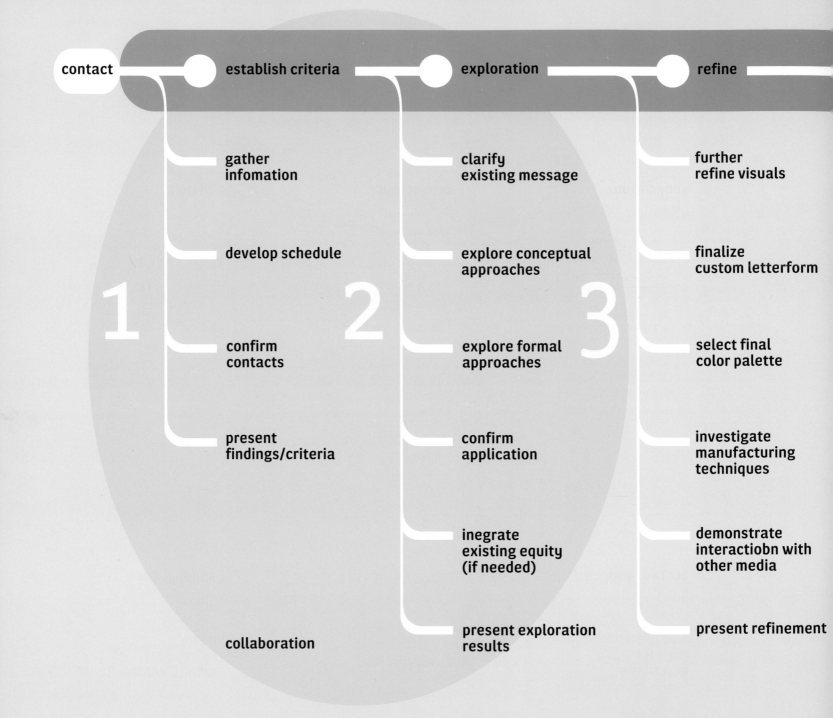

contact

establish criteria

exploration

refine

1

gather infomation

develop schedule

confirm contacts

present findings/criteria

collaboration

2

clarify existing message

explore conceptual approaches

explore formal approaches

confirm application

inegrate existing equity (if needed)

present exploration results

3

further refine visuals

finalize custom letterform

select final color palette

investigate manufacturing techniques

demonstrate interactiobn with other media

present refinement

4

applications

apply approved mark

apply primary and
secondary typefaces

apply
color palette

identify technical
needs of applications

determine
materials and
manufacturing

present applications

5

production

produce
digital files
and specifications

supervise
printing estimates

supervise
printing,
manufacturing

supervise
deliverly

6

system

produce
standards
manual

supervise
implementation
of visual system

coordinate with all
outside
consultants

coordinate with
in-house departments

modify system as
needed for
usability

collaboration

Typography

Typography is pictures of words. The letterforms work together to convey a message. In the same way that we decipher imagery, we decode typography. The attitude, history, and culture of a company are conveyed with the letterforms of the logo. Choosing the appropriate typeface for a logo is a complex task. The shape of the letters in combination must be considered, as well as the legibility and distinct sound of the word when spoken. Certain typefaces will lend themselves to better legibility with upper and lower case.

Often, a type study is conducted to examine options. Once a general typographic direction is established, a letter-style will be created. There are instances when an existing font will work adequately, but proprietary and unique letterforms provide greater value. This is either a modification of an existing typeface, or a completely original typeface. While most nongraphic designers will not recognize the difference between Helvetica and a custom font, it is the unique attributes of the custom font that give ownership to the client. A word of warning, however; the further the letterforms depart from the original recognizable forms, the more quickly they will date.

1470 • Nicolas Jenson • Venice   Humanist

Centaur
ABCDEFGHIJKLMNOPQRSTUVWXYZ
abcdefghijklmnopqrstuvwxyz
1234567890

1495 • Aldus Manutius, Francesco Griffo • Venice   Old Style

Bembo
ABCDEFGHIJKLMNOPQRSTUVWXYZ
abcdefghijklmnopqrstuvwxyz
1234567890

1532 • Claude Garamond • Paris   Old Style

Garamond
ABCDEFGHIJKLMNOPQRSTUVWXYZ
abcdefghijklmnopqrstuvwxyz
1234567890

1757 • John Baskerville • Birmingham   Transitional

Baskerville
ABCDEFGHIJKLMNOPQRSTUVWXYZ
abcdefghijklmnopqrstuvwxyz
1234567890

1768 • Giambattista Bodoni • Parma   Modern

Bodoni
ABCDEFGHIJKLMNOPQRSTUVWXYZ
abcdefghijklmnopqrstuvwxyz
1234567890

1845 • R. Besley & Co. • London — Slab Serif

Clarendon

ABCDEFGHIJKLMNOPQRSTUVWXYZ
abcdefghijklmnopqrstuvwxyz
1234567890

1954 • Adrian Frutiger • Deberny & Peignot • Paris — Lineale or Sans Serif

Univers

ABCDEFGHIJKLMNOPQRSTUVWXYZ
abcdefghijklmnopqrstuvwxyz
1234567890

1984 • Doyald Young • Esselte Letraset, Ltd. • London — Script

Young Baroque

ABCDEFGHIJKLMNOPQRS
TUVWXYZabcdefghijklmnopqrstuvwxyz
1234567890

1929 • C.H. Griffith • London — Graphic/Decorative

Poster Bodoni

ABCDEFGHIJKLMNOPQRSTUVWXYZ
abcdefghijklmnopqrstuvwxyz
1234567890

1993 • Robert Kirchner • Austria — Digital

Isonorm

ABCDEFGHIJKLMNOPQRSTUVWXYZ
abcdefghijklmnopqrstuvwxyz
1234567890

Typographic Classification

Humanist
calligraphic forms
Centaur, Verona

Old Style
refinement of calligraphic forms
Bembo, Garamond, Caslon

Transitional
proportional refinement
Baskerville, Fournier, Bell

Modern
heavy contrast
Bodoni, Modern, Walbaum

Slab Serif
heavy, square-ended serifs
Rockwell, Memphis, Clarendon

Lineale or Sans Serif
without serifs
Grotesque, Helvetica, Univers

Script
cursive
Palace Script, Young Baroque

Graphic/Decorative
decorative fonts
Poster Bodoni, Hobo, Dom Casual

Digital
digital forms
Oakland, Isonorm, Modula

Letterforms can be thought of as clothing.
A good pair of khakis and a white shirt will
always be classic and will never look out of
date. The addition of a unique tie or scarf will
make the outfit personal. Long lived,
classic typefaces are perceived in the same
way. Alternatively, orange plaid pants and a
pink tank top may get attention now, but as time
passes they will become the focus of jokes when
friends look at old photos. Trendy typefaces
often suffer the same fate.

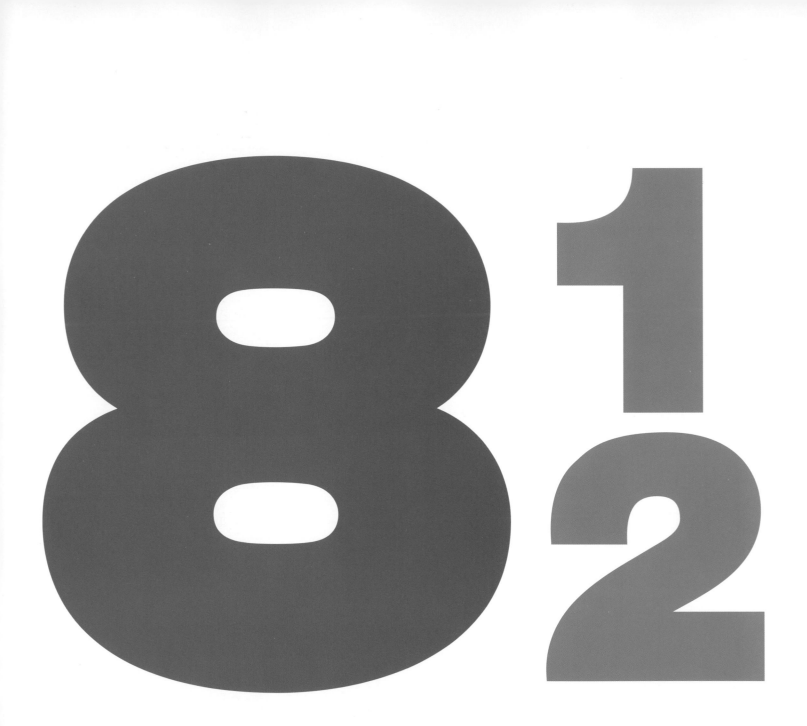

44

44 (opposite)-45
Brasserie 8 1/2, the restaurant at 9 West 57th Street, references the large three-dimensional figure "9," which is a famous New York City landmark in front of the building. The curves of the beautifully drawn custom letterforms of the Brasserie 8 1/2 logo have been simplified; the shapes of each letterform echoes the shapes of the others. Chermayeff & Geismar

46
The Architects Alliance is an amalgam of several architectural practices. The Trade Gothic letterforms are clear, confident, and minimalist in their creation. Concrete

47
Goût du Jour is a Japanese cake and bread bakery chain. The letterforms are hand-drawn and communicate an attitude of spontaneity and joyfulness. Anthon Beeke

48
Gizmo, a board game, is a combination of various forms based on the slab serif font Geometric 703. The dingbats simulate the action of this game about creating mechanical "inventions." The shift of letters on the baseline forces the viewer to "hear" the word. Tom and John, A Design Collaborative

49
Based on the classical font Firmin Didot, the ITC Didi letterforms used on the Bocconi logo exaggerate the terminal of the "c," which echoes the dot on the "i" and creates a proprietary element. Pentagram UK

50
The Design Exchange promotes connections in cultural identity and design innovation. The name is simplified into an iconic language with minimal means. The letterforms are based on Gill Sans. Concrete

51
Lowe and Partners is one of the world's leading advertising agencies. Taking advantage of the possibilities inherent in each letterform, a custom letterstyle was developed with a square as the primary guide. Carter Wong Tomlin

52
MTVI Group, the online division of MTV Networks, connects three online businesses. As opposed to using the MTV logo, heavily modified versions of News Gothic and Venus were used, while the three dots of the "i" relate to the composition of the division. AdamsMorioka, Inc.

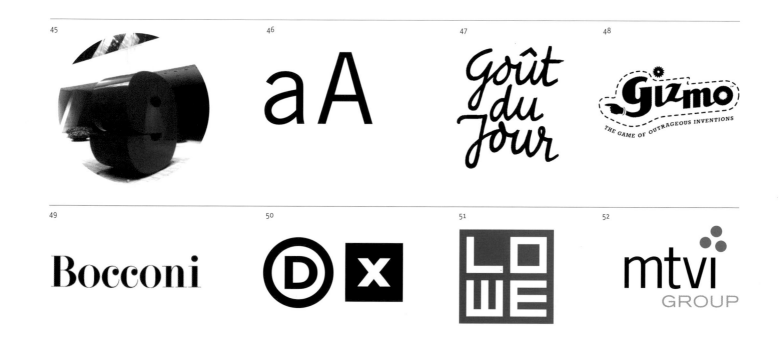

Color

Color is subjective. There are emotional connections that are personal to each color we see. In relationship to logo design, color is integral to mnemonic value. It also conveys the tone of a company. Although certain colors have accepted meanings in Western European culture, there are multiple meanings across other cultures. In the United Kingdom, white is considered pure and positive. In China, white is used in mourning, symbolizing heaven. Red is connected with strength and life, but is taboo in financial communities. In these instances, the color acts as a signifier of ideas.

The idea of "owning" a color is one of the highest priorities of a logo and subsequent identity. Orange has been associated with Nickelodeon for almost two decades. PMS 659, a deep dark blue, is used on the Gap identity, and was also the name of their fragrance. Subverting standard definitions can help to make a color proprietary. Wells Fargo Bank's use of red was considered heretical by the financial community, but has given Wells Fargo a clear identity above the multitudes of financial institutions with blue logos.

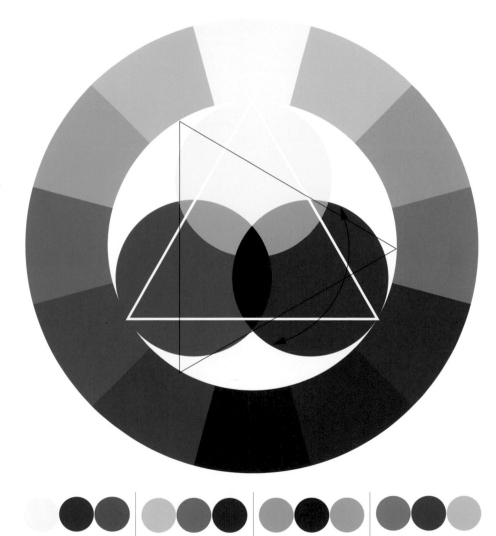

The triangle rotates to identify harmonious color combinations.

Hue:	The color itself, ranging from yellow to blue to red
Saturation:	The purity of a color from gray to the most intense color value
Value or tint:	The brightness of a color from black to white

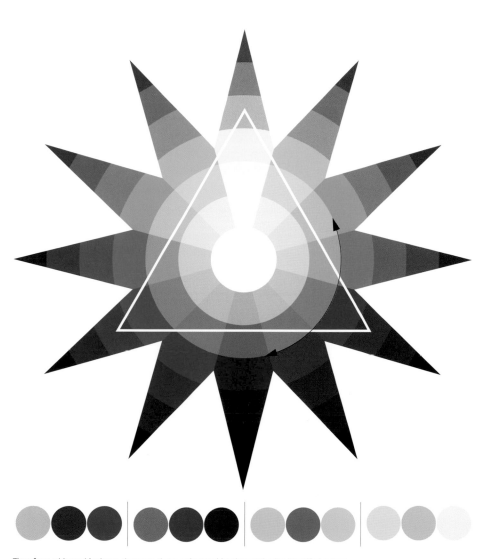

Tints from white to black use the same three-point combination method to identify harmony.

Color Meanings
The human eye and brain experience color to produce a mental and emotional response. As a result of this, colors themselves have meanings. The exact symbolism is often a cultural agreement. Listed below is a sampling of color meanings in the U.S.A., Canada, and Western Europe. We recommend the investigation and consideration of a particular color's meaning when using it in an identity system.

Red
Passion, Anger, Stop, Battle, Love, Blood

Yellow
Joy, Intellect, Caution, Cowardice, Youth

Green
Fertility, Money, Healing, Success, Growth

White
Perfection, Purity, Wedding, Clean, Virtue

Blue
Knowledge, Tranquility, Calm, Peace, Cool

Black
Fear, Negativity, Death, Evil, Secrecy

Purple
Royalty, Wisdom, Spirituality, Imagination

Orange
Creativity, Invigoration, Unique, Energy

Grey
Neutrality, Uncommitted, Uncertain

53
Red and gray were selected as the colors for architectural lighting fixture manufacturers Gotham. According to designer Clive Piercy, it was chosen because these colors are "prettywittysoftiespecial." Ph.D

57
Information, Advise and Guidance Network, or IAG, is an organization, that is committed to helping people with training, career counseling, and job placement with regional offices throughout the United Kingdom. The chartreuse color makes this logo both visible and memorable.
blue river design limited

54
When the logo was redesigned, electronics retailer Good Guys asked Pentagram to continue to use their exhisting colors of red and black for branding continuity. Pentagram SF

58
Vodovod-Kanalizacija Ljubljana is the town's water supply service. Blue is an obvious choice to represent water. The "V" for Vodovod and the waves combine to create the dynamic shape of this logo. KROG

55
The color palette for the pan-European graphic design conference Grafic Europe is not restricted to one combination. The colors are intended to change to reflect each city chosen to host the conference. This logo is for the conference in Barcelona, Spain.
Lippa Pierce

59
Steel blue grey and sans serif typography create a solid minimalist logo for polygon. Lippa Pierce

56
Sonic Fruit is a sound design company. The logo's colors are a modern interpretation of classic corporate colors. The colors—red, blue and a touch of orange—reflect the hip nature of the client's business. Volker Dürre

60
Holland Festival is an annual avant-garde cultural festival in Amsterdam. The "HOLND" is red and the "FSTVL" is blue, which results in a logo that resembles the Dutch flag. Anthon Beeke

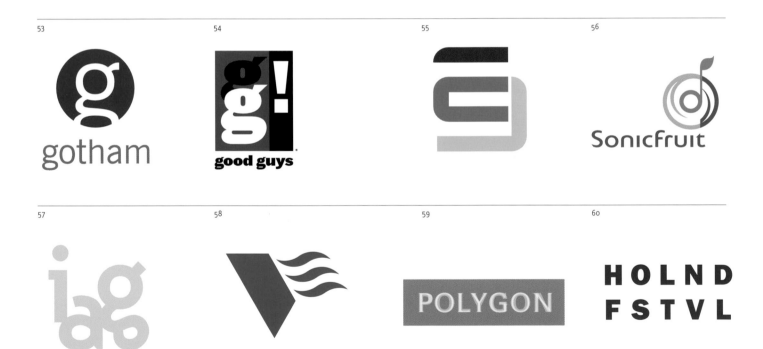

53

54

55

56

57

58

59

60

61
Developmentor is a company that trains software engineers and developers. Their logo is black and orange to give a twist to the traditional corporate colors. Ph.D

62
Green typography with red circles above the l's suggest a growing plant for Geo. J. Ball—growers and distributors of seeds of plants. Chermayeff & Geismar

63
The primary blue of the VH1 logo references multiple musical ideas: the blues, Blue Suede Shoes, Blue Note Records. AdamsMorioka, Inc.

64
"The official VT color is blue, any blue. Why? Because research has shown conclusively that blue is America's favorite color," says designer John Bielenberg. John Bielenberg

65
Blue was chosen for Mediabolic, a company that provides home entertainment networking systems, to be an unexpected nature-based color instead of a slick high-tech one. Tom and John, A Design Collaborative

66
Danes Oblikujem Jutri means Today I Design for Tomorrow. This logo was created for a Slovenian conference on sustainable development, with green selected because of its connection to nature and the environment. Kontrapunkt

67
Eneos is the gasoline service station brand of Nippon Oil Corporation. The radiating spirals of red and orange convey energy, innovation, and provide visual impact. Landor Associated International Limited

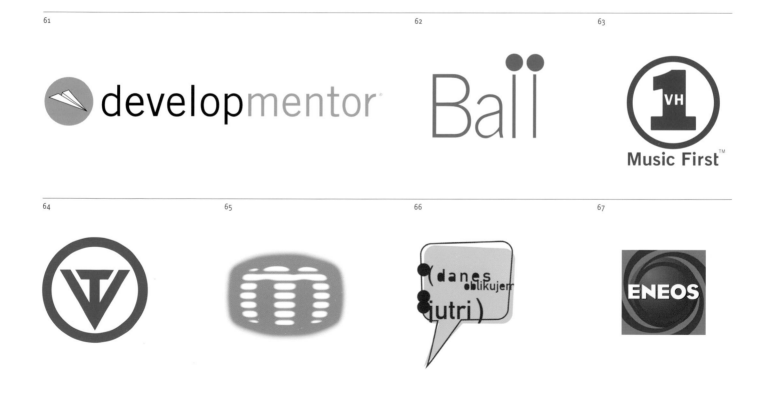

61   62   63

64   65   66   67

Image/Iconography

When we talk about iconography here, we are discussing its role in the context of logo development. Icons are loaded. They can be very powerful and convey a large amount of information quickly. They can, conversely, be oblique and neutral, allowing for a broad range of meaning. The style of execution impacts the tone and meaning. An icon created for a logo does not need to be a hard-edged, flat drawing of an abstract shape. While direct illustration of the subject matter is a mistake, various representational techniques can be utilized.

An apple acts as both a symbol of New York and of education. This may seem like a cliché, but clichés are, intrinsically, very recognizable. Such symbols should not be disregarded but, rather, presented in a fresh form. The iconography should engage the viewer. Seeing recognizable signs in a unique form is a good way to achieve this goal.

As society and culture change, the meaning of imagery and iconography shifts. Aunt Jemima was an acceptable image in the 1930s, but has since been modified to better represent an African-American woman as an individual, not as a stereotype. Responsibility for understanding the meaning(s) of an image lies with the designer.

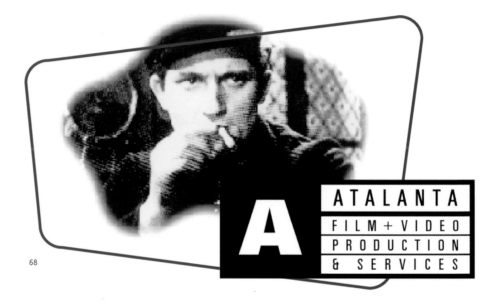

68

68
The representational technique of photography is used for the Atalanta Film + Video Production logo. The execution (photography) evolves from the subject matter—film—and does not rely on a purely graphic solution. Kontrapunkt

69 (opposite)
The stationery for Paul Vonberg Architects plays with the concept of space. The yellow block creates a horizon on which the word "architects" stands. The viewer can move through the type in the same way a person can walk through a building. Lippa Pierce created a typographic landscape, steeped in classicism, especially with the use of the font **Didot.** Lippa Pierce

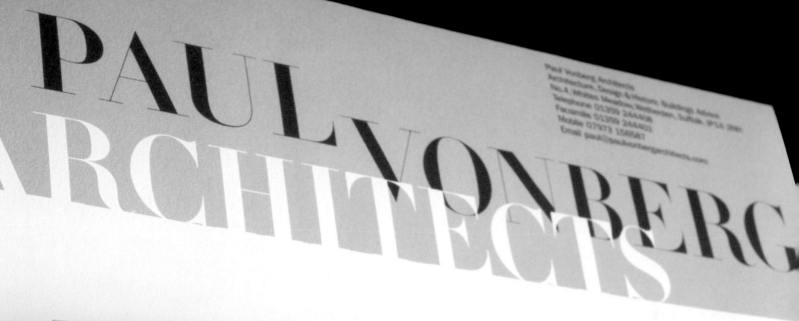

PAUL VONBERG
ARCHITECTS

Paul Vonberg, Architects
Architecture, Design & Historic Buildings Advice
No.4, Whites Meadow, Netherton, Suffolk, IP14 3NH
Telephone 01209 244406
Facsimile 01209 244401
Mobile 07973 106561
Email paul@pbulvonbergarchitects.com

PAUL VONB
ARCHITECT

Paul Vonberg, Arc
Architecture, De
No.4, Whites M
Telephone 012
Facsimile 012
Mobile 0797
Email paul@

Types of Icon

Diagrammatic
Icons are simple representations of the structure of the subject matter. The process of thinking is conveyed by an asterisk in the Spark logo.

Metaphoric
Icons are based on conceptual relationships. A hat for a talent agency communicates trust, honesty, and old-fashioned values.

Symbolic
Icons are abstract images that have no clear relationship to the subject. Their only connection is their proximity to the subject. A nonrepresentational mark next to the name of a shopping center is a symbol.

70
The photograph of surfboards for Quicksilver Edition is an image. It represents the tone of the company and serves as an icon for the lifestyle Quicksilver serves. Ph.D

71
The drawing of the head and asterisk communicate the process of thinking for the Spark logo, as opposed to a representation of a thought. The action is communicated with a diagrammatic icon. BIG, Ogilvy & Mather

72
Since entertainment industry talent agents seem to wear a lot of hats in their work, metaphorically speaking, a hat makes a great icon for the company. Ph.D

73
The logo for Pabst City is a skillful blend of letterforms and an abstract shape. The shape conveys multiple meanings (energy and light). It acquires meaning, however, only with its relationship to Pabst City. SamataMason

74 (opposite)
Bloom, a Dutch magazine, relies on a logo that is a simple typographic form combined with an image. The image in this instance takes the place of an icon connected to the logo. Anthon Beeke

70

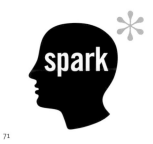

71

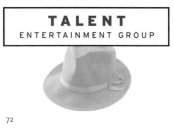

72

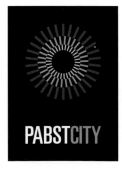

73

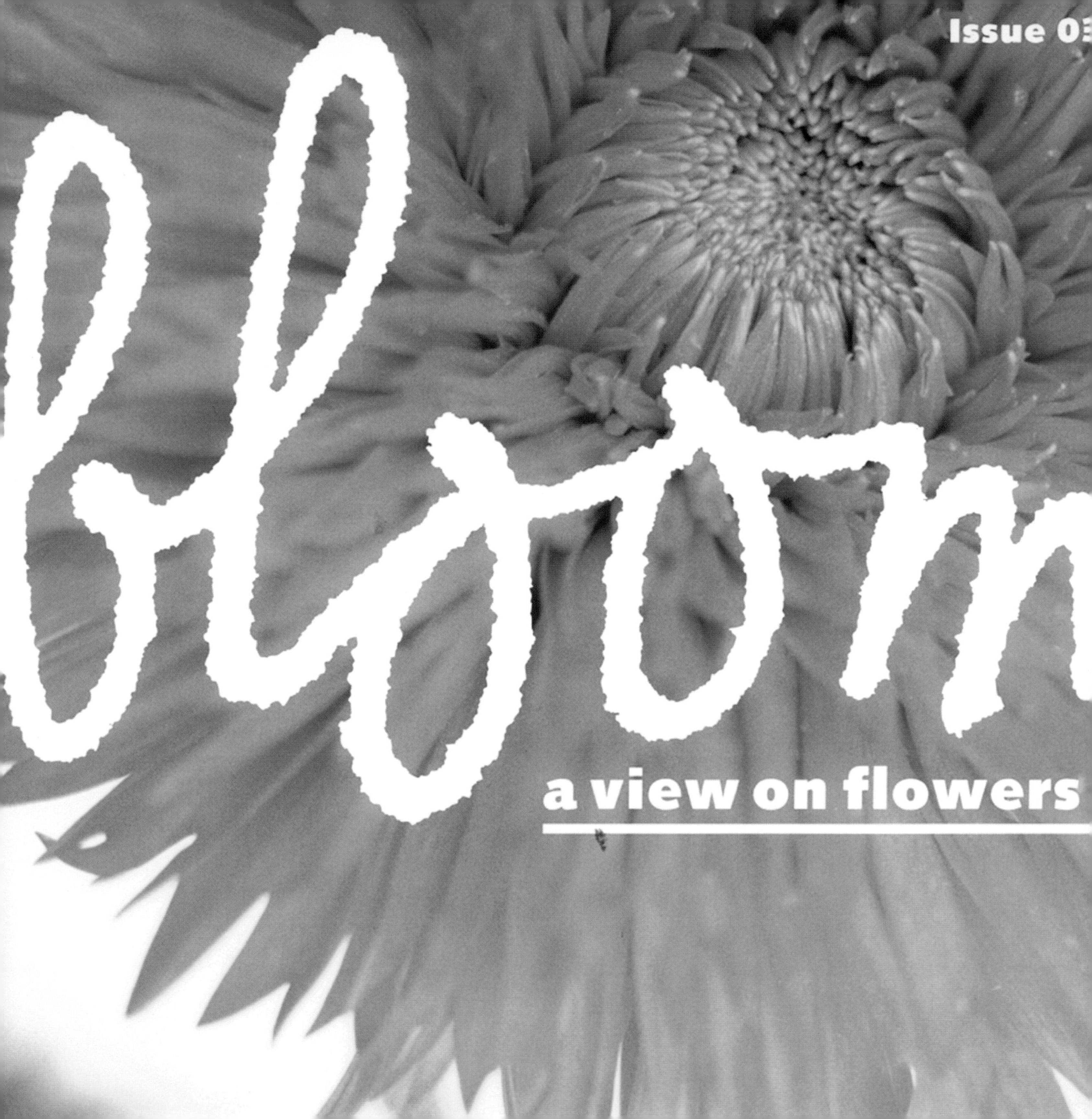

bloom

a view on flowers

Shape

A good logo will involve a shape that is appropriate and memorable. Shape is at the core of mnemonic value. Although it would be easy to say that a circle is the most successful shape for a logo, it would be untrue. There are logos made with squares, ellipses, triangles, and other unique shapes that are equally successful.

It is also wrong to think that all logos must be contained within a shape. The overall form of a logo should comprise a shape. This is achieved by the letterforms and icon being constrained within a shape. Alternatively, the letterforms and icon can create an implied shape.

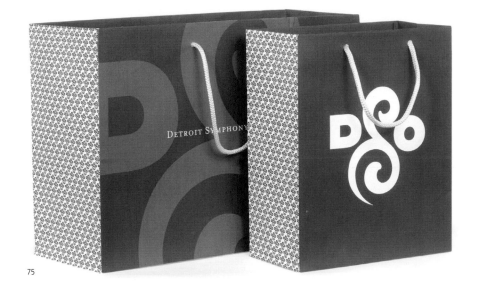

75

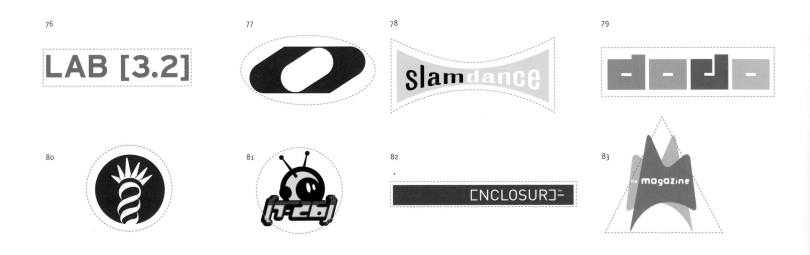

76

LAB [3.2]

77

78

Slamdance

79

80

81

82

[NCLOSUR]™

83

The magazine

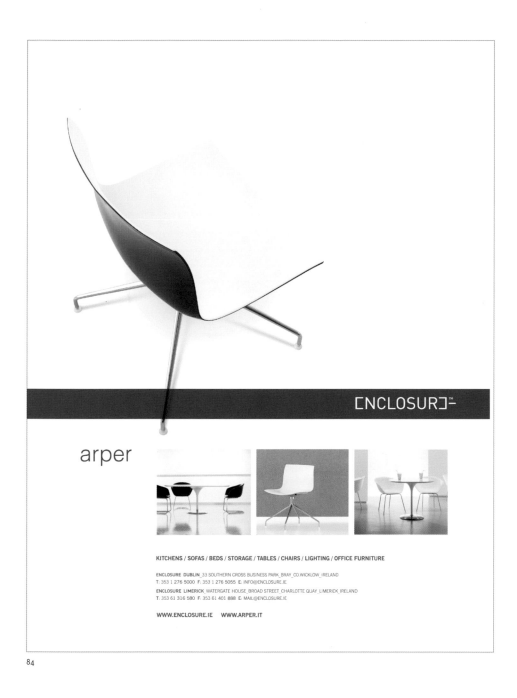

75
The counters of the "O" and "D" of the DSO logo echo the shapes of the curvilinear "S." The negative shapes within the lower portion of the "S" are as well considered as the positive shapes. Pentagram NY

76
The LAB [3.2] logo is primarily a rectangle. The brackets around 3.2 and the "L" reinforce the strong horizontality. KINETIK

77
The strong mechanical shape, a chain link, symbolizes Gruppo Principe, an Italian heavy industries group. R&Mag

78
The bow-tie shape of the Slamdance logo refers to filmic technologies like VistaVision and Cinemascope. AdamsMorioka, Inc.

79
Dodo's logo is composed of identical rectangular forms with slight variations. The repetition of the rectangles provides unity and power. Carlos Segura

80
The La Bella del Golfo logo features a sceptre contained in a circle. The shape also suggests the curved lines of the female form. R&Mag

81
The logo for T26 creates an implied circle. Each element—the eyes, head, and letterforms—echo the circle. Carlos Segura

82, 84
The Enclosure identity is designed to complement the fluid forms of the furniture it represents. The applications take advantage of the strong linear shape of the logo as a counterpoint to the product's nonlinear lines. Dynamo

83
Overlapping shapes play a prominent role in the logo developed for ESPN's publication, "The Magazine." Carlos Segura

84

Hierarchy and Scale

Myth: Everyone likes everything bigger. This might be true at a Burger King drive-through, but it is rarely true in design. A logo must be able to exist as a twenty-five foot sign on a building, but it must also function on a business card. Intricate, complex, and layered forms might look incredible on the computer screen at 400 percent, but will become a jumbled mess on a CD label. Obviously, simple forms reduce best. Conversely, bad curves or sloppy kerning are only exaggerated on a fifty-foot billboard.

The issue of hierarchy and meaning are interconnected. Is an individual product more important than the parent company? This depends on two questions. First, will it be advantageous for the client to be associated with the product? Second, will it be disadvantageous? If the connection with a product will position the client inappropriately, there's a much bigger problem that needs to be addressed than just the size of the logo.

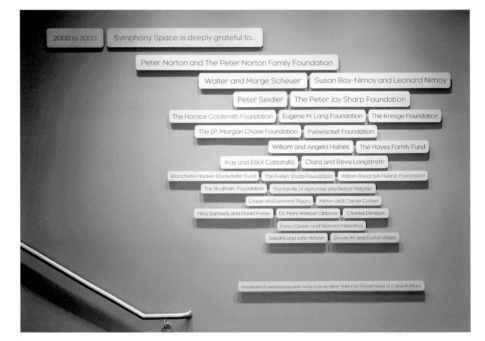

85

85-86
Symphony Space is a community-based arts organization that presents a diverse range of programming in music, film, dance, literature, and theater. The new logo needed to work in environmental and print applications. The logo usage ranges in scale from 1/4" (0.6 cm) to two-story building-sized signage.
Pentagram NY

86

symphonyspace

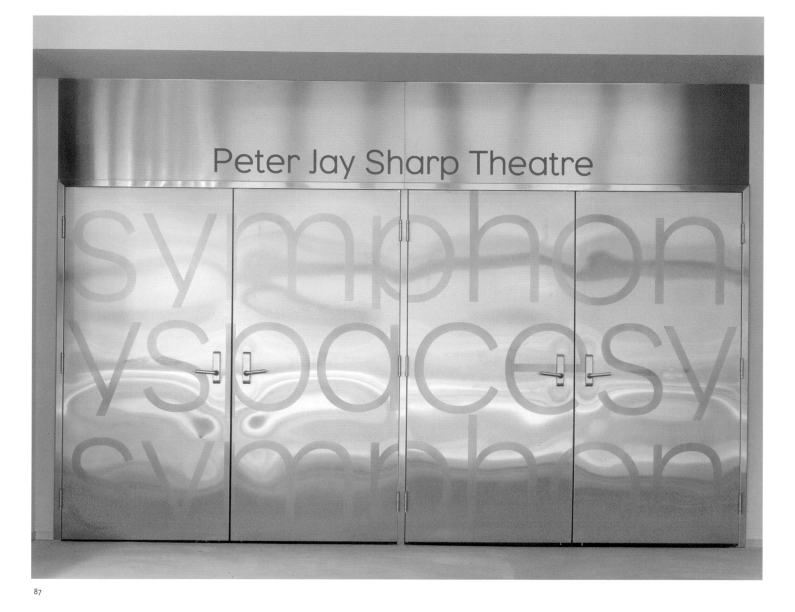

87

87
The donor signage system reflects the new Symphony Space logo's aesthetics. Pentagram NY

88 (next spread)
The exterior marquee visually connects Symphony Space to the adjacent Thalia Theater by extending its reach out over the corner of 95th and Broadway in New York City. The use of the building's architecture and graphics at this scale cause a direct dialog between the street and this cultural center. Pentagram NY

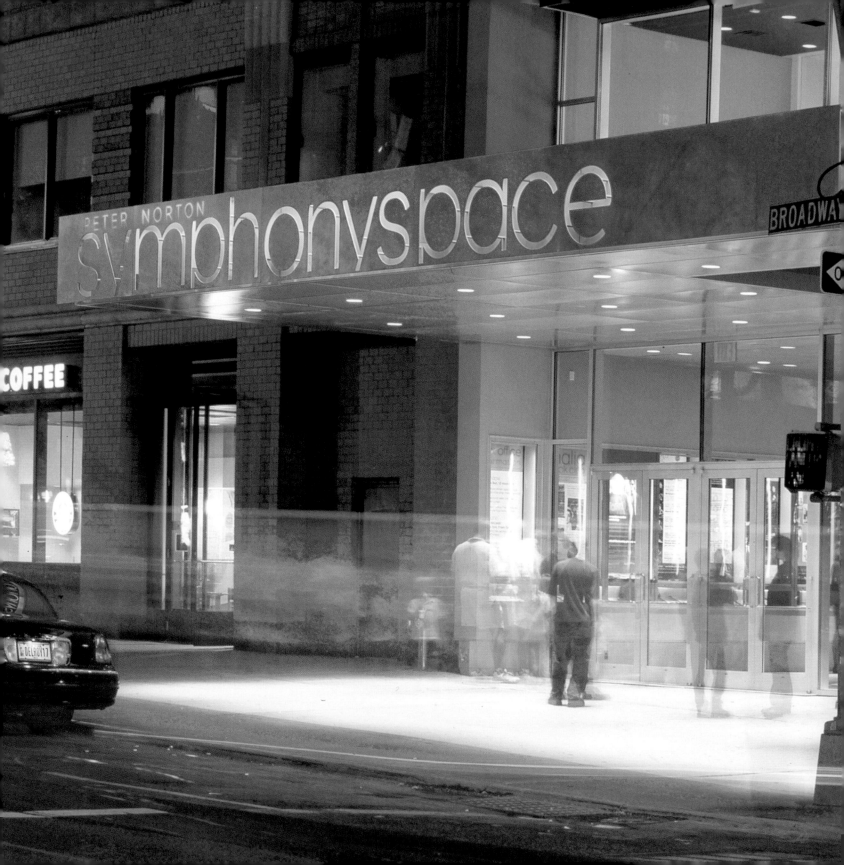

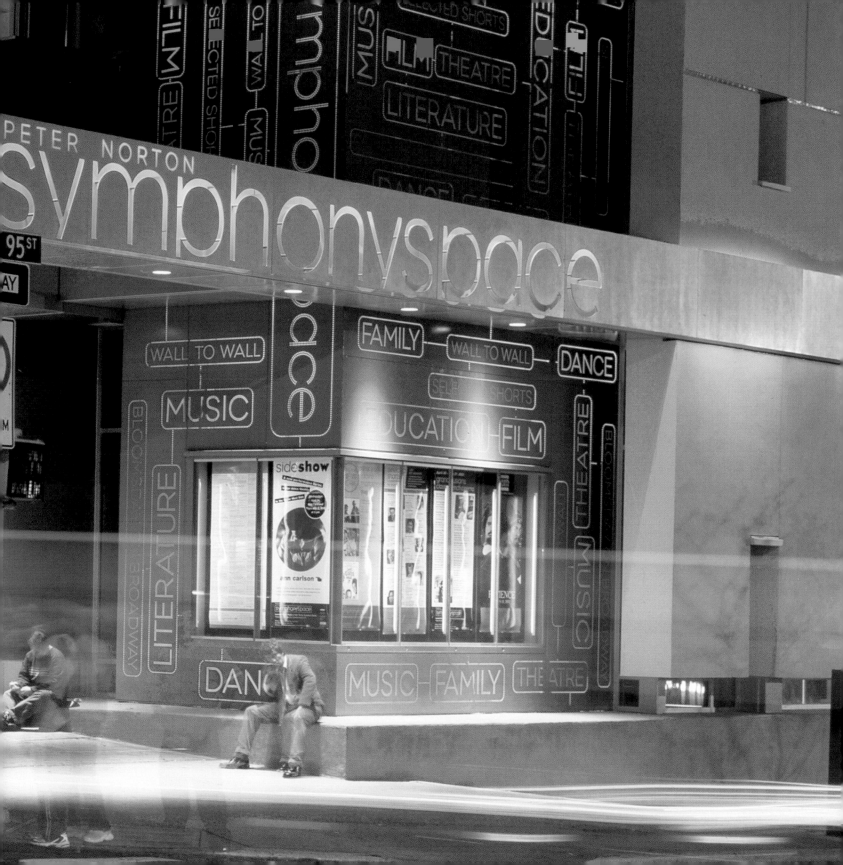

Static vs. Changeable

The logo must serve as a central tool providing a cohesive voice for a wide range of applications. This does not necessitate that the logo be an intransigent, immutable object. Twenty years ago, the idea of designing a logo that could mutate was heresy. As the delivery systems of information have expanded into television and new media though, the desire for logos to move, change, or just plain "do something" has increased. We now expect a logo on the bottom right corner of the television screen to animate. An accompanying audio cue is also expected. Whether it was meant to move or not is irrelevant; somewhere along the line, someone will make it spin.

Rather than allow someone else to make decisions about the changeable qualities of the logo, the designer should presuppose this scenario. Providing guidelines for motion, audio, and print is as important as choosing color. Once again, however, the message is at the heart of the decision-making process. It might be possible to have a logo twirl, flash, and bubble to the tune of "Surrey with the Fringe on Top," but it is not wise unless it is appropriate for the product. The action and reaction of the logo should reinforce the overall criteria and concept.

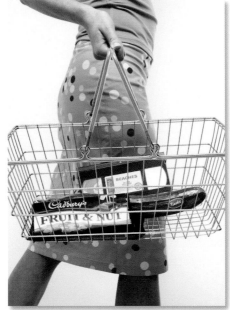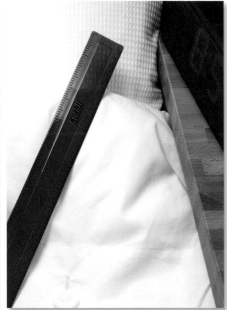

89

89-91
Creative director Michael Johnson says, "The girls at Kushti are hard-drinking, twenty-first century women. We call them 'laddettes' over here. So we wanted to find something that expressed what being 'Kushti' (i.e. sorted) meant to modern women. So it seemed that the modern, sorted woman would always pull in bars, never worry about her weight or waistline, had well-endowed boyfriends, and enjoyed a night in with chocolate, cucumbers, and a chick movie." All these images form the basis of a series of promotional pieces illustrating this kinetic branding concept.
Johnson Banks

92 (opposite)
London-based firm Johnson Banks developed a lot of visual ideas for their client Kushti, an all female PR/communications consultancy. It seemed too limiting to just have one logo, and much more fun to have six. The client liked the idea, and it suited them well. Johnson Banks

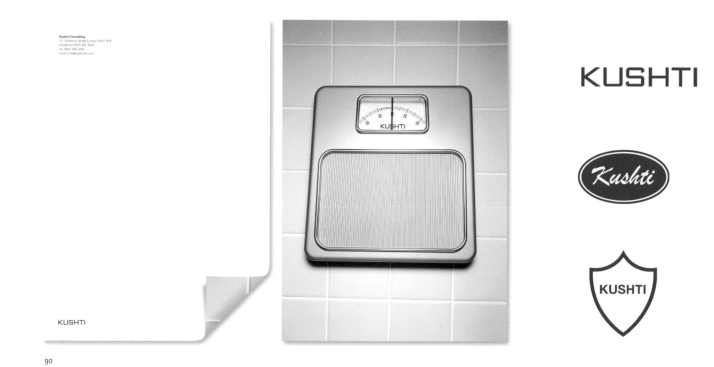

90

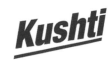

91

KUSHTI

KUSHTI

Kushti

KUSHTI

KUSHTI

Kushti

Kushti

92

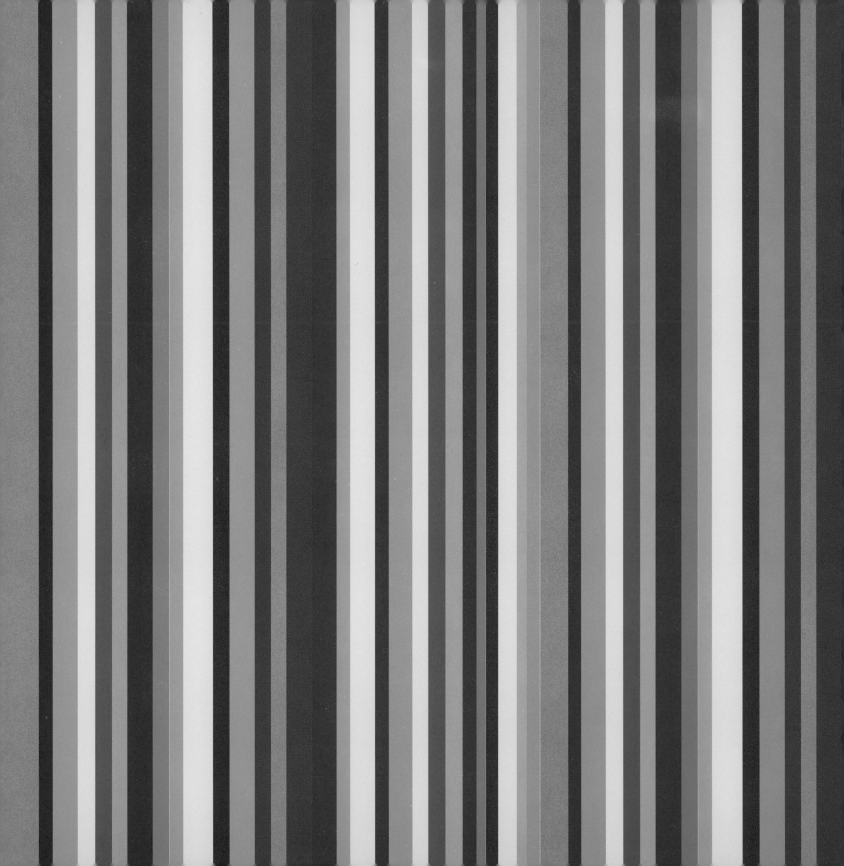

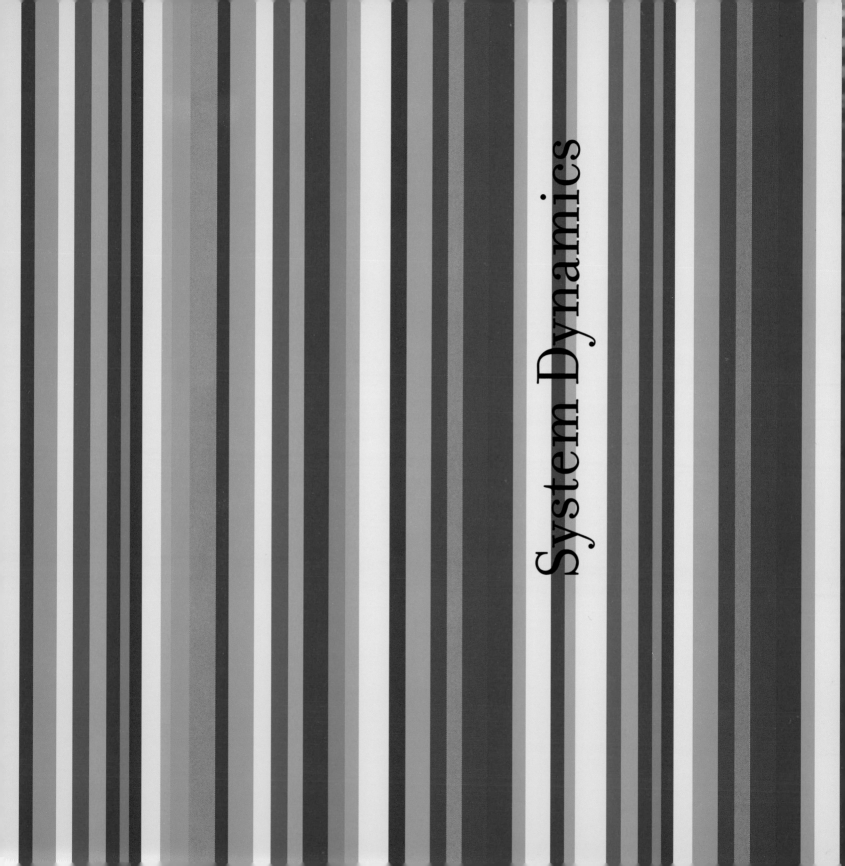
System Dynamics

Creating a kit of parts

Identity design must be fluid. When the logo is complete, many more elements need to be created to make the logo truly usable in a variety of applications. An identity system needs to be designed that will be dynamic enough to allow for the ever-changing needs of the client. Therefore it is essential that designers create logos with flexibility in mind.

CONSISTENCY OF CONCEPT

It is important that the identity system functions as a cohesive group of visual and verbal elements that serve to continually identify the client to its target audience(s). Consistency is central to effective branding. This does not preclude creativity. An identity system will fail if it is predictable and lifeless. Power, clarity, and freshness must accompany consistency.

CLARITY OF MESSAGE

The role of the identity system is to provide a visible and obvious shorthand that supports the intended image of the client. To achieve this, every graphic element within the identity system must clearly support the logo.

ACCOMMODATING TO THE CLIENT

When the system is developed, the designer must understand who will use it and how they will use it. With this information, the designer will be able to create a system that is graphically appropriate, and capable of both accommodating the requirements and reflecting the personality of the client. The designer must create a system that can be customized within the constraints of the client's needs.

FLEXIBILITY FOR USERS

The identity system must allow for an individual user's own modifications. As much as the original designer may not wish it, other creatives will use the identity system. Plan for enough variables in the system to keep the identity fresh.

What is a kit of parts?

Quite simply, it is all the core aspects of a complete identity design program. All these elements must be thought through and carefully determined:

Logo & Variations
- What is the main mark or signature? (e.g., icon only, icon + type)
- Are there variations? (e.g., horizontal, vertical)
- What changes get made to vary size? (e.g., redrawn for large scale use)
- What happens to the logo in various media? (e.g., thicker line weights for TV use)
- How are brand extensions handled? (e.g., a product logo)
- How does the logo work with other related logos? (e.g., trademark icon)

Color Palettes
- What is the primary color or color combination for the logo?
- Are there acceptable alternative colors?
- What about black and white usage?
- Can the logo be reversed? Reversed out of a containing shape only?
- What are the exact Pantone Matching System (PMS) numbers and CMYK, RGB values?

Containing Shapes
Is the logo designed to be contained within a particular shape? Always? Or only in specific circumstances?
- If so, what shape?
- Does the shape ever change?
- Does the shape contain anything other than the logo?

Typography Selection
- What is the primary typeface?
- Are there secondary fonts?
- Does the client need a range of weights? Italics too?
- What changes need to be made to the type selections in order to accommodate different media? (e.g., is the primary typeface a default font for web use or does an alternative need to be specified?)

Taglines and Modifying Copy
- What is the primary tagline?
- Is there a secondary or alternative tagline?
- What typeface are these set in?
- What is the size ratio of logo to tagline?
- Are there any other modifying copy or symbols required? (e.g., copyright symbol)
- Are there any legal lines or other mandatory copy which must be incorporated?

Imagery Specifications
If images, photographs, and/or illustrations are considered to be part of the identity system concept:
- How are they used?
- When are they used?
- In what size ratio and proximity to the logo?
- Is there an image library? Where does it exist? How is it accessed?
- What if additional images are required in the future?

Sound Signature
If the identity will be used in broadcast or web environments there will most likely be a sound component to develop:
- Is there a musical or tonal signature or sting? (e.g., Intel's chimes)
- When and how will sound elements be used?
- Will there be music? If so, what kind?

Animation
Again, if the identity will appear in other media besides print, especially broadcast or web environments, it may need to be animated:
- How will the logo behave when it is in motion? How does it move?
- How does it react with other visual and audio elements?
- When and how will the animated version of the logo be used?

logo palette

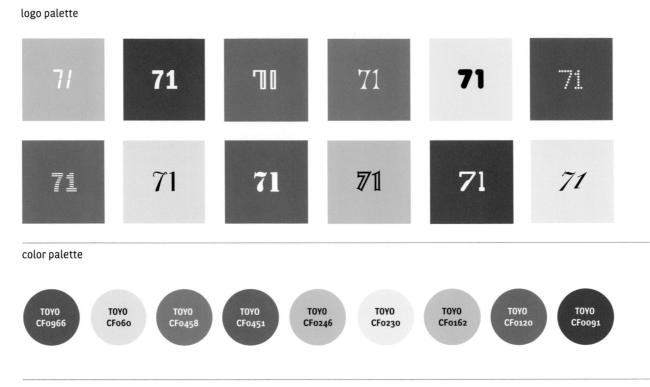

color palette

TOYO CF0966 TOYO CF060 TOYO CF0458 TOYO CF0451 TOYO CF0246 TOYO CF0230 TOYO CF0162 TOYO CF0120 TOYO CF0091

type palette

Franklin Gothic Condensed Demi

ABCDEFGHIJKLMNOPQRSTUVWXYZ
abcdefghijklmnopqrstuvwxyz
1234567890

Franklin Gothic Condensed Medium

ABCDEFGHIJKLMNOPQRSTUVWXYZ
abcdefghijklmnopqrstuvwxyz
1234567890

Franklin Gothic Condensed Demi Italic

ABCDEFGHIJKLMNOPQRSTUVWXYZ
abcdefghijklmnopqrstuvwxyz
1234567890

Franklin Gothic Condensed Medium Italic

ABCDEFGHIJKLMNOPQRSTUVWXYZ
abcdefghijklmnopqrstuvwxyz
1234567890

93

Hotel 71

Liska + Associates created an identity system for Hotel 71 that is fresh, fun, savvy, and inviting. Hotel 71 is a 450-room boutique hotel in Chicago. The designers were charged with reinventing the way travelers perceive the hotel experience. At the heart of the assignment was the creation of a brand image that would appeal to people looking for more than a bland, predicable lodging experience. The logo needed to be anything but predictable as well. In addition, the identity needed to work when applied to everything from the hotel's website to guest room incentive items to marketing materials to staff uniforms.

The Hotel 71 logo consists of a solid square of color, in one of twelve approved colors, with the numeral "71," in one of the twelve approved typefaces, reversed out of it. The various combinations of typography and block colors can convey a wide range of tones and messages—some serious, some more playful. This variety of choices allows any creative user working with the Hotel 71 system the ability to implement their own individual expression, as well as to maintain consistent branding.

93 (opposite)
The identity system developed by Liska + Associates emphasizes Hotel 71's unrepeatable experience and dynamic atmosphere. It specifies a set of changing colors and typefaces, allowing the hotel some flexibility in terms of the image it chooses to present. The identity also projects the idea that the hotel is welcoming rather than exclusive.
Liska + Associates

94
A series of direct mail postcards were created to provide Hotel 71 with a way to communicate information to existing and potential travel guests. The postcard set here includes four different postcards, which the hotel's sales department can use for printing information about its latest offers. Liska + Associates

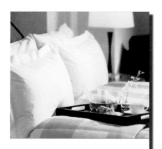

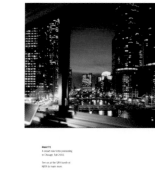

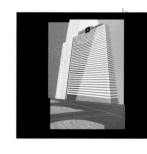

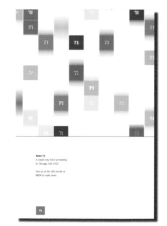

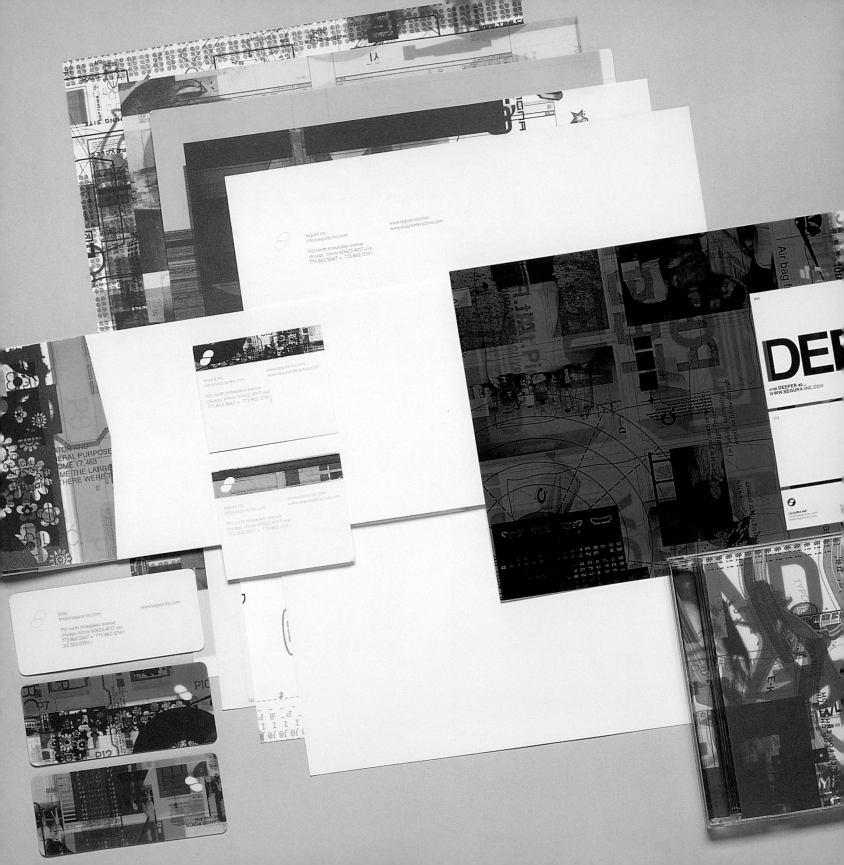

Segura, Inc.

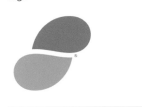

Segura, Inc. is an innovative design and advertising firm located in the United States whose principal, Carlos Segura, also heads T-26 Digital Type Foundry and 5-Inch CDs. Segura, Inc. needed to convey their own unique brand of creativity. The designers created a lush identity system, which has a heavy emphasis on photographic-based image patterns. These patterns appear on the backs of all corporate business materials required by the firm, while the logo itself is treated as a small, subtle visual element.

The Segura, Inc. identity system has an unusual, eclectic feeling that captures the brand image the firm wishes to convey. There is a visual reference to printers' "make-ready" test sheets that offset lithographers run through their press to set the machine and prepare for a print job. Being your own client is a huge challenge for many designers, but Segura, Inc. was clearly able to successfully rise to the occasion.

Sample Alphabet

ABCDEFGHIJKLMNOPQRSTUVWXYZ
abcdefghijklmnopqrstuvwxyz
0123456789

Patterns

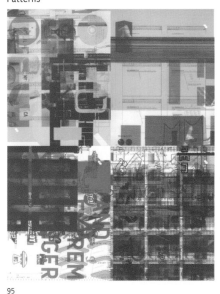

95

95
The Segura, Inc. identity system's kit of parts includes logo, typography, and visual patterns. Segura, Inc.

Photos, type, illustration, and color all combine to create an elegant and eclectic series of patterns in the identity system. The logo itself plays a more secondary role as can be seen in the Segura, Inc. business papers shown opposite. Segura, Inc.

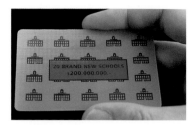

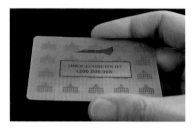

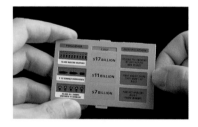

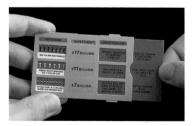

96

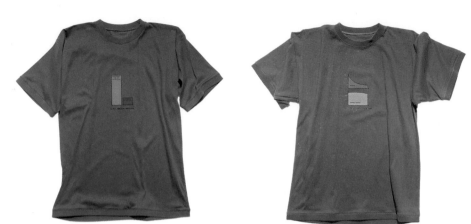

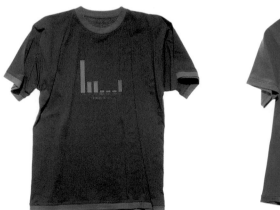

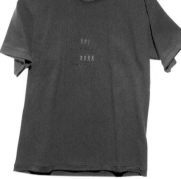

97

96
Sagmeister's goal of surprising people into consciousness is achieved with an interactive card that slides to reveal a comparison chart of government spending. The card illustrates such things as how many schools can be bought for the price of one jet. Sagmeister Inc.

97
The Move Our Money identity system pictured here contains a serious message within its fun, colorful graphics. This contemporary example of powerful graphic design conveys the client's opinion that the U.S government is spending too much money on its military, and that those funds should, instead, be diverted to health and education programs. The T-shirt graphics show various versions of the information graphics. Sagmeister Inc.

Move Our Money

Ben Cohen, of Ben & Jerry's Ice Cream, heads a political action group called Business Leaders for Sensible Priorities. The group launched "Move Our Money" as a nonprofit organization created to raise the consciousness of ordinary American citizens about the way their government allots huge amounts of its discretionary budget on military spending. Designer Stefan Sagmeister, who met and bonded with Cohen at a conference, volunteered to develop an identity system that clearly illustrated the facts, and disclosed how the money was being spent. Sagmeister created a pie chart logo as well as a series of simple charts and graphs, all designed to allow the viewer to grasp the message instantly.

Sagmeister used the system to design unique and accessible communication vehicles for communicating Move Our Money's various messages to its target audience. Nontraditional, simple, and playful media was used to impart serious messages: lenticular printing, a pen that pulled apart to reveal the American flag, huge inflatable plastic graphs, a traveling bus, and a mini-lapel. Sagmeister's goal was to try several different tones to convey the same message, which resulted in a deliberately kinetic identity system. Move Our Money has since taken on broader international issues and has morphed into a group called True Majority.

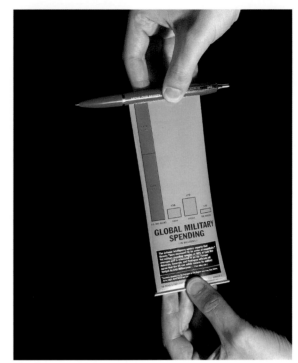

98

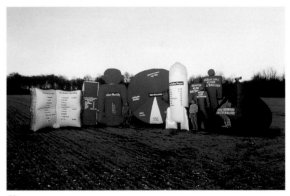

99

98-99
A ballpoint pen and large inflatables are clever ways, developed by Sagmeister Inc., of getting the Move Our Money message across to American citizens. Sagmeister Inc.

OK

Mr. Keedy, a type designer and CalArts graphic design faculty member, developed this dynamic identity system for OK. Located in Los Angeles, OK is a retail shop specializing in modern furnishings. The store is known for offering well-designed, and in some cases, rare, objects for home and personal use. It's a resource for good design, and Mr. Keedy was challenged to be just as unique and resourceful with his design.

The identity system is a collection of logos and text that are designed to work together as interchangeable elements rather than as fixed graphic images. This collection of idiosyncratic choices allows a variety of interpretations of the OK brand, which results in a fluid identity. The letterforms are innovative, with a wide variety of ideas—crazy and abstract, blocky and bold, clean and modern. Bursts and bars also work with the letterforms to create unique and interesting patterns.

OK is a variable identity system with a large range of approved logo and typographic elements. Each one of these elements is designed in, and is native to, Fontographer. Using a typography design software program such as Fontographer allows the logo to be a typeface rather than a traditional digital file (eps or tiff file). With a locked font, the designer eliminated the need for the client to own high-end graphics software to work with the identity. Mr. Keedy also circumvented the Macintosh/PC platform problems since the logo is a font that works in any program. All the identity elements are contained within the "font." This allows the client to easily use the logo, applying it to a variety of disparate applications.

100-102
All of the OK identity system is dynamic. Created in Fontographer, the system offers nearly infinite possibilities for combination. At right are various OK symbols, and opposite, are OK's address graphics. All these various elements are designed to fit together no matter what combination is selected (just like the letters in the typeface fit together.) Basically, Mr. Keedy delivered a graphic language, not a traditional logo that the client uses and evolves. It is a simple example of what Mr. Keedy thinks may be the future of branding. Mr. Keedy

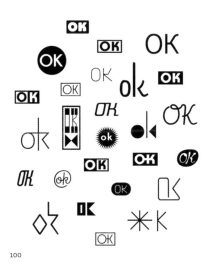

100

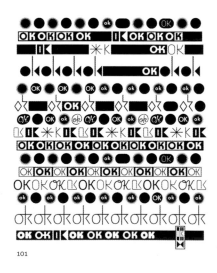

101

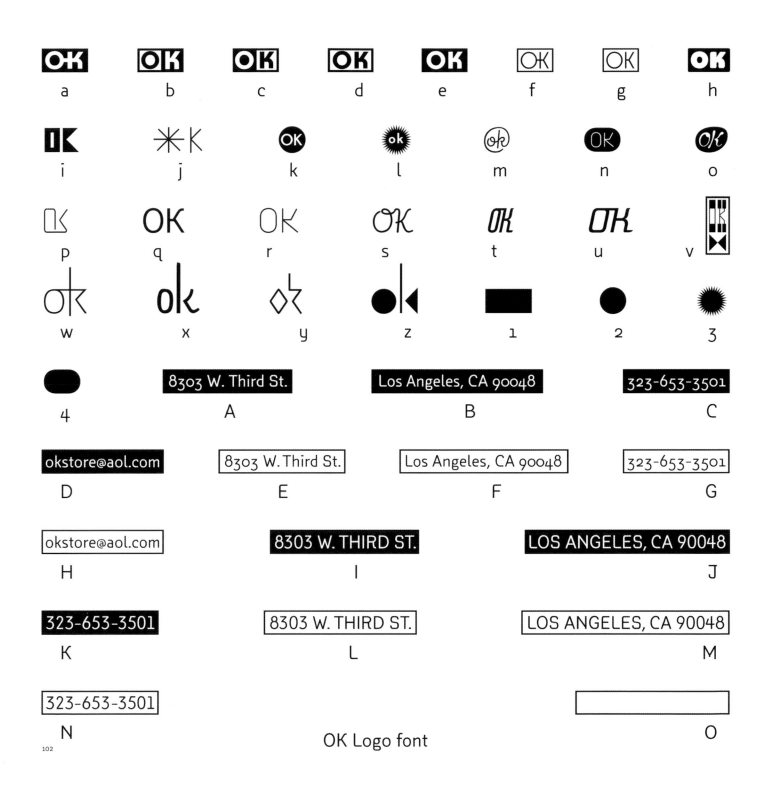

a   b   c   d   e   f   g   h

i   j   k   l   m   n   o

p   q   r   s   t   u   v

w   x   y   z   1   2   3

4

8303 W. Third St. — A

Los Angeles, CA 90048 — B

323-653-3501 — C

okstore@aol.com — D

8303 W. Third St. — E

Los Angeles, CA 90048 — F

323-653-3501 — G

okstore@aol.com — H

8303 W. THIRD ST. — I

LOS ANGELES, CA 90048 — J

323-653-3501 — K

8303 W. THIRD ST. — L

LOS ANGELES, CA 90048 — M

323-653-3501 — N

O

OK Logo font

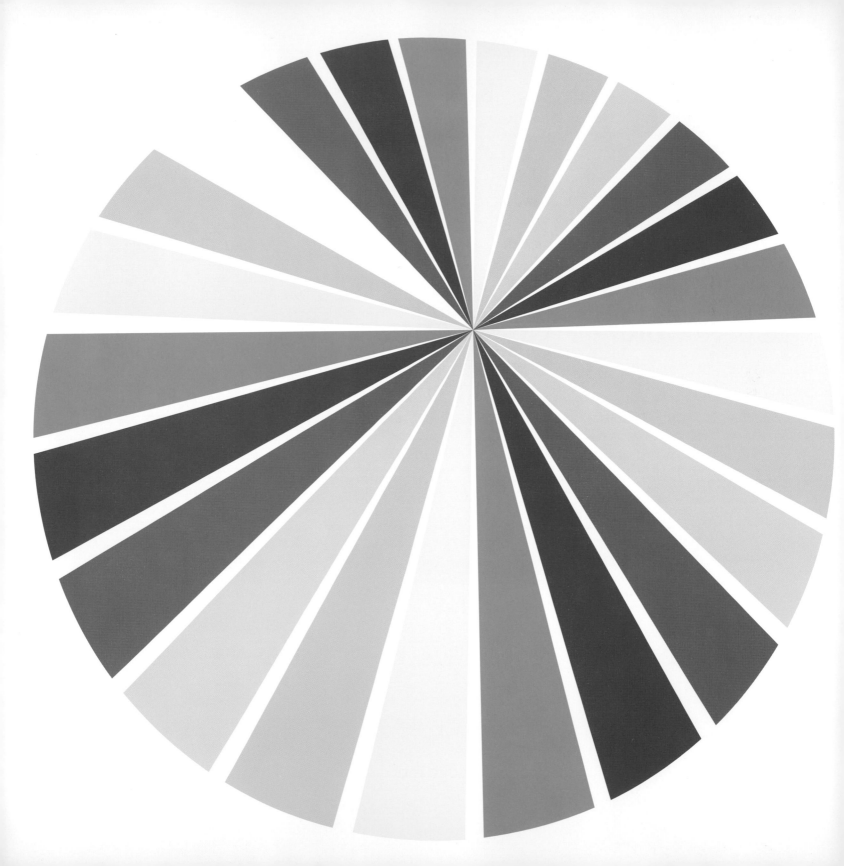

Implementing Logos

Rollout: process and best practices

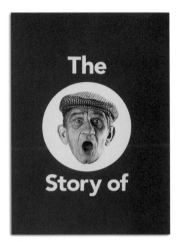

103

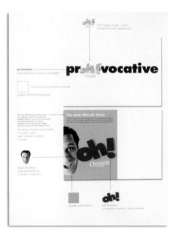

104

Now that the logo is created, an identity system is designed, and everything is approved by the client, the next step is rollout. Rollout means actually putting the logo to use in real-world scenarios. In order to prepare for these various applications of the logo, designers create identity standards manuals. This allows the original designer to visualize all the information needed to implement the logo successfully. It requires thinking through every possible use of the logo, and providing specific guidelines for those uses.

A comprehensive yet concise list of directions will save time, forestall bad design, and result in an effective message, even when designers new to the business are added. To paraphrase Milton Glaser, design which has been given minimal thought will have little value in the long run. Since the word design means to formulate a plan, creating a road map in the form of a standards manual is a key step in the process of designing a logo.

Standards manuals or guidelines allow identity systems to be managed properly—because they serve as the ultimate resource for consistent application of the logo throughout all communication and visual materials required by the client. Manuals function to ensure that the standards and ideas developed by the original designers are systematically and consistently reproduced in the same manner every time. It is vital that the logo be used properly over its lifetime, not only for the first six months of rollout when the original designer creates the first round of materials. Designers who take these extra steps are invaluable to their clients. This is one of the primary reasons that major corporate clients work repeatedly with design consultants who understand implementation and the role of identity guidelines. Informed clients, for example, understand the confusion and disorganization their brand image will suffer when something as simple as inconsistent color is used in the printing of their business cards.

103-104
The Oxygen Television Network's Oh! logo manual was designed in the form of two slim volumes—one covering print communications and the other providing guidelines for broadcast on-air usage—thereby allowing two completely different in-house creative departments to use the manual. AdamsMorioka, Inc.

Manuals must be created to be useful to the widest possible group of logo users. Often, in larger companies, there is an identity or branding coordinator who assures continuity and accurate use of the identity by following the graphic standards manual. In-house design departments are often the primary users of a graphic standards manual, but not all clients are large enough organizations to have such groups. All out-sourced designers will use the manual. Other in-house departments and related consultants that need the manual include: advertising, public relations, marketing, investor relations, merchandising, licensing, printers, package manufacturers, signage fabricators, vehicle and uniform supply companies, and all purchasing departments responsible for any of the above.

Getting all creatives and related consultants to use the standards manual will be of primary importance. A CEO that supports the new identity system is critical. Many manuals begin with a CEO letter. This letter states the support of the CEO, briefly explains the need for the identity, and directs the employees to support and correctly use the identity. This, in effect, makes brand stewards of the employees. If a designer has been able to lay the groundwork for acceptance, success is attainable.

The Politics of Rollout

Get buy-in for the identity system early in the development process. Seeds of discontent are sewn early, usually by the designer's failure to allow involvement from the people who will actually be using the logo day to day. When the logo is finished and ready for rollout, these users may find subtle (and sometimes not-so-subtle) ways to sabotage the new program. It is important to allow for participation and consensus-building during the creative process. Try to make sure that every stakeholder is heard from (typically this is done by requesting that they answer the briefing questions; see page 23) even if it is only a small team or one individual who actually interfaces with the design consultants.

Here is a strategy for successfully negotiating the politics of rollout:

- Allow everyone who has input into the development, approval, or implementation of the logo to voice their opinions up front—ideally in a structured manner.

- Present the logo at appropriate development stages to all relevant individuals so that they do not see only a finished logo at the end of the process.

- Empower the client coordinator with all relevant, as well as irrelevant, thinking, information, and rationale regarding the logo so that they can be an advocate for the new design.

- Create a user-friendly manual that is complete, concise, and flexible so that other creatives will enjoy working with the system.

- Provide technically refined identity elements in a central, well-known location so that users can work with the logo.

- Ask the CEO or department head to publicly endorse, explain, and validate the identity system.

- Stay in touch with the client, be available for questions, additional work, and periodic identity reviews/audits.

Graphic standards manuals can be slim and concise or multipaged behemoths, depending on the personality and needs of the client. Whether they are printed and bound pieces or whether they exist only on the client's intranet, identity guidelines are the key to consistent use of a logo.

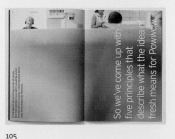 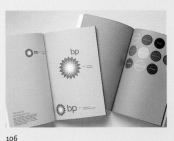 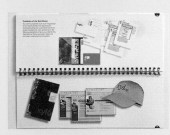

105   106   107

As a point of reference, we suggest you include any/all of these things in a graphic standards manual:

A. Introduction

CEO Letter
Brand Image Message
How to Use This Manual

B. Primary Identity Elements

Brand Overview
The Mark: Symbol & Logotype —————— **Can the logo be separated into a wordmark and symbol?**
Should it always remain connected?
Typography
Color Palette
Imagery/Iconography —————— **Do you use color, black-and-white, or special doutone images?**
Do you use illustration? If so, what type?
Shapes
Staging Requirements
Sizing
Acceptable Usage
Grids

C. Selected Identity Applications

Business Cards
Stationery
Business Forms —————— **Fax form, invoice, transmittal, etc.**
Environments
Signage: Interior & Exterior
Vehicles
Uniforms
Advertising —————— **How is it used on a billboard, full-page ad, or direct mail piece?**
Promotions —————— **Is it okay to put the logo on a backpack, cup, or toilet plunger?**
Marketing Materials
Corporate Communications
Online —————— **How does the logo work online? Does it animate?**
On-Air

D. Additional Information

Contact person & information —————— **Who should someone call when they are confused about usage?**

Standards manual pages from (105) Pow Wow designed by Wolff Olins, London;
(106) BP designed by Landor Associates, San Fransisco; and (107) XYIO designed
by Girvin, Seattle, are pictured at left.

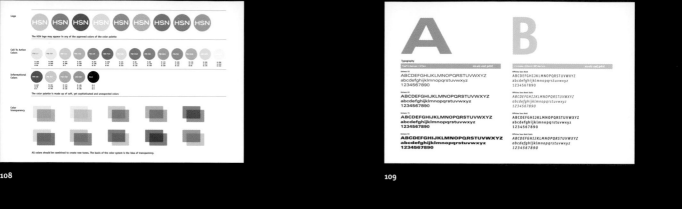

A manual can be as small as a one-page pdf file showing the logo, type, and color palette, or as large as

a 300-page printed and bound book with a companion CD full of the same information in digital form. It

can be printed with limited edition laser printouts or four-color process offset. The idea is to design a set

of guidelines that serves the needs of both the identity system and the client. After the logo designing

process, a designer will understand the work process and personality of thier client. This information will

help decide which format will be most successful.

Having a printed manual, or printing one on demand, allows the client to have a physical object which

makes the guidelines seem more real to most users. Additionally, putting the entire manual, or appropriate

segments, on the client's intranet or extranet is a smart idea for large, multiuser enterprises. Consider that

the implementation of the logo will grow and possibly change, so creating a three-ring binder style manual

that allows for additional pages to be added in the future is also a good idea. The exact length of the manual

will be determined by the specific needs of the client, but should contain representative pieces illustrating

how the logo has been applied. The size and scope of a graphics standards manuals is also heavily impacted

by budget considerations. Designers need to understand what these parameters are, and develop a manual

that works within these limits. The goal here is to be thorough yet flexible.

metropolitanmarket

110

SamataMason, a corporate identity and communications design consultancy based in Chicago, created the identity for Metropolitan Market, Food Markets Northwest, Inc.'s new retail store venture. Metropolitan Market is a collection of neighborhood grocery stores originally known as Thriftway. When the business model changed from a discount provider to a gourmet destination, SamataMason was asked to capture and project the organization's growing and unique character. The client needed an identity that was a quick read with fresh graphic appeal, a visual language that would speak to the active, urban, and upscale customer in a distinctive contemporary fashion. It was important that the branded personality said to its young, adventure-shopper customer base, "this is your place."

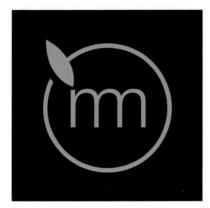

111

108-109
The identity system standards for the Home Shopping Network is depicted in a single sheet format. AdamsMorioka, Inc.

110-111
Metropolitan Market is a chain of high-end, urban boutique grocery stores whose identity reflects a name change and a new business model for the client. SamataMason

112-113
SamataMason understood the importance of buy-in for the new identity program. They helped to ensure company-wide acceptance and appropriate usage of the identity by developing a graphic standards manual that contains both a letter from the CEO endorsing the program and a statement explaining the importance of consistent standards.
SamataMason

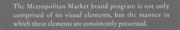

112

113

Brand Overview

With this new brand, a distinctive image program is launched to set Metropolitan Market apart from the competition, while providing a recognizable "face" to the organization, its services and dedicated people across the area.

Consistent application across many mediums and throughout the organization's many service communities is key to its success.

The core system elements (mark, signature, color palette and typography) are specifically integrated throughout the program.

MARK

COLOR PALETTE

| Pantone 618 | Pantone 425 | Pantone 422 | Black | Metallic Silver |

TYPOGRAPHY

Stempel Garamond Family
AaBbCcDdEeFfGgHhIiJjKkLlMmNnOoPpQqRrSsTtUuVvWwXxYyZz
!@#$$%^&*()_+=-123456789

Helvetica Neue Family (both Condensed and Regular)
AaBbCcDdEeFfGgHhIiJjKkLlMmNnOoPpQqRrSsTtUuVvWwXxYyZz
!@#$$%^&*()_+=-123456789

Metropolitan Market Graphic Standards

Brand Mark and Signature Display

The three-color brand signature represents the organization on all corporate communications materials (i.e. corporate stationery, shopping bags, brochures, collateral and advertising) and should be displayed in the following manner:

Reverse Usage – Preferred

MARK "circle m" Pantone® 618, or reversed to white.
LOGOTYPE "metropolitan" reversed out; "market" solid Pantone® 422 grey (for two color applications use a 40% screen of black).

Positive Usage – Acceptable

MARK ONLY "circle m" Pantone 618, Pantone Silver, Pantone 425 Grey or black.
LOGOTYPE "metropolitan" solid Pantone 425 grey; "market" solid Pantone 422 grey (for two color applications use a 50% screen of Pantone 425)

REVERSE USAGE – PREFERRED

Dark background is preferred, with a minimum 60 percent color tint.

POSITIVE USAGE – ACCEPTABLE

White background is preferred, with a maximum 30 percent color tint.

Metropolitan Market Graphic Standards

114
Metropolitan Market's founder, CEO, and president Terry Halverson's unique vision and creativity moved SamataMason to its fresh, focused, and personality-rich brand solution. Theirs was an open and collaborative identity development process. SamataMason

115
The Metropolitan Market visual brand strategy is presented in the form of a 102-page book that is laser printed and spiral bound. The graphic standards are also available in pdf form for review on screen or for laser printing. To maintain viewer interest, the manual is interspersed with photographic duotone image pages displaying a variety of fruits and vegetables. It is divided into eleven sections: Introduction, Brand Elements, Business Papers, Typing Templates, Exterior Signage, Interior Signage, Labels (because this is an extensive program within itself, this manual refers users to a separate labels-only manual), Customer Promotions, Advertising, and Uniforms. SamataMason

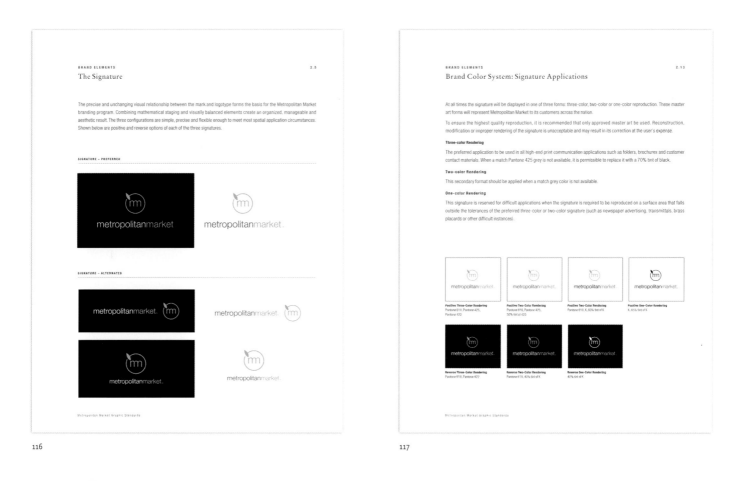

116

The graphic standards manual works to provide direction, guidance, and rules that best project and maintain the identification platform in a clear and friendly manner. It is obvious from the professionalism displayed in the document that a strict branding program exists and that specific guidelines must be upheld for the identity program to succeed. SamataMason

117

SamataMason requests that creative users of the new Metropolitan Market System carefully study and adhere to the guidelines they have established for the brand. Through use of this document they have been able to effectively communicate the essence of their identity while conveying the personality of the client, consequently building brand champions out of the staff users. A "Brand Overview" page provides an at-a-glance view of all core identity elements. The entire manual is written in simple language that even nondesigners can easily comprehend. SamataMason

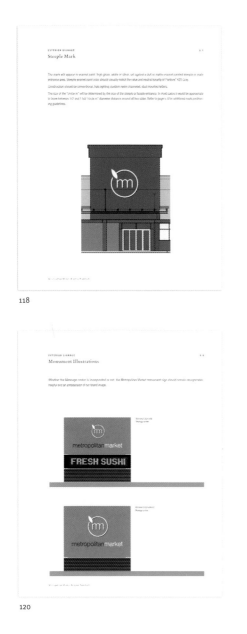

EXTERIOR SIGNAGE
Steeple Mark

118

INTERIOR SIGNAGE
Chalkboard Header Examples

FLOWER GARDEN   PRODUCE

DELI

119

EXTERIOR SIGNAGE
Monument Illustrations

metropolitan market

FRESH SUSHI

metropolitan market

120

EXTERIOR SIGNAGE
Examples of Locations

metropolitan

metropolitan

metropolitan

121

118-122
The Metropolitan Market in-store visual experience is colorful and active, providing almost too much visual stimulation. To counteract the busy atmosphere, SamataMason chose a muted olive color with an accompanying neutral palette, and designed clean, modern, fashion-driven graphic elements that would appeal to the younger high-end urban customers.

The new Metropolitan Market logo (or "circle m") represents a sense of organized artisanship that is meaningful and rich in texture. The strict mathematical relationship of the "circle m" logo elements may not be altered or modified—it is a precise and unchanging ratio. A page such as "Brand Mark and Signature Display" helps users understand the relationship between the identity elements, and illustrates preferred and secondary usage options.

"The Signature" manual page explains the rationale behind the staging and visual balance of the identity elements. It shows three configurations, all of which are simple, precise, and flexible enough to meet most spatial applications. Offering options to users is a key strategy in designing a logo that works in the real world of communication.

The Metropolitan Market graphic standards includes a "Brand Mark Color Usage" page, which provides a quick reference to the approved colors, not only by listing the Pantone numbers, but by showing an example of what the logo looks like in each color version. The entire "Brand Elements" section of this manual contains very detailed information on: Staging Requirements, Sizing, Acceptable and Unacceptable Usage Variations, Positioning Methodology, Color Systems, Signature Applications, Typography, Design Motifs, Photographic Themes, and Grid Systems— all in an easy to use layout. This thorough yet accessible approach virtually eliminates confusion on how to use the Metropolitan Market identity system.

Directional Signs

All directional signage in the parking lot will utilize the Helvetica Neue family of typefaces:

MAIN MESSAGE   Helvetica Neue Condensed Light, caps and lowercase

SUPPLEMENTAL MESSAGE   Helvetica Neue Condensed Medium, caps and lowercase

TYPE SIZES AND LAYOUT   Apply the universal grid and size all type appropriately, as illustrated below; refer to page 2.20 for
                        universal grid information

Other sign specifications:

SIGN HEIGHT   Preferred – 60", if variance is required, size appropriately to meet local sign ordinances

SIGN PROPORTIONS   1:2 ratio (direction or informational)

SIGN FACE COLOR   A visual exterior, enamel paint color match to Pantone® 425 Gray

STRIPED BAND   Vinyl to match Pantone® 425 Gray; refer to page 5.7 for specifications

TYPOGRAPHY/SYMBOLS   White (non-illuminated: white vinyl; internally illuminated: poly carbonate, routed and flush fitted letters)

SIGN ILLUMINATION   Preferred—internally illuminated

MANUFACTURING   Painted aluminum, routed and flush fitted plexi lettering, concrete footing mounted

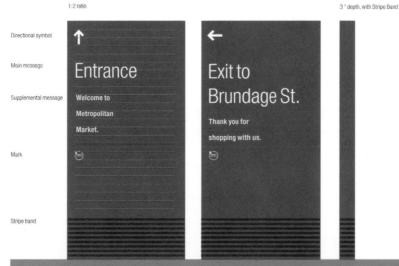

Worth the Time and Money (Even if Both Are Limited)

Creating a great graphic standards manual can be a long and difficult job, but effectively launching and rolling out a new logo and identity system requires an intelligent set of standards and guidelines. A client who values design and understands its impact on business will invest in a design consultant to manage a well-planned identity rollout. This will save time, money, confusion, and frustration. And it will maintain the desired message in other hands. A designer should always include the development of a graphic standards manual as a separate line item in proposals for an identity project.

In some cases, the rollout of the new identity system must be done swiftly, with many applications designed and produced within a compacted time frame. This allows no time to create a formal printed manual. AdamsMorioka created the logo and identity system for the 2003 Sundance Film Festival, which is only a two-week event, but it is announced and promoted globally over a six-month period. There were at least one hundred pieces using the Sundance Film Festival logo, including printed booklets, catalogs, direct mail, advertising,a website, movie trailers, badges, swag, merchandise, signage, and tickets— all created within approximately three months. The identity system had minimal elements, and simple guidelines, which were shared with a variety of creative consultants simultaneously.

AdamsMorioka developed a one-page set of identity guidelines as a poster, and a pdf file on the AdamsMorioka ftp website. A "Matrix of Applications" was created, which included an image of each individual application, specifications, and schedule information. This allowed everyone working on the festival to hang up two posters in their offices and be able to understand the entire system and its applications.

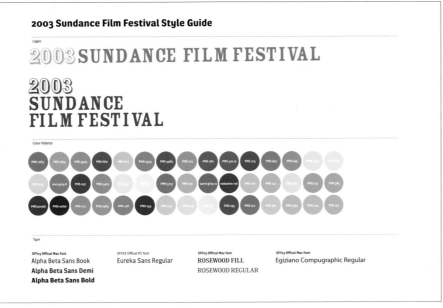

2003 Sundance Film Festival Style Guide

Logos

2003 SUNDANCE FILM FESTIVAL

2003
SUNDANCE
FILM FESTIVAL

Color Pallette

Type

SFF03 Offical Mac font
Alpha Beta Sans Book
Alpha Beta Sans Demi
Alpha Beta Sans Bold

SFF03 Offical PC font
Eureka Sans Regular

SFF03 Offical Mac font
ROSEWOOD FILL
ROSEWOOD REGULAR

SFF03 Offical Mac font
Egiziano Compugraphic Regular

123

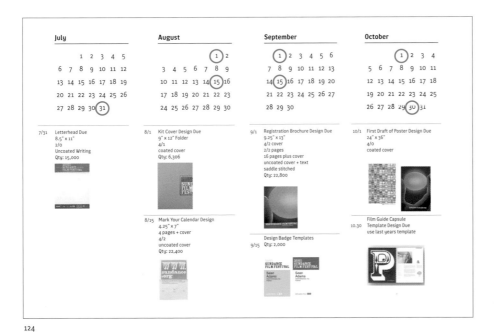

July

		1	2	3	4	5
6	7	8	9	10	11	12
13	14	15	16	17	18	19
20	21	22	23	24	25	26
27	28	29	30	31		

August

					1	2
3	4	5	6	7	8	9
10	11	12	13	14	15	16
17	18	19	20	21	22	23
24	25	26	27	28	29	30

September

1	2	3	4	5	6
7	8	9	10	11	12	13
14	15	16	17	18	19	20
21	22	23	24	25	26	27
28	29	30				

October

1	2	3	4
5	6	7	8	9	10	11
12	13	14	15	16	17	18
19	20	21	22	23	24	25
26	27	28	29	30	31	

7/31 Letterhead Due
8.5" x 11"
2/0
Uncoated Writing
Qty: 15,000

8/1 Kit Cover Design Due
9" x 12" Folder
4/1
coated cover
Qty: 6,306

8/15 Mark Your Calendar Design
4.25" x 7"
4 pages + cover
4/2
uncoated cover
Qty: 22,400

9/1 Registration Brochure Design Due
9.25" x 13"
4/2 cover
2/2 pages
16 pages plus cover
uncoated cover + text
saddle stitched
Qty: 22,800

Design Badge Templates
9/15 Qty: 2,000

10/1 First Draft of Poster Design Due
24" x 36"
4/0
coated cover

Film Guide Capsule
10.30 Template Design Due
use last years template

124

123-124
The Sundance Film Festival requires a range of materials to be developed in a relatively short period of time. AdamsMorioka simplified the identity standards to create two posters. This maintained a common understanding of the rollout of the Sundance Film Festival identity. AdamsMorioka, Inc.

Cityplanning
1980 : : : 2001

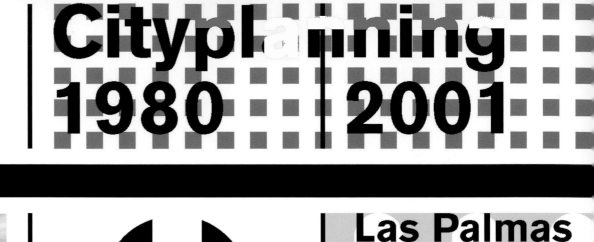

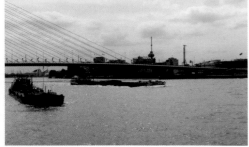

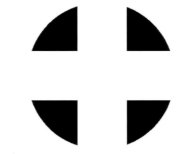

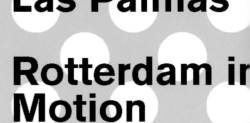

Las Palmas

Rotterdam in Motion

Reading 'Charlene'
Interpictorial Dialogue
Kelly vs Johns

Havens & Heerlijkheden

City of Rotterdam

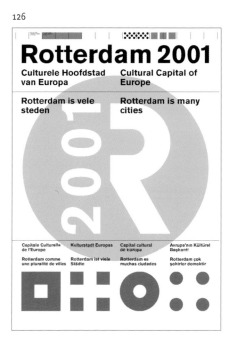

125-126
The identity by the design team of Linda van Deursen and Armand Mevis for the multicultural City of Rotterdam was designed to connect and promote arts and cultural institutes to residents and visitors. Mevis & van Deursen

A variety of graphic elements are presented in a page from the City of Rotterdam standards manual. Mevis & van Deursen

Mevis & van Deursen, in collaboration with the cultural department of the City of Rotterdam, accepted the challenge of branding an entire city. The goal was to promote the cultural aspects of the city and enhance the perception of the city's attractiveness, both to citizens and visitors. Rotterdam is considered to be one of the cultural capitals of Europe, and the city's mayor sought to utilize this association.

At the heart of the design problem was the need to develop an identity that would connect all the various cultural activities in Rotterdam. The identity had to function as a logo system, and it needed to be flexible enough to allow other designers to use it. Users needed to receive clear guidelines in order to be able to "play" with the system.

Mevis & van Deursen designed the logo system knowing that it would be handed off to many other designers, so a graphic standards manual was created. Mevis & van Deursen worked with the logo system through the implementation of the stationery and the first series of posters. Subsequently, numerous other designers became involved with the project. Mevis & van Deursen were aware that this dissemination would occur, and created a user friendly, "damage proof" system. A large range of successful pieces were created, but certain items were designed in a manner Mevis & van Deursen disliked. At a certain point though the original designer must give up control of the creation. Although it may be difficult, it is inevitable. All of which reinforces the need for good a graphics standards manual.

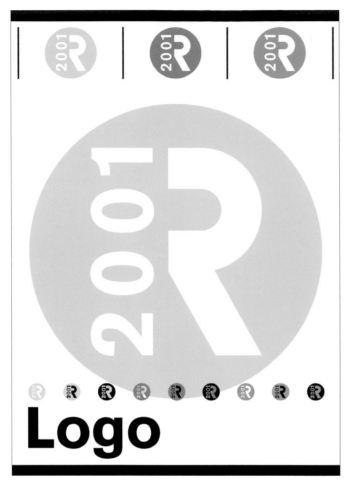

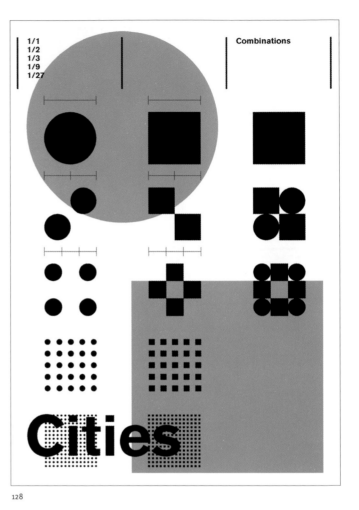

127
The City of Rotterdam identity system is targeted at a vast audience, made up of a diverse population living in a large, multicultural city. Despite this, Mevis & van Deursen chose to use the visual language that is traditionally directed to a culturally aware audience.

Although Mevis & van Deursen had relevant experience with culturally themed assignments (they had done work for theater, art, design, and architecture organizations), they did not have much experience with complex identities until the City of Rotterdam project. The designers exceeded expectations and developed an innovative, fresh, kinetic identity system and a template for a comprehensive print program. For the design of the city's website they collaborated with Mauritz de Bruijn.

128
Conceptually, the designers combined multiple ideas in creating the identity system. Formal needs, such as schedules and logistics, drove the visual form of a white information banner that appears on all print materials. The banner can be interpreted as a river of information, an idea referential to the river Maas in Rotterdam.

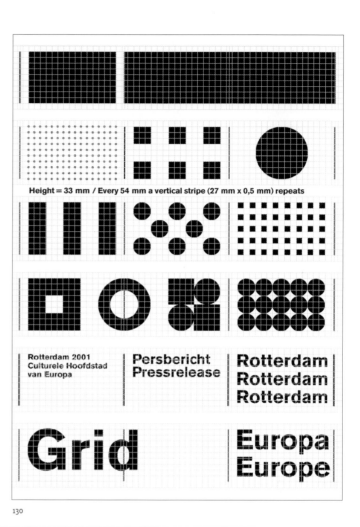

129

In creating an identity system for the city, Rotterdam's cultural director, Bert van Meggelen, chose to integrate the idea that Rotterdam is actually composed of many cities; a theory based on Italo Calvino's book, *Invisible Cities*. Following this idea, the designers used either dots or squares to represent these "cities" on a map. A collection of repeating dots and squares was subsequently developed, which could be recombined to form abstract logos symbolizing multiple cities.

130

According to Mevis & van Deursen the colors used in the City of Rotterdam identity system were not specific to conceptual ideas. Rather, practical considerations dictated the color palette. Because most of the logo applications would be printed in four-color process CMYK, the designers chose magenta and cyan as the main colors. In Mevis & van Deursen's opinion, green can be problematic in a four-color process; accordingly they tried to avoid using it in the system. Two key components in the logo system were grids and the typography selection, Berthold Akzidenz Grotesk, chosen for its clarity and versatility. The identity system designed by Mevis & van Deursen works to represent the actual, as well as the aspirational, image of the City of Rotterdam.

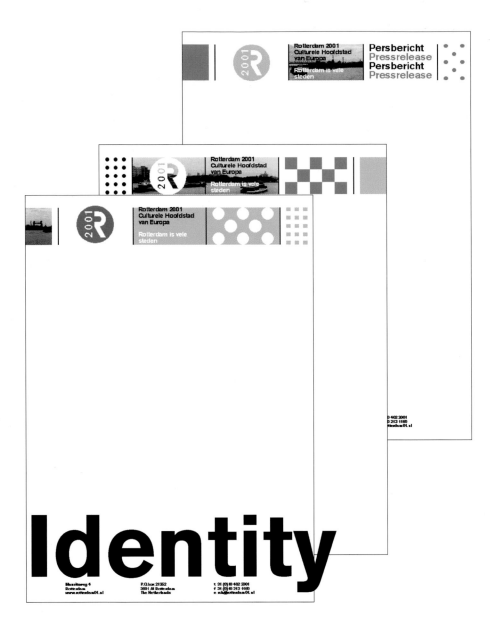

When all the graphic elements are combined, as seen in the samples of the stationery and business cards, the City of Rotterdam logo system comes together as a lively and contemporary visual solution, rich with layers of meaning. The city's identity system is a tool box. The graphic tools provided were fairly fixed, but the creative users of the system could manipulate them to create a variety of forms. With this flexibility, the designers created a nontraditional manual that clearly conveyed the visual concepts of the identity system, and provided a wealth of typical application samples.

It is important to remember that even if a designer has created a great logo, designed a complete, yet flexible, identity system, put it all in a well-conceived, well-presented graphics standards manual, the client (and/or other creative users) can still develop items that would never be approved by the original designers. Make the work as "foolproof" as possible, but understand that creative people may feel compelled to subvert the system in order to assert their creativity. Remember the advice of designer Tibor Kalman: "Rules are good. Break them." Allow for change. Expect it.

Staying Involved: Auditing Systems

Once the development and rollout phases are complete, the designer should stay involved with the client to monitor the identity programs they have created. Some designers continue working with the client, designing everything required, which ensures brand continuity. If that is not an option, try to secure a consulting arrangement with the client. Typically, a designer will provide intensive, on-site art direction in the first few months following the launch of a new logo. They may then taper off to monthly, quarterly, and perhaps, annual reviews.

At these periodic implementation reviews:

- Specifically review any benchmarks that were set up.

- Do a visual audit of the client's communication materials and other applications of the identity.

- Review consistency of usage in design and messaging.

- Determine if the identity assets are being managed well. Is the system available to all users?

- Interview users. Hear what their issues and concerns are, or simply collect platitudes on how well the identity system works.

- Problem-solve solutions for cases in which the new identity system is not working.

- Review the quality of the printing, fabrication, and manufacturing of items using the new identity system to ensure that suppliers are adhering to guidelines. See how well the identity is holding up technically. Note quality-control issues.

- Check that the identity system is evolving to meet the client's expanding needs.

- Alert the client to any changes in the competitive landscape that might impact the identity system.

- Evaluate how well the client is doing with the new identity. Note what is exceptional (both good and bad).

- Put your findings into a written report and/or follow up with an analysis presentation meeting.

- Validate great creative thinking. Identify successful applications and the people involved.

- Empower those in charge of the identity system to help ensure accountability. Make sure that they have implemented a method that works to maintain the system.

- Express your commitment to ongoing excellence, and stress your availability for consultation.

- Determine additional opportunities for working with the client.

- Request an invitation to provide a bid/proposal for new projects. Use this as a sales opportunity.

Nickelodeon

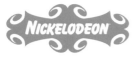

Nickelodeon, a children's entertainment company owned by Viacom, had been growing organically over fifteen years to become a multifaceted global brand. In the process, however, it had become disjointed and was losing some of its cohesion. The original logo, designed by Tom Corey, needed an update and expansion. AdamsMorioka was brought in as identity consultants with a goal of bringing together Nickelodeon's brand extensions, as well as unifying the company's messages and visual vocabulary across all media. Overall, the brand needed to be more accessible and less oblique to Nickelodeon's external, as well as internal, audience.

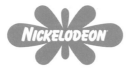

AdamsMorioka designed a simple identity toolkit based on the original logo. The identity system was intended to refocus Nick's internal creative departments on the core promises and messages of the brand, and encourage creative thinking and execution.

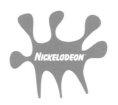

AdamsMorioka designed the Nickelodeon Visual System Basics as an explanation of the new visual system. The thirty-eight page book is a 10" x 10" (25 cm x 25 cm) spiral bound booklet with several short sheets and a gatefold. It contains a CD with digital files for the system. The manual reflects the identity and message, is lively and nontraditional, and focuses on positive inspiration. A list of the creative sources that may inform some of the system's ideas is provided in the manual. This encourages the Nickelodeon creative services department to look at new sources, from Paul Rand and Alvin Lustig to Andy Warhol and Alexander Calder. Rather than using these sources as forms to slavishly copy, they provide insight into basic ideas of modernism. The manual is bright, fun, concise, and easy to follow.

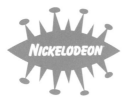

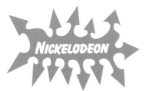

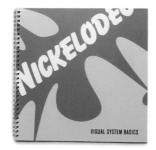

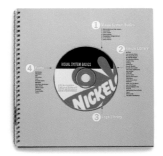

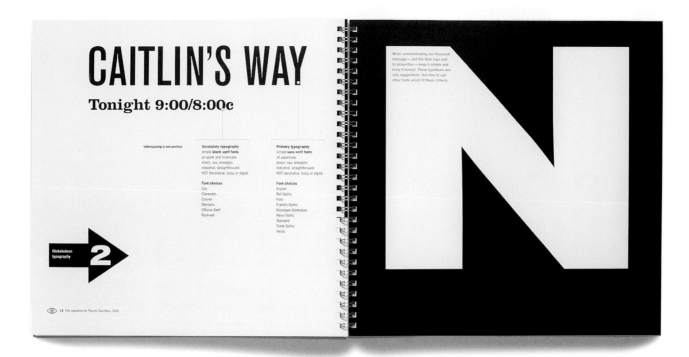

CAITLIN'S WAY

Tonight 9:00/8:00c

letterspacing is not perfect

Secondary typography
simple **black serif fonts**
all upper and lowercase
direct, raw, energetic
industrial, straightforward
NOT decorative, fussy or digital

Font choices
City
Clarendon
Courier
Memphis
Officina Serif
Rockwell

Primary typography
simple **sans serif fonts**
all uppercase
direct, raw, energetic
industrial, straightforward
NOT decorative, fussy or digital

Font choices
Airport
Bell Gothic
Folio
Franklin Gothic
Monotype Grotesque
News Gothic
Standard
Trade Gothic
Venus

Nickelodeon typography → 2

When communicating our focussed message — and the Nick logo and its properties — keep it simple and keep it honest. These typefaces are only suggestions; feel free to use other fonts which fit these criteria.

13. Title sequence for Psycho. Saul Bass, 1960.

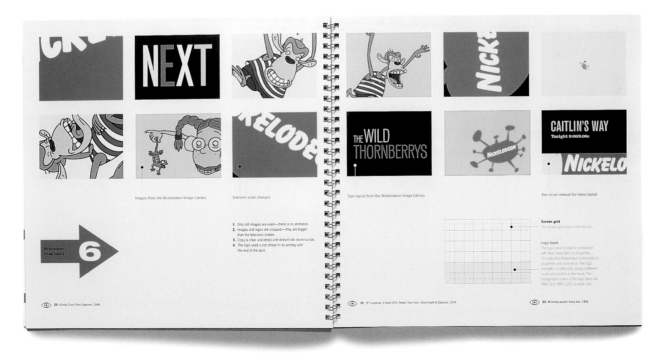

Images from the Nickelodeon Image Library

Extreme scale changes

1. Only still images are used — there is no animation.
2. Images and logos are cropped — they are bigger than the television screen.
3. Copy is clear and direct and doesn't talk down to kids.
4. The logo used is not shown in its entirety until the end of the spot.

Nickelodeon on-air basics → 6

Type layout from the Nickelodeon Image Library

See on-air manual for menu layout

Screen grid
The screen grid uses a field division.

Logo band
The logo band is used in conjunction with Nick characters or properties. This links the Nickelodeon brand with its properties and vice-versa. The logo animates, in stills only, using a different scale and position in the band. The background colors in the logo band are PMS 116, PMS 1205 or black only.

20. Along Chair. Eero Saarinen, 1948.

21. "9" sculpture, 9 West 57th Street, New York. Chermayeff & Geismar, 1974.

22. Milantes poster. Herb Itoh, 1954.

Case Studies

Case Study Contents

| AdamsMorioka, Inc. | Creative Directors: Sean Adams, Noreen Morioka | Designers: Jennifer Hopkins, Volker Dürre |

CALARTS

CalArts is a multidisciplinary college encompassing fine art, graphic design, photography, film and video, theater, music, and dance. Founded by Walt Disney in 1971, the school quickly formed a reputation as an epicenter of the avant-garde. The original logo, however, had been considered too stifling and not representative of the school's attitude. Lacking a clear identity, the CalArts community—potential students, faculty, and donors—was being lost. To get the school back on track it was decided that a logo and visual system that included the multidimensional attitudes of the school's diverse population and that also spoke confidently to potential donors was needed.

The design process, which included approvals from the heads of each school (music, art, etc.), was complex. Over the course of six months and numerous meetings, a firm criteria was eventually developed. An internal sense of ownership was critical. The final mark, in two-dimensional form, can be utilized in a conservative fund-raising context; alternatively, the three-dimensional mark and multifaceted color palette can be used on communications to other audiences, such as potential and current students. The form of the mark is purposefully neutral, allowing the surrounding context to supply meaning. The decision to simplify the name California Institute of the Arts to CalArts and add the school names was made to facilitate development and enrollment.

The Calendar of Events newsletter prototype utilizes the three-dimensional version of the CalArts idenity.

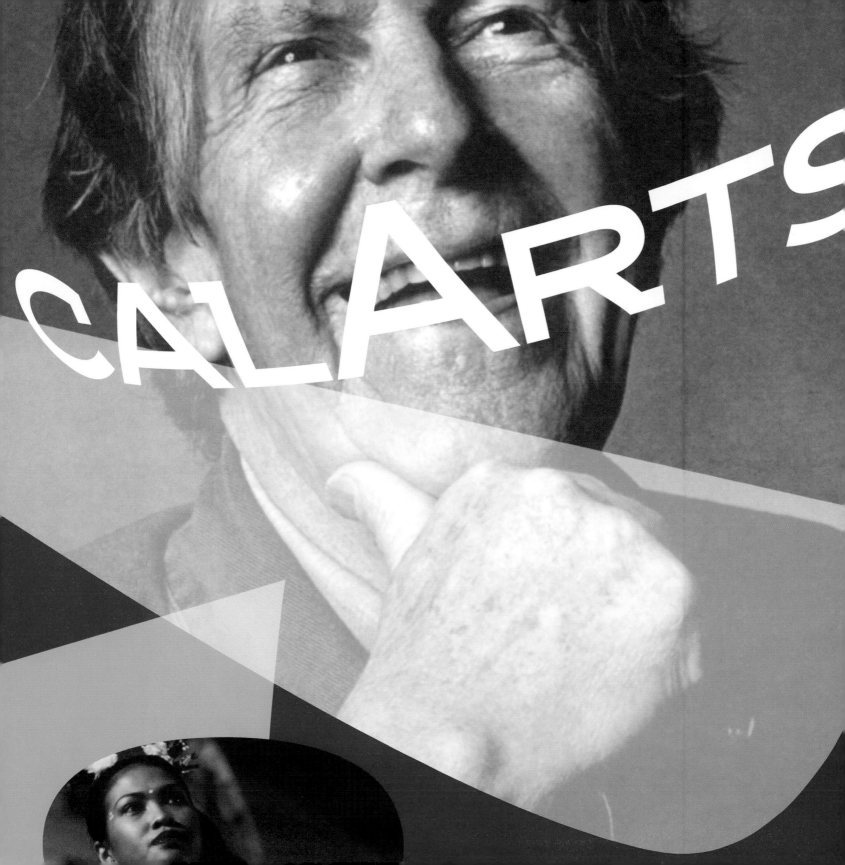

CALARTS

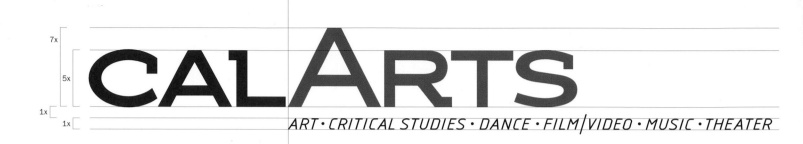

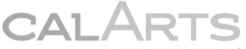
ART·CRITICAL STUDIES · DANCE · FILM/VIDEO · MUSIC · THEATER

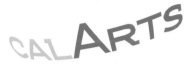
ART·CRITICAL STUDIES · DANCE · FILM/VIDEO · MUSIC · THEATER

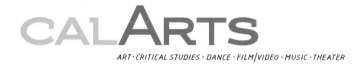
ART·CRITICAL STUDIES · DANCE · FILM/VIDEO · MUSIC · THEATER

ART · CRITICAL STUDIES · DANCE · FILM/VIDEO · MUSIC · THEATER

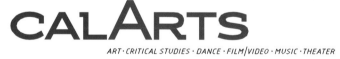
ART·CRITICAL STUDIES · DANCE · FILM/VIDEO · MUSIC · THEATER

ART · CRITICAL STUDIES · DANCE · FILM/VIDEO · MUSIC · THEATER

The three-dimensional logo "lives" on a sphere, allowing its user to rotate the mark in space. The sphere is never revealed, it exists only as a hidden underlying structure that informs the shape of the logo.

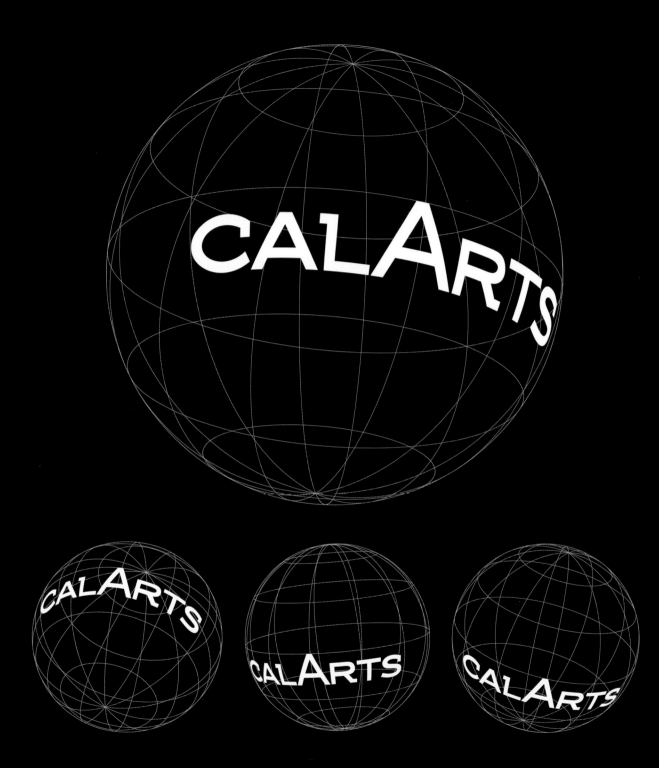

The Blue Gallery

The Blue Gallery is an independent gallery providing a venue for young contemporary artists, as well as a platform for the exploration of other aesthetic avenues, such as the relationship between science and art. Over a ten-year period the gallery had grown, relocated three times, and had undergone three identity revisions—all designed by Atelier. Currently, the gallery's logo is formed from the fusion of a "b" and a "g." The resulting abstraction is always recognizable, even when it has to compete with the most striking work of an artist—a key issue when designing an invite, press advertisement, poster, or catalog.

In many respects, the personality, culture, and brand attributes of The Blue Gallery are expressed through the fresh new work continually emerging from their artists. In this case, it would have been wrong for Atelier to help define a set of values and to impose an appropriate graphic structure onto all The Blue Gallery communications. Instead, the energy and creativity of the artists themselves make up the identity of The Blue Gallery.

The primary target audience that Atelier was designing for was the art buyers. It was important for this audience to recognize and become familiar with every item of communication from the gallery. Prospective buyers needed to be constantly updated on new exhibitions, and they needed to form the impression that the gallery was very much alive, with an essential vibrancy. The secondary target audience, the art critics, was a more difficult lot to cater to because the critics are quite savvy, and many artists and galleries compete for their attention. The final audience the design needed to resonate with was the artists themselves. For designer Ian Chilvers, this was the joy of working with the gallery— the chance to collaborate with artists, the most challenging people when it comes to design. After spending years preparing for a show, and after the exhibition has been shown and sold, often all the artist has left is a catalog. So what designers do is really important to fine artists, by both creating a record of, and interest in, their work.

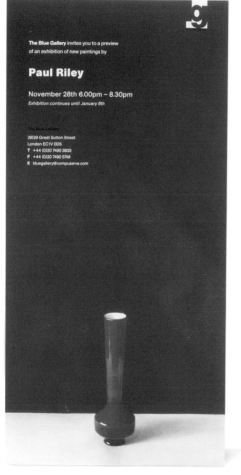

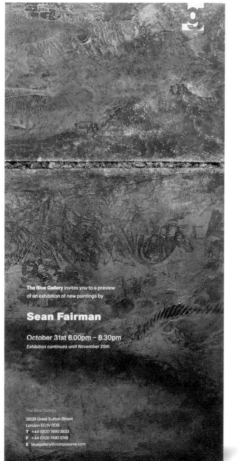

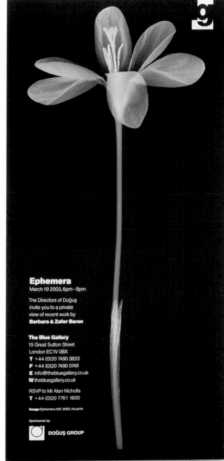

Show Posters, seen above, are very
important applications of The Blue Gallery
identity. In these pieces, the logo must
stand out but not compete with the
images of the artists' work.

When Atelier first started working with the gallery, there didn't seem to be any independent galleries with strong identities; they all had their stand-alone logos, but never seemed to make it beyond a letterhead. Atelier was determined to bring a synergy to all The Blue Gallery communications, and they achieved this by using a single typeface and adopting a reverential respect for the work of every artist. With this attitude, the gallery owners left the designers alone to work directly with the featured artists.

The logo is compact and graphically simple. It looks the way it does because it functions purely as a marker, reminding clients of the gallery. The logo had to work on many applications: invites and catalogs (where it acts as a "tag" on the artists' work), press advertisements (where it has to work in very crowded surroundings and often with low screen values), and on the gallery's website (where it has to work digitally). Atelier has refrained from applying it directly onto the gallery, as this is where the artists' work should prevail.

Because the gallery is always in a state of evolution, its identity can never be considered complete. As mentioned above, this is the third development of the logo in ten years. For some this may be heresy, but for The Blue Gallery it is important to be continually refreshed.

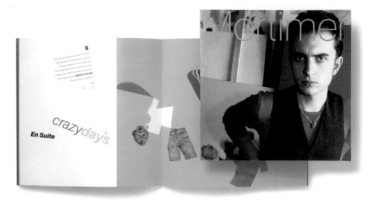

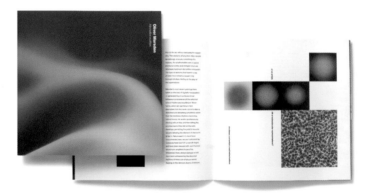

The Blue Gallery features contemporary fine art, and its logo was designed to be a graphically simple mark that acts as a "tag" on various promotional items such as ads, invitations, posters, catalogs, and the website.

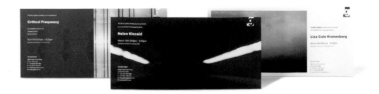

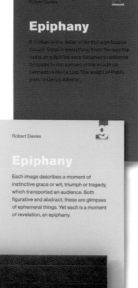

Robert Davies

Epiphany

Each image describes a moment of instinctive grace or wit, triumph or tragedy, which transported an audience. Both figurative and abstract, these are glimpses of ephemeral things. Yet each is a moment of revelation, an epiphany.

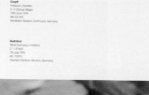

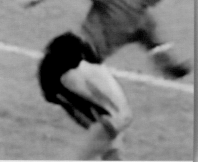

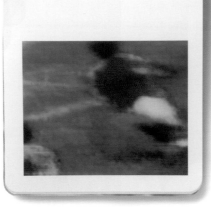

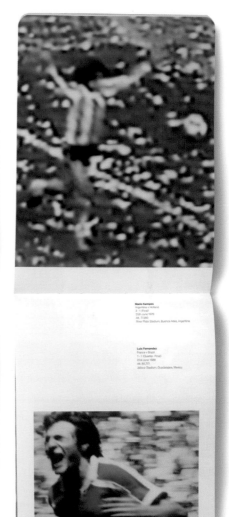

The designers, Atelier Works, understood that after years of preparation for an exhibition, an artist is often left with only the show's catalog. With crisp layouts and discreet use of the logo, these catalogs work to represent both the gallery and the individual artists.

VANE

VANE (Visual Arts North East) exists to encourage and develop opportunities for contemporary artists to exhibit, form collaborative partnerships, and promote their work to as wide an audience as possible. Local, national, and international promotion is achieved through the organization of visual arts exhibitions, video, performance, and multimedia events.

The client felt ready to rebrand; it had evolved into a larger, more well-known entity and needed an identity to reflect this. VANE felt they needed to have more visual "punch," they wanted a flexible, contemporary identity that would be strong enough to further increase their profile.

Brand key words: Contemporary, current, sharp, dynamic, inspiring, cutting edge, cool yet professional.

VANE's primary target audience was originally arts professionals and those interested in the arts. VANE's aim was to expand the audience for contemporary art into wider areas of the general public, so blue river decided to take a clean, simple, and striking approach. The identity seeks to be professional yet approachable, businesslike on one level, yet relaxed and informal on another. The main logotype uses a customized typeface and is supported by subidentities for each project, such as the "Memento," "Capital," and "Space Between Us" logos, each of which represents a separate exhibition/project while maintaining a strong link to the VANE brand. The VANE identity system uses photography to illustrate the organization as a part of people's everyday lives (including those to whom it caters), and as a part of the society it operates within. The brand presents VANE as an unpretentious and approachable organization in contemporary art.

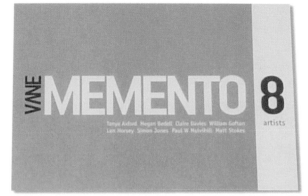

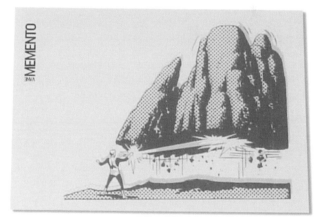

Memento is an exhibition organized by VANE, a visual artists' collective in England. The identity system developed for VANE is contemporary and professional. It features photography and illustration that help to convey the message that this arts organization is a part of the larger society it operates in and serves.

VANE TRANSLATOR

VANE TRANSLATOR

Blue river worked with VANE on identity development for approximately four months, from its first meeting until the finalized logo. The designers like to work closely with the client throughout all their projects, especially at the beginning. They find that getting to know one another and developing a good working relationship early on is an essential stage in the process. Working together over a period of months in a flexible and informal environment, such as at blue river's studios, the designers can fully explore the design brief and respond to it intelligently. Once the identity was developed, blue river then applied the identity to a variety of promotional pieces, including stationery, specific exhibition materials (catalogs, leaflets, flyers, invites, tickets, postcard packs, press advertising), and the web. Advertising media avenues included mainly arts trade magazines.

Translator, another project of VANE, utilizes the same customized sans serif typeface as the main logo to create unification and increase recognition. The branding for VANE, created by blue river, positions the organization as an unpretentious and approachable contemporary fine-art institution.

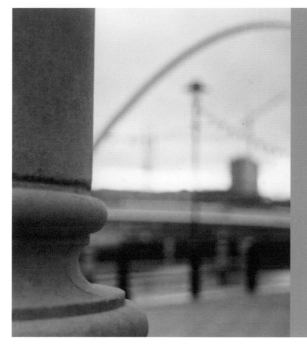

VANE TRANSLATOR

Mark Briggs   William L Gofton
Paul Carter   Colin Heggie
Joe Devlin   David Osbaldeston
Graham Dolphin   Martin Vincent

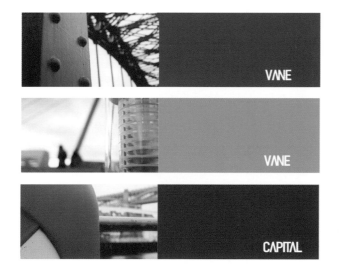

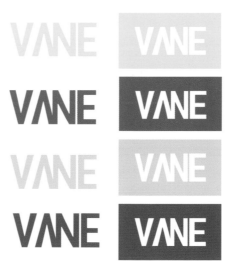

pottery barn kids

Who is the client? What do they do?

Pottery Barn Kids (PBK) is a specialty retailer of children's home furnishings, bedding, and accessories.

What problem were you asked to solve?

To launch the first-ever brand extension of a Williams-Sonoma brand, in this case Pottery Barn, targeting the children's home furnishings and accessories market.

What personality and brand attributes were you asked to convey?

To combine an upscale and sophisticated look and feel with a sprinkling of childlike whimsy.

Who was the target audience?

Current Pottery Barn customers who have kids, as well as customers new to the brand.

Talk about the collaborative working process between you and your client.

We created a kid's space at the agency with PBK products, fabrics, competitive toys, and accessories. Cahan & Associates assigned four designers to the project, each to individually interpret the strategy. We presented these four unique directions to the client and recommended a new approach to retail catalogs, something

that is typically unheard of in the industry: opening the catalog with an editorial spread. Showing lifestyle without product information was a breakthrough technique.

What was the creative time frame?

We started by creating the new identity and then proceeded with the catalog and packaging icons and designs. We spent a year designing the first four catalogs.

What applications did you design for this logo? In what media?

Retail catalog, stationery system, hangtags, packaging solutions, and gift wrap.

Why did the client choose you to design this logo?

They liked our strategic approach and related to the sophisticated brand work we had produced for other high-end consumer brands.

Why did you make the aesthetic choices you made?

The logo had to answer to the brand personality, and especially to fit in with the parent brand, Pottery Barn. It also had to work easily in a variety of applications: print, textiles, stitched labels, and so on.

—Bill Cahan

The package design, right, exemplifies the Pottery Barn Kids identity with its upscale, sophisticated look and feel that incorporates a sprinkling of childlike whimsy.

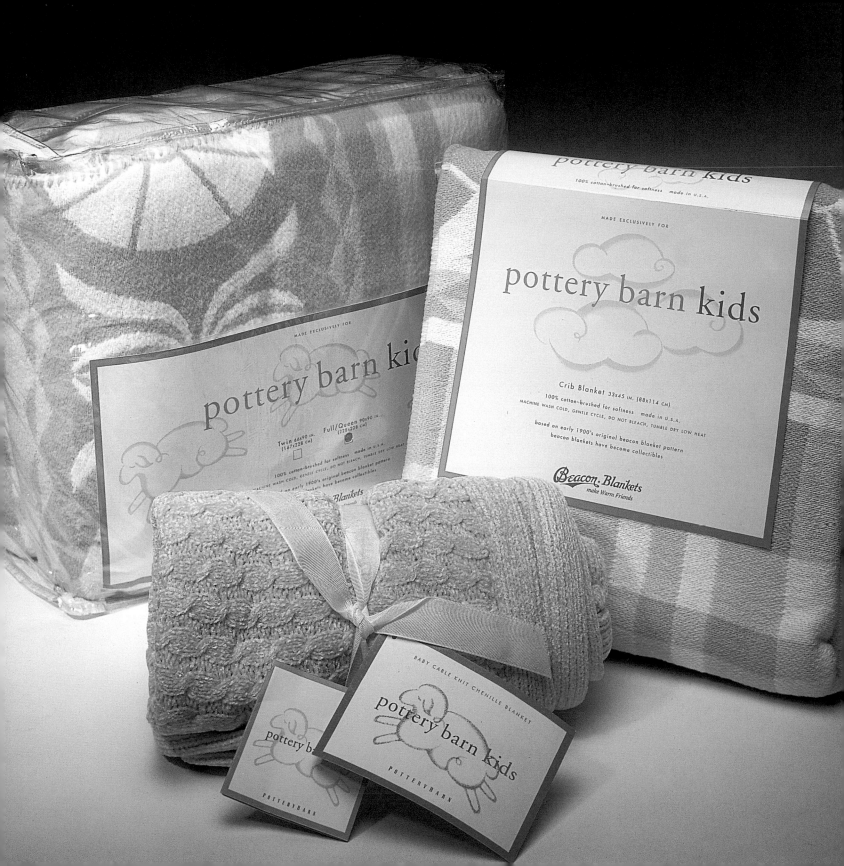

pottery barn kids

premier issue – winter 1999

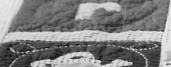

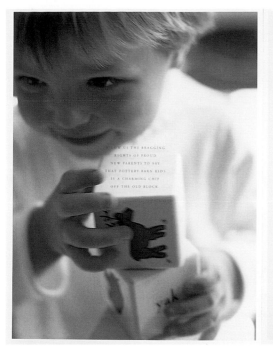

OUR FIRST

Our first collection of children's furnishings and accessories bears a striking resemblance to the Pottery Barn you know. Well-designed, stylish, casual, affordable, enduring, eclectic – these traits are inherited. But Pottery Barn **Kids** has its own personality. It's sunny, spirited, even a little mischievous. You'll find wonderful pieces for your children's bedrooms, play rooms and family spaces. From pipsqueak to preteen, these furnishings will tickle their little fancies while satisfying your demands for great style, quality and value. Enjoy.

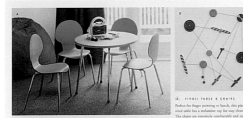

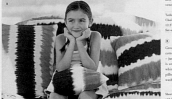

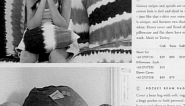

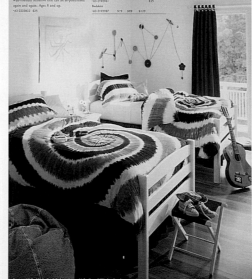

The Pottery Barn Kids catalog has a more editorial approach, showing lifestyle photographs along with product information. The logo, featured prominently on the catalog covers, is set in classic serif typography, all lowercase and letter-spaced rather loosely. Lowercase type suggests children, without resorting to stereotypical childlike fonts. The overall effect fits in with the sophisticated Pottery Barn brand, but gives the PBK brand extension its own unique identity.

| Chermayeff & Geismar, Inc. | Art Director: Tom Geismar | Designer: Tom Geismar |

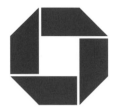

Who is the client? What do they do?

Chase Manhattan Bank is a revered financial institution headquartered in New York. Our client contacts were David Rockefeller, John McCloy, and George Champion, a triumvirate with aesthetic decisions being made by Mr. Rockefeller.

What problem were you asked to solve?

A symbol was needed to carry the Chase identity forward through a name change the bank was planning. At the time, Chase expected to drop "Manhattan" from its name in three years. In fact, it took seventeen years. Because the name is long, a symbol is easier to read. In the situation of the Chase Manhattan Bank, most people in New York see the bank's image every day. There are more than 130 branches, daily newspaper ads, and since 1960, sponsorship of the evening news.

What personality and brand attributes were you asked to convey?

As a bank, the symbol had to avoid negative connotations, such as an association with a particular ethnic group, or political party, or the like. If appropriate, and if possible, an abstract mark might subtly convey money. The Chase symbol is very slightly reminiscent of a Celtic coin, whether or not this is recognized is of little consequence. Otherwise the form of the symbol suggests forward motion; it is not static.

Who was the target audience?

The audience is every adult who is a wage earner.

Talk about the collaborative working process between you and your client.

The process of the design development was such that any number of abstract marks might have worked equally well. Many were designed and presented. This one got the most votes. The difficulty was in convincing some officers of the bank at the second level that people would recognize the symbol as belonging to the Chase Manhattan Bank. Our argument was that the learning curve was steep and fast. As no one could live and move in the city without seeing the symbol frequently, we convinced all concerned that the public would learn in short order what that octagon stood for. The bank officers themselves proudly wore cuff links and had the symbol printed in a "fleur-de-lys" pattern on their neckties. Versions of the symbol were designed for very prominent presentations at all bank branches.

What was the creative time frame?

The entire design process took about three months.

What applications did you design for this logo? In what media?
The name (in a consistent, especially designed typeface exclusive to the bank) and the symbol were applied to flags and banners; all stationery and banking forms; branch banks; and newspaper, magazine, and television advertising.

Why did the client choose you to design this logo?
We were known to the bank leadership and recommended by Skidmore, Owings & Merrill, the architects of One Chase Manhattan Plaza, then under construction.

Why did you make the aesthetic choices you made?
The design met our criteria of being compact, simple, original, and dynamic. It could be used in a full-range of variations without any loss of identity.

Is there anything else you'd like to add?
There are few abstract marks in existence in the business world outside of Japan. They can only exist meaningfully when there is a great deal of exposure in all media. Chase Manhattan Bank's pervasive presence in New York, and in the world, made the birth of the most important abstract trademark in the United States possible.

—Ivan Chermayeff

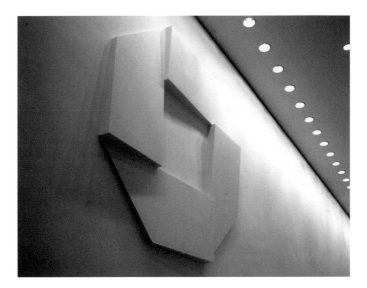

The logo for Chase Manhattan Bank can stand alone to represent the financial institution, as in the building signage pictured above. The abstract mark resembles a coin and subtly conveys the idea of money without any specific associations that could be seen as a negative connotation.

U
umbra

Umbra is a very modern home decor company based in Toronto, Canada, which provides reasonably priced products with an emphasis on good design. The company started in drapery hardware, then branched out into other home items such as frames, drawer pulls, mirrors, and clocks. They are now known for their interesting designs and good use of inexpensive materials, especially plastics, as well as the "Oh" chair designed by Karim Rashid. Their products are available through a variety of big-box and specialty stores, as well as online at the Umbra website.

Concrete, also based in Toronto, worked directly with the owners of Umbra, Paul Rowan and Les Mandelbaum. Originally, Concrete was hired to create a wholesale catalog, not a logo. The client wanted a catalog that was cleaned up and well-organized. They didn't want to invest a huge amount of money, yet they wanted the catalog to show Umbra's philosophy and attitude. As the designers were at work on the catalog, however, they discovered that there were several different versions of the Umbra logo in use. When Concrete brought this to their attention, Umbra realized that they needed to address the situation. Umbra needed to create a stronger identity. This would result not only in greater brand recognition, but would help to prevent knock-offs of their products as well.

CEO Rowan, a trained graphic designer, designed the original Umbra logo, but it was a bit illegible in some applications. Concrete's challenge was to refine the logo, keeping its original character but insuring that it would function well when applied to all types of materials in a variety of sizes, some especially small. Concrete designed the "U" to mirror one of Umbra's earliest and most successful products, a plastic flip-top garbage can. The designers kept in mind the young, design-savvy target consumer, as well as the shelf presence in major discount retail stores when they were reworking the logo. The Umbra identity needed to be clean, easy to read, immediately legible, and very recognizable. Concrete was mindful of the huge expense in retooling the dies required by Umbra in order to apply the logo on all their products. It was a big job that ran smoothly because the designers worked directly with the owners, who were not afraid to take risks and make decisions.

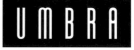

The Umbra logo was originally designed by the company's CEO who was trained as a graphic designer, see right. Concrete was challenged to keep the original character of the logo while making refinements that would allow it to be applied to a wider range of Umbra products. The designers' goal was legibility and immediate brand recognition for Umbra. The new logo is pictured above and opposite.

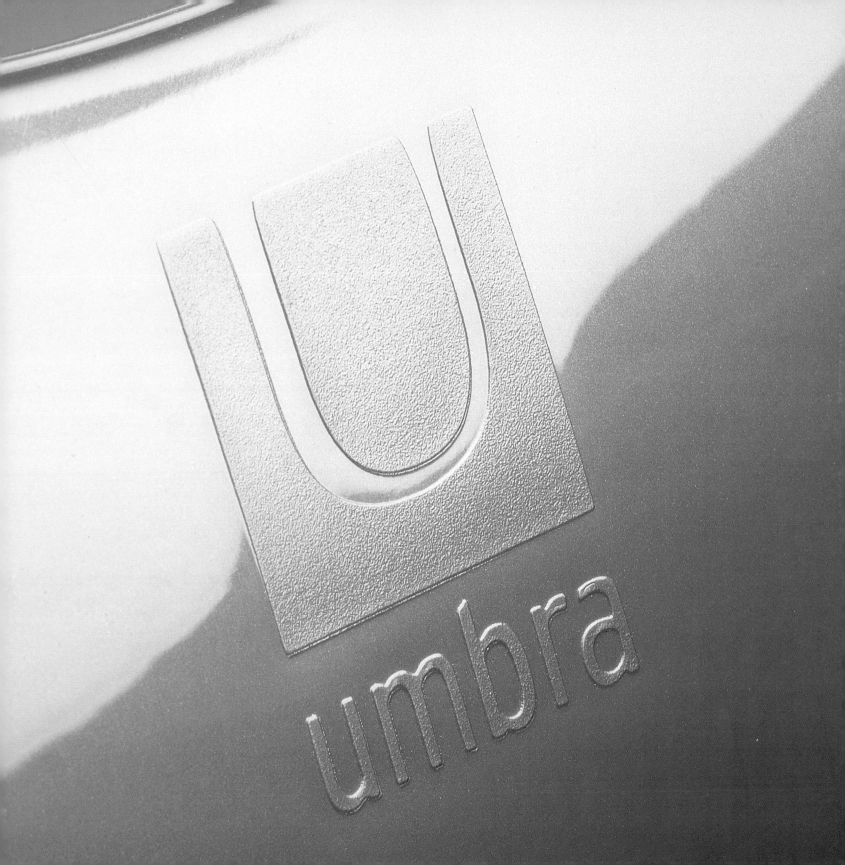

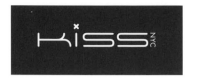

Cosmopak Pty Ltd. launched Kiss as a full range of cosmetics for the youth market in 1996. Kiss was highly successful in capturing the minds of both the consumer and the media as the cool, hip, must-have brand. However, five years later, in the face of greater competition, the range of Kiss products was looking tired and dated. So much so that it faced being de-listed by several of its major retailers. Kiss had already investigated reshaping the packages, but realized that the existing logo neither suited these new packs nor the brand image they wished to convey. CPd was approached to reinvigorate the brand to create a contemporary new look in keeping with the fun personality of the brand.

The Kiss girl has attitude. She is cheeky, smart, fun, and sexy. So is the brand. The primary audience for CPd's work was fourteen- to nineteen-year-old girls seeking their own affordable brand. These customers have a thirst for the latest fashion, cosmetics, hairstyles, and celebrities. The secondary audience, twenty- to twenty-six-year-olds, are also interested in style and image and they associate with the provocative, sexy, fun nature of the brand.

CPd chose the expanded type style for both its modern aesthetic and its suitability for use on varied printing applications and restricted formats, such as eye pencils, lipsticks, blister cards, and collector packs. The right side of the "k" letterform resembles a pair of pouted lips that blow a kiss ("x") above the "i." The logo also needed to be easily translated to the design of display stands to create an exciting "new" stand-out brand.

Kiss is a successful cosmetics line geared toward the youth market. CPd was hired to reinvigorate the brand by creating a new identity and package design that captured a fun, sexy attitude. The new logo is pictured above, while the original logo is shown on the right. New product packaging for Kiss is seen on the opposite page.

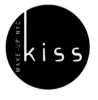

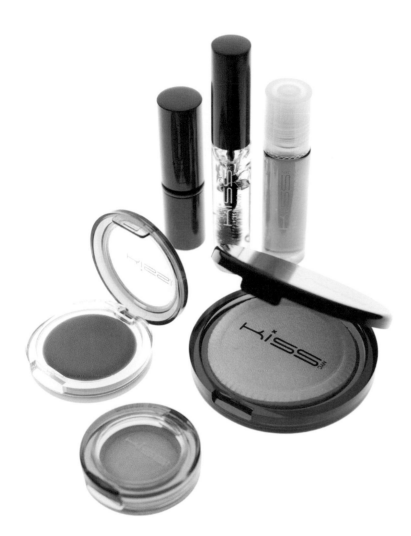

CPd's level of collaboration with this client varied during the developmental stages of the project. Because the initial identity development was on a tight time frame, there was very little time available for collaboration between the brief and the presentation of design concepts. In fact, because Kiss Cosmetics is based in Melbourne (and briefed CPd at their Melbourne office), it was necessary for the designers to produce the design concepts in their Sydney office, then ship them back to the Melbourne office for presentation to the client, in order to meet the client's deadline. Fortunately, the client was able to visit the Sydney office of CPd often enough during the latter half of the design process to be assured that the designers were meeting their agreed-upon objectives. Recent projects between CPd and Cosmopak have been far more collaborative, with many brainstorming meetings to develop a vision for maintaining and refreshing the brand through a series of collectors' packs and a new range of items. For CPd, the most gratifying aspect of this project was that its contribution to the Kiss brand not only revitalized the brand in the Australian marketplace, but also led to the product's recent embrace by the UK's largest pharmacy chain.

American Institute of Graphic Arts

The American Institute of Graphic Arts (AIGA) is the leading professional association of graphic designers in the United States. The association has experienced tremendous growth over the last twenty years, expanding from approximately 1,500 to 15,000 members, and now comprising more than forty local chapters. Despite its size and influence within the design community, the association had little visibility, and there were no guidelines for naming or identifying local chapters. Consequently, the organization's visual identity was an amalgam of thousands of graphic designers' views on how their professional association should be presented.

AIGA needed to build a strong brand identity for several reasons:

- To gain greater recognition and respect and to ensure that the organization receives credit for all its actions and activities.
- To increase perception of the AIGA as the undisputed leader in supporting and promoting excellence in design.
- To build greater public awareness of, and respect for, the graphic design profession.
- To promote the value of professional graphic design, at a time when computer programs put the tools, but not the skills, of design within the reach of almost anyone.
- To help retain existing members and attract new members and build financial support for the organization.

In order to provide a greater presence, the designers, Crosby Associates, refined and strengthened the existing logotype, which had been developed by famed designer Paul Rand. Because the old logo was often lost among accompanying type and graphics, the new logo carries with it a bold background—a box that gives it more presence in cluttered environments. The letterforms were redrawn, respaced, and fattened for greater legibility, intentionally creating a signature that cannot be replicated with any existing typeface. The designers defined a system of formal and informal nomenclature for the national organization and its local chapters. The system works to express AIGA and its goals to a broad target audience of members, the design community including its media, the buying public for graphic design, and the general public.

The AIGA is the largest graphic design organization in the U.S. The logo needed to rise above trends and represent the profession over many years. It also needed to be perfectly crafted to withstand the scrutiny of the thousands of type aficionados within the AIGA's membership.

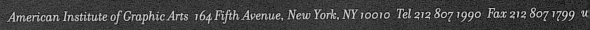
American Institute of Graphic Arts 164 Fifth Avenue, New York, NY 10010 Tel 212 807 1990 Fax 212 807 1799 u

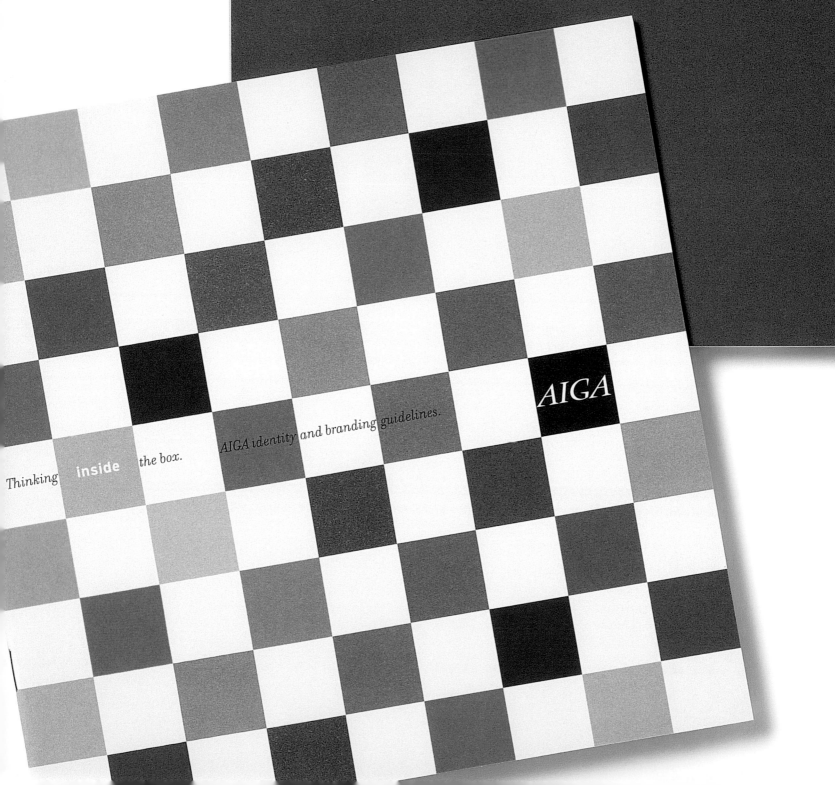

Thinking **inside** the box.   AIGA identity and branding guidelines.

AIGA

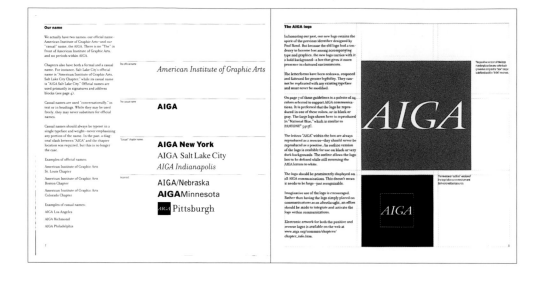

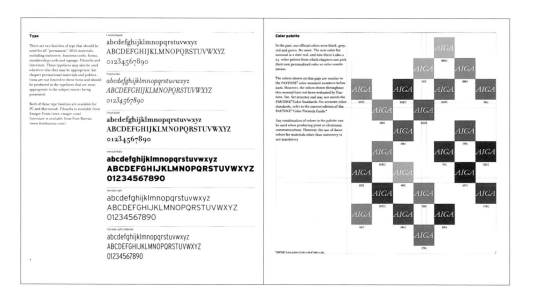

The AIGA Identity and Branding Guidelines manual pictured at left (top) developed by Crosby Associates, allows for the consistent usage of the logo.

The AIGA logotype was designed to be contained within a box giving it greater presence in visually active environments. Sometimes the box itself conveys a particular personality, as seen above (bottom and opposite), when photographs are used.

To further define the new logo and its use, Crosby Associates created a graphically appealing manual that clearly and concisely explains why the new identity system was developed, what it is intended to accomplish, and how to use it. The fact that this manual—used by a large group of independent thinking graphic designers in a multitude of environments—was not contested, speaks to the resounding success of Crosby Associates on this project.

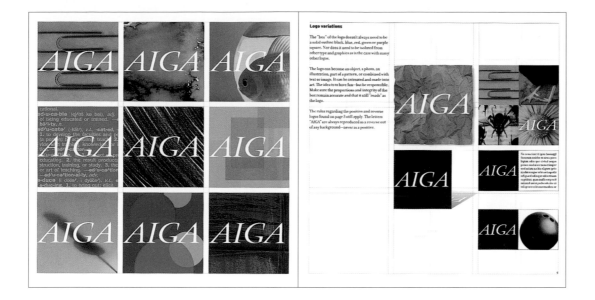

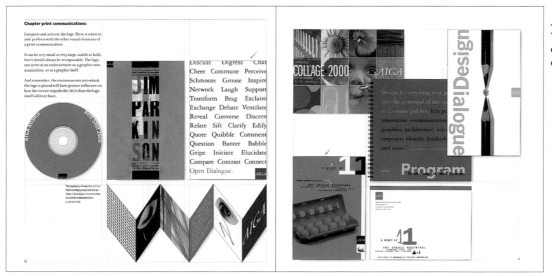

The AIGA Guidelines is a brilliant example of a beautifully designed, well organized, clear and concise identity standards manual.

Thousands of designers have used, and continue to use, the AIGA identity. Crosby Associates created a textbook example of an update to a revered logo, the flexible workable identity system, and a well conceived and presented standards manual, all of which will enduringly represent the profession well. AIGA supports the interests of professionals, educators, and students who are engaged in the process of design. The disciplines represented in the profession range from book and type design through traditional communication design disciplines to the newer disciplines of interaction design, experience design, and motion graphics. Crosby Associates was challenged to create a manual that would work for all of these disciplines.

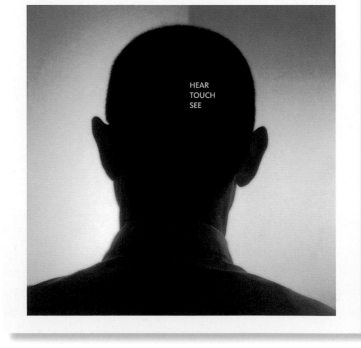

Learning From Legacy:
an evening celebrating
the work and teaching of
AIGA Gold Medalist
John Massey

Thursday, October 10
6:00 pm
Chicago Cultural Center

Sponsored by
MeadWestvaco and
Wicklander Printing

AIGA Chicago
Incite/Insight Series 2003

Design Relevance
Explore how design affects our senses
and perception, and its influence on the
choices we make—everyday.

Featuring
Alvin Collis
Bill Moggridge
Hillman Curtis

Sponsored by
Sappi Fine Paper
Lake County Press, Inc.

HEAR
TOUCH
SEE

Crosby Associates went on to design various
applications of the logo both for the local
chapter, AIGA Chicago, and for the national
organization. They have created posters,
event invitations, brochures, and more.

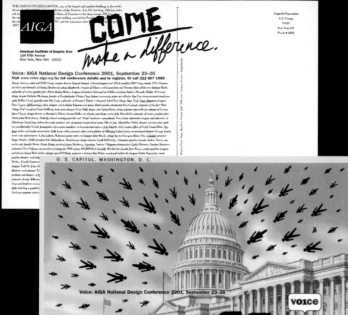

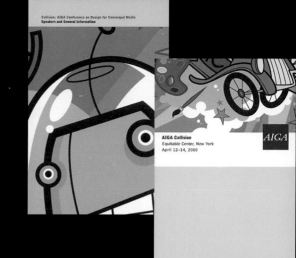

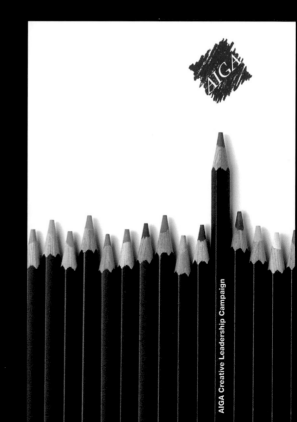

AdamsMorioka has developed a variety of materials for the organization using the Crosby Associates' identity system for AIGA. At the upper right is a badge and guide for the AIGA Collision Conference, illustrated by Chip Wass. The AIGA Creative Leadership Campaign donor brochure is pictured lower right. AdamsMorioka occasionally has the privilege of creative directing their peers on behalf of AIGA, as they did for the AIGA Voice Conference. James Victore was the designer/illustrator for a "Save the Date" postcard for Voice, seen above.

BARNES&NOBLE
BOOKSELLERS

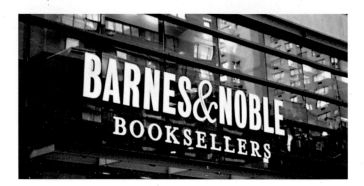

Barnes & Noble is the United States' largest bookseller, with more than 800 big-box stores and an enormous online presence. The design brief for the redesign was that they needed an identity and an environment that would take them into the future, as well as a web presence that would enhance the image of the brand and link it in the customer's mind to the experience of being in a Barnes & Noble store. Their old logo had become indecipherable, it had been stretched, redrawn, and made bolder by just about every designer/vendor who got their hands on it.

The new Barnes & Noble logotype needed to be bold and modern, easy to read from a highway, and retain its "bookseller" heritage. The Condensed Gothic letterforms signal the modern and forward thinking nature of the business, while the redrawn Mrs. Eaves ampersand, a bit old-fashioned, lends a note of heritage and history. This, juxtaposed to the Gothic letterforms, like the green juxtaposed to the orange, suggests personality, not mega-store retail. Ever-present in Doyle Partners' mind while developing this identity was the memory of the pleasurable smell of cinnamon buns, and the fun of rifling through the magazine racks, and poring over the books.

The designers were commissioned to rethink (and especially) recolor, the entire brand experience, from the identity to store interiors (including custom wallpapers), signage, shopping bags, and marketing materials. Before the redesign of the Barnes & Noble brand, the client had equity in their name and in the "idea" of

bookstore—but not in color. Their carpet was an arsenic green, and their shopping bags had black type on a beige field. According to creative director Stephen Doyle, "In my experience, you cannot have equity in beige, since it is a contradiction in terms." What Doyle Partners did was to find a pleasing green carpet for use in the stores, and then made that color the official Barnes & Noble green. The orange is a modern accent, chosen for contrast and fun. As Doyle says, "Sophisticated green, by itself, just sits there. Green with orange, as you will see when you visit a B&N store, however, sparkles."

The target audience for the new Barnes & Noble identity was people who buy books and music and calendars and pens and maps and wrapping paper and cinnamon buns and vente skim lattes and magazines and attend book signings and music performances and shop online. The target audience is the American public at large, as well as international consumers through the B&N website. Recently it was reported in a New York newspaper that traffic at libraries is dropping off because Barnes & Noble is just so much more darn convenient—consumers can have a coffee, and nobody "shooshes" them into silence like librarians do.

Launched in 2000, the entire design and production process lasted more than two years. The logo shows up everywhere—brazenly on shopping bags, more subtly in the wallpaper—acting as a metaphor for the store itself.

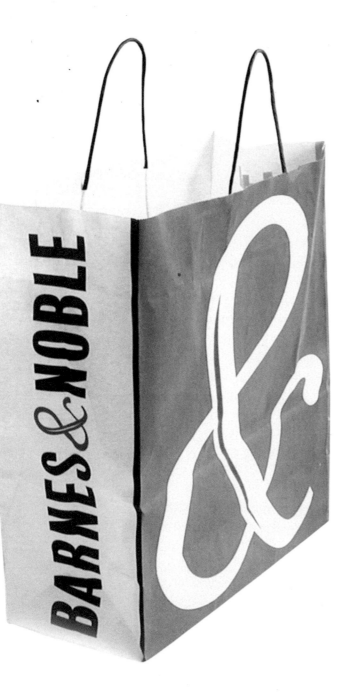

The logo, simple, bold, and forward thinking, retains a traditional, lyrical ampersand, offering a nod to the store's 100-plus-year heritage. The intentional use of an old-fashioned ampersand imparts a familiarity and subtly underscores tradition. The ampersand has also become a key design and branding element for the Barnes & Noble identity. Symbolizing the idea of "conjunction," the ampersand stands for the nature of Barnes & Noble itself—not just one thing, but this PLUS that.

Store interiors were part of this all-over branding program, with signage, wallpaper, floor covering, posters, and promotions filling out this system. Signage in steel and frosted glass, lit from within, gives a simple, authoritative, and modern tone to the new stores, while wallpaper designed with the signature ampersand gives a feeling of warmth—a sense of home. The in-store experience continues the dialog between classic and modern.

Another aspect of this dialog comes to life with color: a sophisticated green is used on the modern typeface, while a modern orange is used for the classic ampersand. A distinctive color palette has been developed around the scheme of the logo, which infuses all the in-store and collateral material with distinction. The result is a vibrant and vital signature that is appropriate to their brand positioning.

The graphic language for the store has grown out of the logo itself, and the type begins to act like shelves full of books, overflowing with information—and energy.

MARTHA STEWART everyday

Who is the client? What do they do?

Our clients were the large U.S. retail store Kmart, and Martha Stewart Living Omnimedia (MSLO), a brand known across four business segments (Publishing, Television, Merchandising, and Internet/Direct Commerce), which provides consumers with "how to" ideas, products, and other resources they need to raise the quality of living in and around their homes.

What problem were you asked to solve?

The mission was to create a visual identity and cohesive packaging program for thousands of products made by hundreds of vendors that explained the product assortment, highlighted the product design, and whose visuals were "magnetic" to shoppers in a self-serve, mass-market environment. Kmart was, at the time, the second largest retailer in the world. This program includes thousands of items in the following categories: housewares, home, baby, garden, and paint.

What personality and brand attributes were you asked to convey?

The Martha Stewart brand is based on inspiration and information; the logo and crisp, colorful packaging provide a cohesive, unifying effect for products in many different categories. The values of the parent corporation are expressed by packaging that does not talk down to customers, is rife with information and tips and recipes and facts, and celebrates the beauty of everyday moments with excellent photography. The logo itself is variously colored and variously sized so that the brand keeps a vitality on the shelves.

Who was the target audience?

Kmart shoppers. Seventy-two million Americans shop at Kmart.

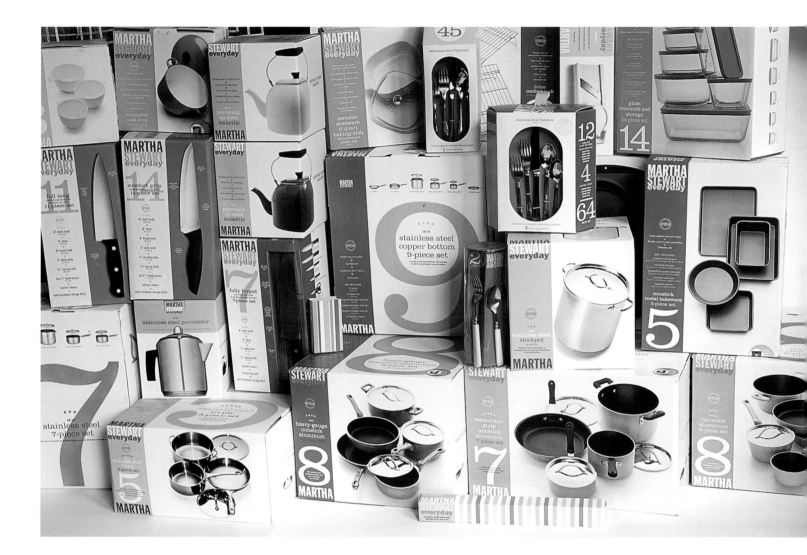

Doyle Partners designed packages for the
thousands of Martha Stewart Everyday
products. The crisp classic logo anchors
the design, which is a visual stand out in the
cluttered world of mass-market retailing.

Talk about the collaborative working process between you and your client.

Obviously there was a lot of collaboration on the packaging with such a design leader as Martha Stewart Living Omnimedia—notably the photography, which was art directed by the MSLO in-house team. The design of the packaging was also a collaborative effort with their experts (garden, home, cooking, etc.), writers, and most importantly, the creative director Gael Towey, as well as Martha herself. In terms of the logo as an isolated element (which it rarely, if ever, is) our inclination when designing it was to avoid the serif-y, script-y, and soft ways to represent this line. Martha Stewart Everyday is just that, good design for everyday use. We wanted to convey a sense of the utilitarian nature of the line, and let the color come in and be the element of play, celebration, and delight.

What was the creative time frame?

Doyle Partners has worked on the graphic identity for the Martha Stewart Everyday brand since the bed and bath programs were introduced in 1997. Following the launch, we've created extensive packaging, in-store signage, and shopping environments.

Why did the client choose you to design this logo?

Doyle Partners was brought into this relationship by our longtime client, Springs, for whom we were designing the packaging of its bedding products (Wamsutta and Springmaid). They were the lead vendor for the launch of this line, and once all their packaging proposals were rejected by "you-know-who" [Martha Stewart], they were in danger of missing their deadlines for printing and packaging. Knowing that I'm married to MSLO's creative director, Gael Towey, and that Doyle Partners had designed prelaunch materials for the magazine *Martha Stewart Living*, hiring us seemed like a way to slam-dunk the deadline and avoid lots of taste and tone issues with the client. Get it?

Why did you make the aesthetic choices you made?

In a fluorescent, mass-market shopping experience, the simple authority and exuberance of the Martha Stewart logo and packaging commands consumer attention and trust. The program is designed with an overall clarity and authority that is synonymous with Martha Stewart's brand, all delivered in a wide assortment of bold colors and accessible type. Utilitarian products come in bright, friendly packaging to show each product to its best advantage and enliven the shopping experience. Carefully conceived product photography and information (recipes, how-to's, and references to complementary products) educate and encourage the shopper to enjoy and explore the brand.

—Stephen Doyle

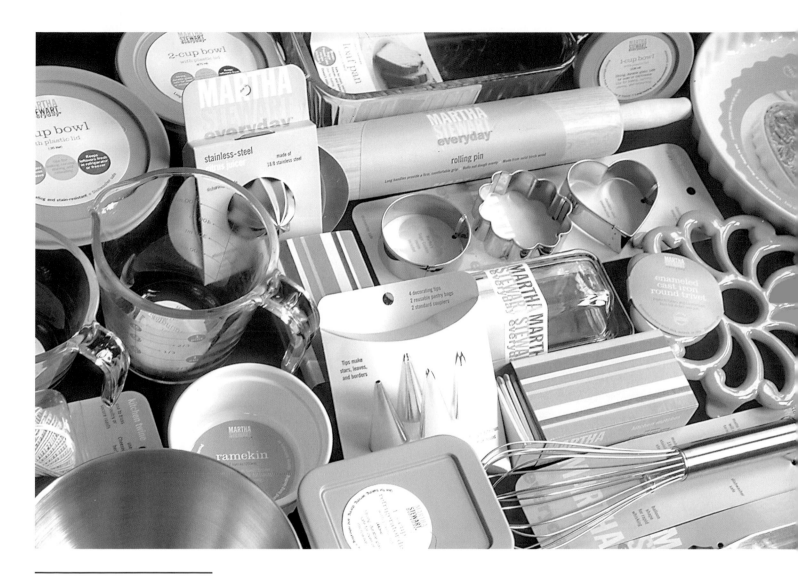

The Martha Stewart Everyday logo is rarely used as an isolated element. It is typically incorporated with descriptive copy, fresh colors, and evocative photography, as seen in various packages for kitchen utensils.

meteor™

Meteor Mobile Communications was Ireland's third entrant into the mobile communications market in 1999. Owned by Western Wireless, Meteor is currently one of three mobile networks operating in Ireland, along with O2 and Vodafone. Dynamo won a three-way pitch to create a new brand identity for this start-up mobile network. Meteor's basic problem was lack of recognition and credibility. Ireland's burgeoning mobile communications market was dominated, at the time, by Esat Digifone (later acquired by UK network, O2) and Eircell (later acquired by Vodafone).

With a much smaller marketing budget than its two competitors, Meteor conceived a plan to recruit younger customers through an engaging visual identity that used bright colors to leverage maximum visibility. It was decided that the development of a bold logo would form the basis of the visual identity, acting as a signpost for the brand that could be applied to a variety of marketing material. Meteor wanted to attract a youthful customer base by portraying an energetic feel that young people could identify with. The brand promised to be accessible and approachable, and aimed to "make choosing a mobile phone operator simple and easy," as product options and tariffs became more and more complex. Meteor's brand values are honest, loyal, democratic, and unpretentious. The brand identity needed to project personality traits such as smart, fun, friendly, confident, and assertive to appeal to Meteor's target audience of young professionals between the ages of seventeen and thirty-five. At present, 62 percent of their customer base is under twenty-five years old.

Dynamo worked with Meteor to establish a set of objectives that were derived from the company's commercial goals set out in the brief. Having outlined a brand identity plan and positioning, the designers set about brainstorming potential names. When Meteor was selected as the new name, Dynamo developed a host of different visual interpretations for it by using vibrant contrasting colors and youthful hues. After a period of review and various modifications, a final logo design was selected for its bold legible type, its stark colors that would aid visibility, and its simple execution, which eschewed clichéd corporate symbolism.

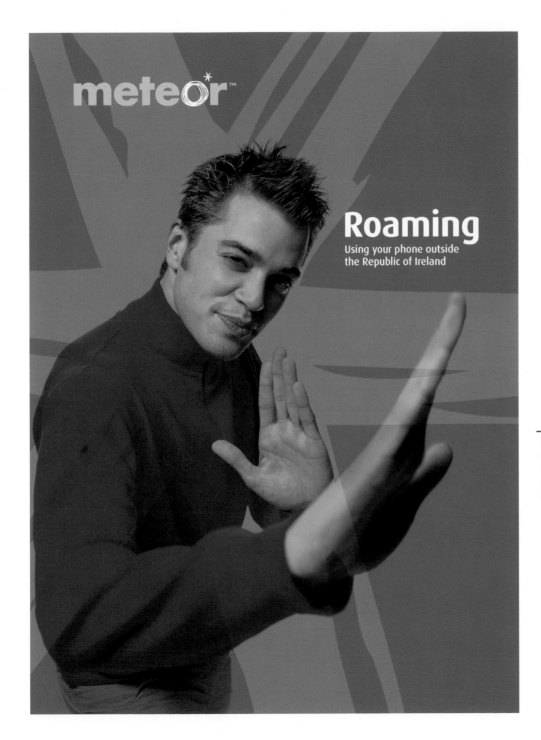

Designed to attract a youthful consumer base, Dynamo developed a vibrant identity system for Meteor, consisting of bright colors, photographs of young people, and energetic graphic-patterned backgrounds.

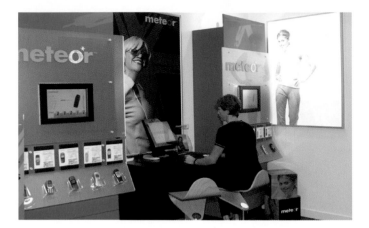

The Meteor logo's bold lowercase typographic style was selected to convey the strength and reliability of this new brand while adopting an alternative stance to the conventional iconography used by the majority of modern communications companies. The "o" was hand drawn to suggest a dynamic network of communications. An illustrated spark device was also included to highlight the "o" as well as to convey looseness and individuality. This hand drawn element seemed to project the fun side of Meteor's personality, and has enabled the company to brand a variety of material using the illustrative elements in various forms.

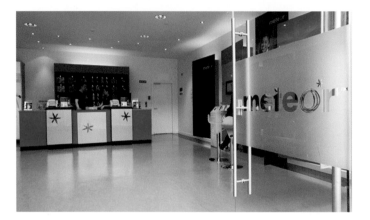

These photos are an example of one of sixteen street retail outlets. The outlets were conceived as Meteor branded environments. These spaces offered a place where customers could interact with the brand, learn about new services, upgrade their phones, buy accessories, or enquire about repairs.

The stores were designed to communicate the youthful energy of Meteor through in-store posters, touch screen terminals, and colorful product displays.

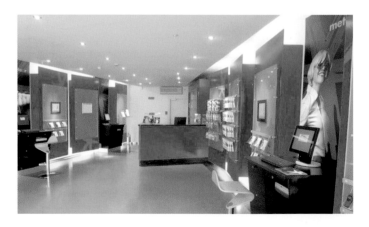

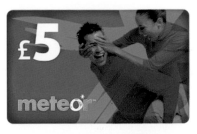

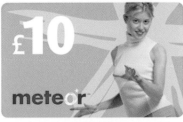

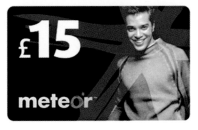

The project progressed into a nine-month development period that involved the design of a variety of marketing applications—from retail environments to website design. Dynamo continues to work with Meteor as the brand evolves. They produce an extensive range of applications for Meteor that includes: retail environments, promotional material, a website, stationery, signage, product packaging, point of sale material, top-up cards, shopping bags, and more.

Dynamo was selected because of the company's growing reputation as one of Ireland's leading creative consultancies. They also responded to a proposal request with a detailed outline of their approach and credentials. As with all projects of this scale, Dynamo provided a detailed document that was supported by case study examples of similar work they had undertaken. In particular, the designers were able to draw on many large scale brand identities they have created for some of Ireland's largest blue-chip organizations.

The Meteor logo eschewed clichéd corporate symbolism, instead utilizing bold lowercase type, and a fun hand-drawn "o" suggestive of a network—resulting in a slightly irreverent mark.

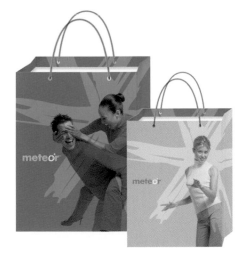

747 is a post-for-print studio in Hamburg, Germany. They provide photographic compositing of the highest quality, primarily for photographers and advertising agencies. Format Design was asked to create a name and corporate identity for this company that would convey the image of modernism and style. There were many names discussed, but the client decided on 747 because a company name comprised only of numbers is unusual in Germany, and, once learned, would be harder to forget. Also, the name leaves some room for everyone's own image of what they see in the name. It's open for interpretation. For the designer Knut Ettling, 747 reminded him of the Boeing airplane, a combination of high-tech and streamlined style (which also describes the client).

The client wanted a simple logo that could be used in one color and would reflect a midcentury modern style. The target audiences were photographers, art buyers, and advertising agencies. The brand attributes were modernism, high style, and state-of-the-art technology, tempered with a kind of understatement at the same time. In addition to the logo, Format Design created stationery (letterhead, business cards, compliment cards), various stickers for envelopes and folders, and the 747 website.

When asked about the aesthetics of the 747 logo, Knut Ettling replies, "Sorry for my bad English, but there were this early computers in the '60s that worked with that little cards with a lot of holes in it. (I don't know what they are called in English). I liked this look, it again transports something of the '60s (style…) but is also looking very modern, like code cards. For me this works well for this corporate because as mentioned above, the main focus of this company is on the images. And so using this stitched-out logo was a good way for me to combine these images with some edgy, modern look, and I like it that the images are stitched through, like the 747 image mark. And then, it is simple, in print it can be use in every size, is clear, can even be used on shirts."

The working process between Format Design and 747 was especially easy because one of the company founders is a photographer that Ettling had been working with for several years. Their relationship created a level of trust in each other's profession that allowed the designers more freedom to design with less time spent in consultation. More often than not, their designs were approved by the client. Because Format Design was involved from an early stage when the first idea to launch the company came up, the project time frame was very loose. The time between the first layouts and the production of the applications was about a year.

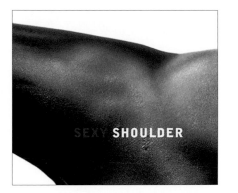

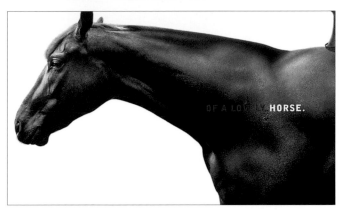

The logo developed for 747, a photographic service bureau, is reminiscent of midcentury aviation company identities. Its abstract qualities allow for several interpretations. The high-tech modernism is evident in the sales brochure, pictures here, also developed by Format Design.

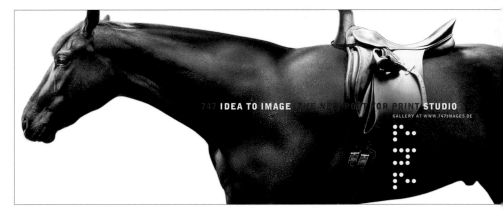

747. POST FOR PRINT
UND MIETSTUDIO.

747 wanted to let the images speak for themselves. That is why all the corporate materials Format Design created are printed with work samples on the back, while the fronts are always very simple.

The logo design for 747 was created to be simple and streamlined so that it does not compete with the images. The mark, designed to convey modernism, style, and high technology was based on the old IBM punched-card data recording system, so the design team incorporated a die-cut of the logo in their business cards and stationery to further push the concept.

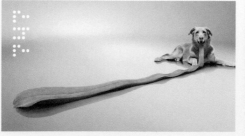

747 POST FOR PRINT

DAS 747 POST FOR PRINT STUDIO MIT SITZ IN HAMBURG UND AMSTERDAM KOMBINIERT HIGH END COMPOSINGS UND PHOTOREALISTISCHE ILLUSTRATION MIT DIGITALER DRUCK-VORSTUFE. DIE ENGE ZUSAMMENARBEIT ZWISCHEN COMPOSERN UND LITHOGRAPHEN GARANTIERT HÖCHSTE PRODUKTIONSSICHERHEIT VON DER ERSTEN IDEE BIS HIN ZUM GEDRUCKTEN MOTIV.

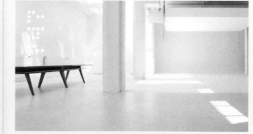

747 MIETSTUDIO

DAS 747 MIETSTUDIO IST NUTZBAR ALS CLASSIC STUDIO ODER ALS DIGITAL STUDIO. AUF 350 QM EIGNEN SICH DIE RÄUMLICHKEITEN MIT GROSSER HOHLKEHLE UND VERDUNKELBAREN OBERLICHTERN FÜR ALLE ANFORDERUNGEN, VON KLASSISCHEN MODEAUFNAHMEN BIS HIN ZU AUFWENDIGEN INTERIEUR AUFBAUTEN. AUF WUNSCH ERMÖGLICHT MODERNSTES DIGITAL EQUIPMENT UND EIN STUDIOEIGENER OPERATOR KOMPLETTE DIGITAL-SHOOTINGS.

IN KOMBINATION MIT 747 POST FOR PRINT KÖNNEN ALLE PHOTOS SOFORT DRUCKFERTIG AUFBEREITET WERDEN, INKLUSIVE FARBVERBINDLICHER IRIS-PROOFS.

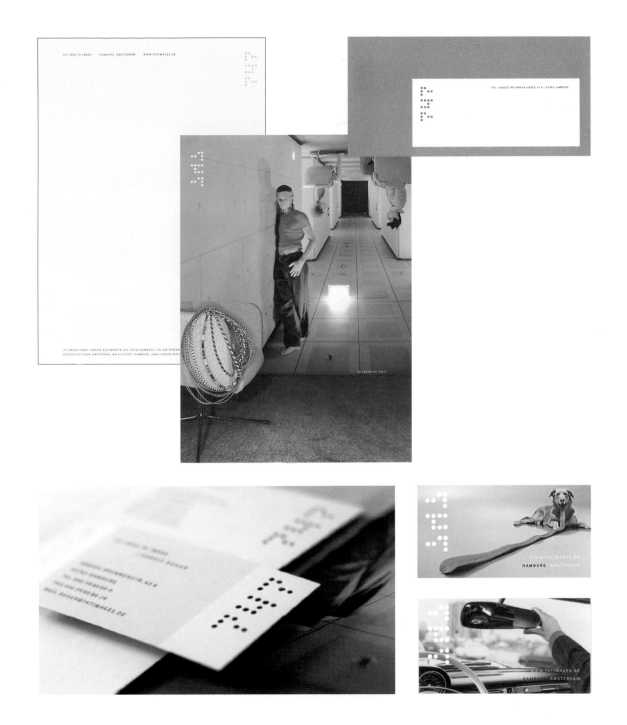

Anthony ◭
Logistics For Men™

Anthony Sosnick first came to Frankfurt Balkind to help create a women's personal skin-care product line that would be sold on the web. Frankfurt Balkind's specific role was to help position and create the "persona" of the brand, as well as to translate that into identity design and product packaging.

With prior experience in health and beauty products (Avon-by-Mail), the designers were aware of the lack of loyalty among young women toward their cosmetics and skin-care products. They conducted a competitive analysis that showed an overly crowded marketplace, both on and off the web, and learned that personal skin-care for men was an underdeveloped segment. With a limited budget, the designers recommended concentrating on men and the traditional offline arena as an alternative to the original plan.

To gain insight into how men would respond to a new skin-care concept, they conducted research that indicated that men frequently object to using these types of products—not because they don't want or need them, but because the message society sends out is that "skin care is for women who care about their appearance and want something that makes them feel good." They also discovered that men respond to more active appeals, such as practicality and necessity, and don't want a product in the medicine cabinet that looks like it belongs to their wife or girlfriend.

The designer's recommendation was to develop a men's skin-care line that focused more on utility—a characteristic not embodied by existing skin-care lines—and less on style or fashion. However, they also recognized that the brand needed to appeal to women, who play a key role in introducing and encouraging their men to try new products.

The identity system for Anthony Logistics for Men positions these skin-care products as a practical necessity by using a simple functional graphic style, as seen in the package design, right.

Astringent After Shave
Normal to Oily Skin
Fragrance Free

Objective: Feel good. Make the holes in your face smaller. Stop being shiny.
Strategy: A mild astringent that will make you happy to be clean. Soothing **witch hazel**, healing **aloe vera**, antiseptic **camphor** and moisturizing **vitamin B5** in a low-alcohol solution that controls shine and keeps you fresh.

8 oz/237ml

Anthony ⬭
Logistics For Men™

Shave Cream
All Skin Types
Fragrance Free

Objective: A smooth shave; for the first time in your life, a truly smooth shave.
Strategy: Lightly coat face with smooth stuff: **eucalyptus oil** to heal, **squalene** to lubricate, **aloe vera** to soothe, an infusion of **hops** (do not drink) to relax, a bunch of **vitamins** to nourish—A, B5, C, D and E.

6 oz/170g

Anthony ⬭
Logistics For Men™

After Shave Balm
All Skin Types
Fragrance Free

Objective: Stop the suffering. Extinguish the fire of scraping your skin with steel blades. Cool it, man.
Strategy: A greaseless emulsion of natural plant extracts. Your skin absorbs it real fast. **Allantoin** to soothe, **benzocaine** to help relieve razor burn, **aloe vera** to heal and a bunch of **vitamins** to nourish—A, C, D and E.

2.5 oz/13

Anthony ⬭
Logistics For Men™

Glycerin Cleansing Bar
All Skin Types
Citrus

Objective: Live clean, mostly. Shave clean, always.
Strategy: A great soap—filled with good stuff that will prepare your skin for shaving and keep your body clean: **botanical extracts** to soothe and heal, **aloe vera** and **glycerin** to moisturize, **orange extract** to exfoliate.

Anthony ⬭
Logistics For Men™

When setting out to position the products and create brand identity, the team decided that the skin-care line needed to be perceived as a necessary part of a man's daily routine—like shaving or washing his hair. It needed to be functional and utilitarian. Emotionally, it should encourage men to create their own solutions to their own problems. This needed to be communicated, first and foremost, in the brand identity—its name, graphic expression, and packaging. And, without a budget for advertising, it was vital that the product communicate with clarity and strength from a store shelf or in a press photograph.

To establish credibility, they chose to associate the product with a real person and marry it to the key characteristics of the identity: clean, simple, functional, and male. From there they explored a variety of naming options, such as Anthony Products, Anthony Tactics, Anthony Strategies, and others that fit within the creative parameters established. Taking a short list of the most promising names into focus groups, the clear winner was "Anthony Logistics for Men." Respondents felt this name best communicated strength, modernity, utility, cleanliness, and masculinity.

After a thorough creative exploration, the chosen visual identity was a strong, clean, and modern wordmark paired with a red dot reminiscent of the Bauhaus. The arrow symbol evokes a map icon "directing" the user to his end objective. Alternatively, this arrow triangle can be seen as an abstract letter "A." The overall feeling: essentially useful, essentially male.

The label was designed to project concise, matter-of-fact simplicity (without seeming clinical), while catching the purchaser's eye in an engaging and entertaining manner. Consistent with the overall attitude, the label uses witty copy in a way that helps the consumer reach his mission with a smile. The "Objective" tells the purpose; the "Strategy" explains the ingredients and their effect; the "Method of Use" explains how to use the product. A deodorant stick invites users to "Laugh at the sun and sneer at the wind!" A shampoo suggests, "Hair so rich it will pay for dinner."

The package—created to be stylish, yet timeless, rather than trendy—uses gray, black, and white utilitarian lines to achieve a clean, masculine look. The bottles are constructed of clear or opaque plastic with off-white coloration, reinforcing the idea that the customer is paying for function, rather than packaging. The products themselves are light in texture and alcohol-free, attributes that proved essential to potential purchasers during testing.

Anthony Logistic for Men is a true success story. They have been able to attract partnerships with established names in the cosmetic, fashion, and personal-care arenas and commitments from specialty stores like Sephora and Fred Siegel, as well as major department stores, including New York's fashionable Barney's, who showcased Anthony products in its windows. The line has expanded to include additional men's products, and sales have exponentially exceeded projections.

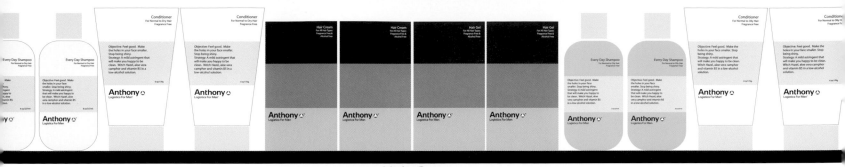

Hair Care

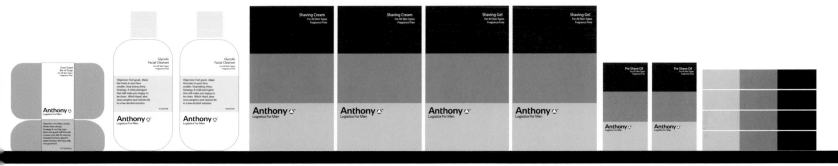

Shave

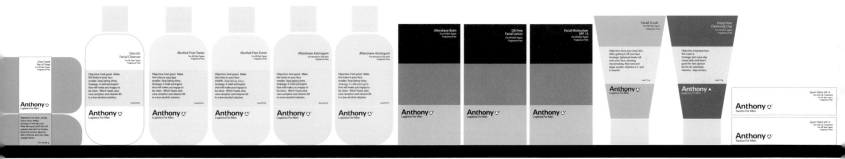

Face

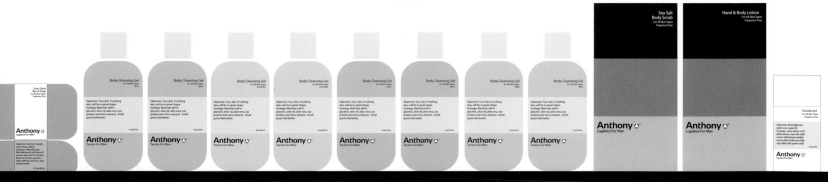

Body

MORE TH>N™

Who is the client? What do they do?

More TH>N was developed as an off-shoot of the large U.K.-based insurance company Royal and SunAlliance (RSA), to provide direct insurance (i.e., by phone, mail, or web) for all sorts of insurance needs—homes, pets, cars, etc. They also offer some financial products and a credit card.

What problem were you asked to solve?

Royal and SunAlliance, itself a merger of two older British insurance and pension companies, had been trying to develop a direct insurance offer, without any great success. The decision was made to create a separate company that would have a new name and brand identity, and RSA would be there to back them up for those worried about heritage and other issues of continuity.

What personality and brand attributes were you asked to convey?

It was pretty clear that the new company had to be modern—RSA is not seen as a "modern" company and thus struggled to compete in the rather fast and furious direct-insurance market. It was also highly desirable to be clear, open, trustworthy, and helpful. The core of the MORE TH>N brand is to help people get their lives in order by letting MORE TH>N take care of all the details.

Who was the target audience?

It basically splits into two, along roughly age-based lines: fifty-somethings with money to invest, and insurance to take out, and then the more critical younger twenty- to forty-somethings, to whom RSA had not previously been reaching out to.

Talk about the collaborative working process between you and your client?

The core of the process was ourselves, the client, and the branding/naming consultants, Brand Guardians. Two names were short listed and initial designs developed, a period of internal and external review took place, then MORE TH>N was chosen as the agreed-upon name and identity.

What applications did you design for this logo? In what media?

To demonstrate the "legs" of the identity, we routinely tested the identity across many media: print, electronic, TV, etc. In this case much of our work was theoretical, used as examples to show other agencies "what it should look like" so they could progress to their own applications. The main output from us was the production of a substantial design manual and regular attendance at design reviews. The applications are carried out by above- and below-the-line specialists: web designers, ad agencies, etc.

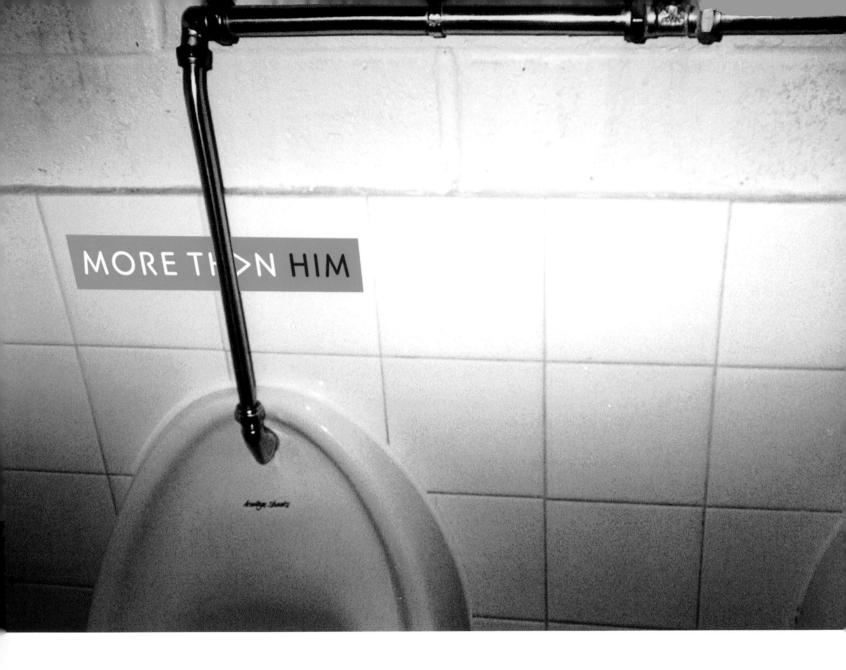

Johnson Banks designed the MORE TH>N logo to set this insurance company apart from its competition. Playing off the name, the designers incorporated the scientific symbol for "greater than" in conjunction with custom drawn sans serif, all-caps type. The theatrically styled photograph above was created to represent an advertising concept that is as unusual as the logo itself.

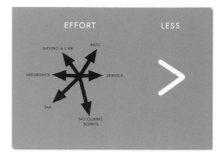

Why did the client choose you to design this logo?

We had had a conversation with them about their plans for a direct insurance arm many years before, and had advised them that the Royal and SunAlliance "brand" wasn't really elastic enough to do the job. The time wasn't right then, but three years later, in conjunction with Brand Guardians, they returned to us for more advice and we were appointed to do the project.

Why did you make the aesthetic choices you made?

The name chosen is a remarkable one really—almost on the first day of work we began drawing logos with more-than or greater-than symbols in them, it just seemed the logical thing to do. And in research no one seemed to have any problems with it either. We were a little worried about the use of a slightly obscure keystroke, but it seems to work well, and it's rare that you can identify a company by creating the logo simply by typing with standard keys, so that it looks like this: MORE TH>N.

The ideas evolved. We began to develop a kind of MORE TH>N language which was very useful when making comparative points (more this th>n that, don't accept less than more th>n, etc.).

The identity worked well using caps, in a rounded typeface that we developed specially for the job with type designers The Foundry. The use of capitals has become a kind of brand property in itself (perhaps as a reaction to the lowercase fever set off by the dot-com thing). We also wanted the company to try and "own" a limited color palette, knowing that recognition would be crucial in this area of direct insurance. We recommended a bright green.

Is there anything else you'd like to add?

Well, it seems to work—unprompted awareness of the brand is already good, and this is for a new brand, only two years old. It seems that even when competing with other analogous products, the MORE TH>N brand is already strong enough to differentiate itself.

—Michael Johnson

Pages from the MORE TH>N style manual, above, demonstrate the use of graphic elements that are naturally derived from the logo, as well as the limited color palette, so unusual for insurance company branding. Johnson Banks designed the manual to be a set of "friendly rules, not restrictions." Therefore the manual contains more do's than don'ts.

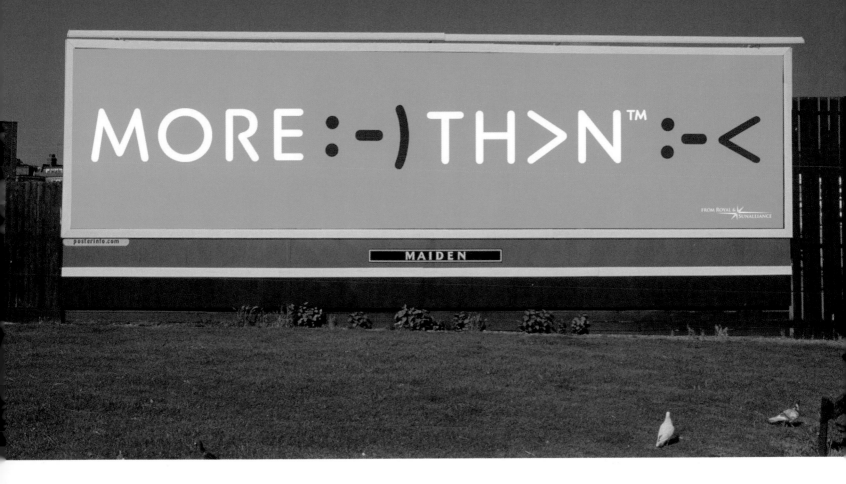

The billboard, above, is another example of the use of iconography borrowed from an industry other than insurance, and incorporated into the logo for a clever, contemporary approach to messaging.

YELLOWBO☒

Yellowbox Studios, a multiple-award-winning sound production house located in Singapore, provides a full range of audio and music services, including music composition and arrangement, and sound design for TV and radio programming, feature films, and documentaries.

Yellowbox Studios needed a logo that would update their image and bring across the professionalism and sophistication for which they were known. The challenge for Kinetic Singapore was to create a simple and strong identity, which would be easily recognized and remembered. The identity needed to convey that the brand is sleek, young, and fun, yet professional and modern. The designers decided on the concept of the "yellow box," a widely recognized international traffic convention, designating that no stopping or waiting is permitted. The symbol is used in many countries mainly to control the traffic and to prevent congestion and chaos. Likewise, Yellowbox Studios believes in getting the job done smoothly and swiftly.

Most of Yellowbox Studios' clients are part of the creative industry—advertising, design, film production, etc. This meant the designers had a very tough job to accomplish—to impress creative people!

Yellowbox Studios knew exactly what they wanted and appreciated what Kinetic Singapore was able to do. It was a relatively seamless process for the designers and a fun collaboration that took about two months to complete.

In addition to the logo, Pann Lim and Roy Poh designed name cards, envelopes, letterheads, CD sleeves, video-tape sleeves and stickers, cassette-tape sleeves, and DAT tape sleeves. These applications became the client's advertisements, all effectively promoting Yellowbox Studios.

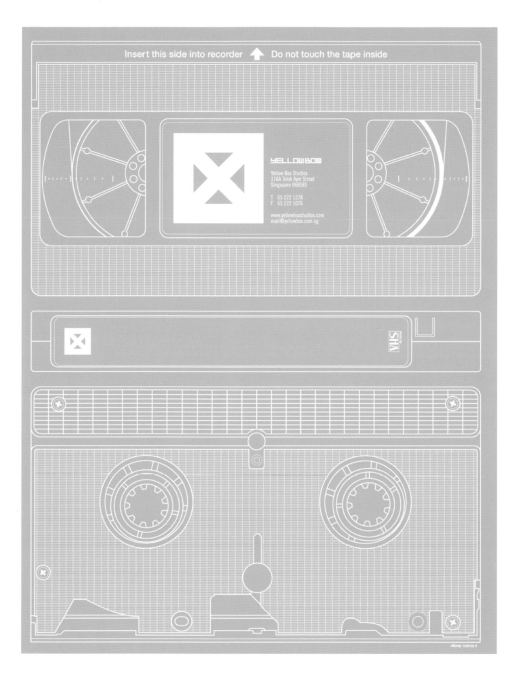

The Yellowbox Studios logo literally incorporates a yellow box containing an "x," which is an internationally recognized traffic symbol for "no stopping or waiting permitted." It is a concept that works well for this sound production company that believes in getting the job done smoothly and swiftly.

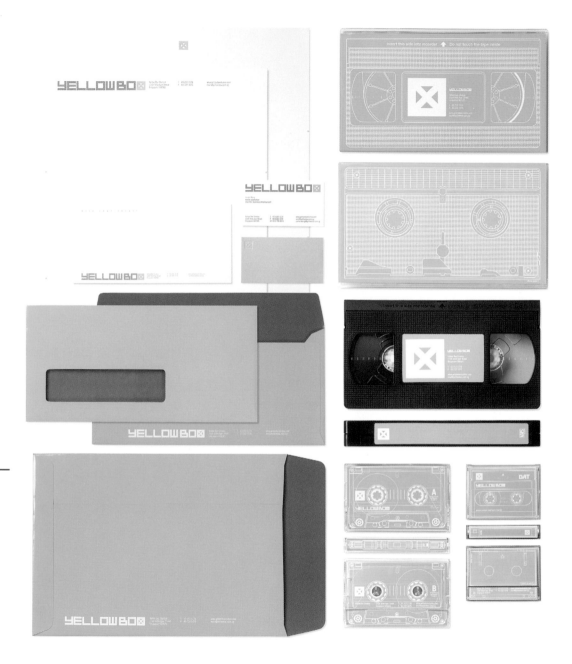

Kinetic Singapore applied the Yellowbox Studios logo to a variety of stationery and video and audio tape labels, as seen right. This approach provided Yellowbox Studios strong brand recognition with standard items required by the client's business.

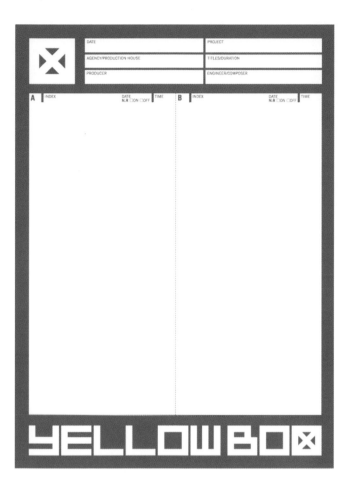

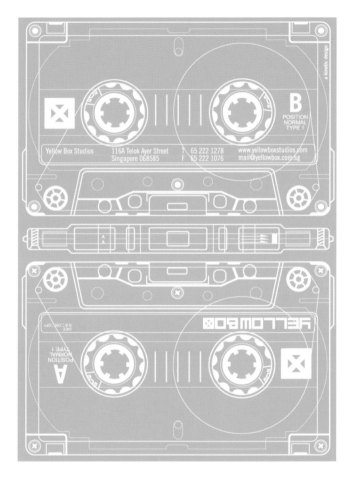

The video-tape sleeves, left, and the video cassette itself, above, became Yellowbox Studios' main self-promotional items by prominently incoporating the fun and easily remembered logo.

ELINK

ELink Communications is a company that retrofits existing buildings with fiber-optic cables capable of delivering high-speed Internet access. They also provide Internet access as a service to the tenants of every building they wire.

ELink was a startup company when they contacted KINETIK. As part of the highly competitive Internet access marketplace, they required a brand that would set them apart. They were interested in a logo that would convey the opposite of startup. Stability, reliability, and creativity were all attributes they asked the designers to consider. KINETIK was charged with creating an identity for a target audience of potential clients that would include building owners and their tenants, investors, and the media. Although ELink did not have the history, establishing a long-term bond with their clients was a core business objective for them.

The company's three founders, as well as their in-house marketing team, were all actively involved in the logo development process from start to finish. They definitely understood the importance of getting their identity right from the beginning and KINETIK was treated as an equal strategic partner in crafting this solution. All work for ELink was done quickly—it took approximately four weeks from kick-off to final mark.

As well as developing the identity, KINETIK created a complete stationery suite and marketing brochure for their client. Web application was handled by ELink's in-house electronic design team using KINETIK 's design strategy for the logo as an inspiration.

In addition to the obvious reference of the linking "Es," the mark is meant to suggest both a three-dimensional structure and the fiber optic "backbone" (their terminology) that ELink installs in buildings.

The Elink logo seen in the stationery package, right, suggests a three-dimensional structure that expresses the company's business of retrofitting buildings with fiber optics to deliver high-speed Internet access.

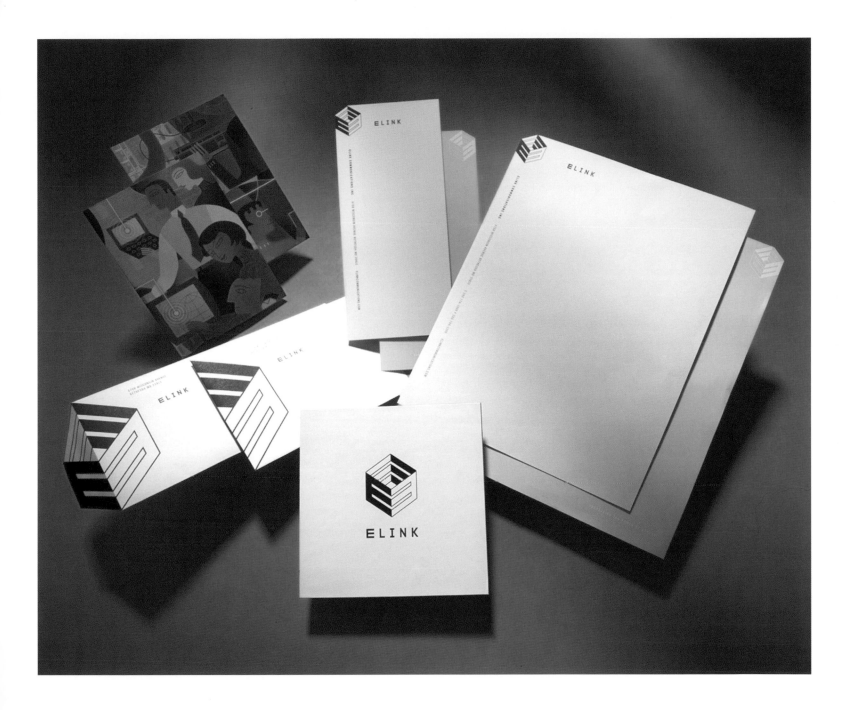

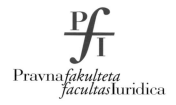

Who is the client? What do they do?

My client was Pravna fakulteta Univerze v Ljubljani, Slovenia, which means in English, The Faculty of Law, University of Ljubljana, Slovenia.

What problem were you asked to solve?

The client didn't have a logo and corporate identity system, but when they moved to a new location, and hired some new faculty, they become aware that they needed a logo. The faculty members of Slovenian universities are perhaps more independent than those in school systems in other western countries. The law faculty in Ljubljana didn't want to get lost among the twenty-six other departments at the university. They wanted to have their own unique identity system. Also, the *Pravna fakulteta* is recognized in the field of law as having a strong book-publishing department. I suggested "Littera Scripta Manet" as the brand name for all publishing activities, because the department is divided into three subdivisions: LITTERA for science articles, SCRIPTA for books and publications on educational programs, and MANET for books with legal themes. Within the Pravna fakulteta Univerze there are also several institutes (e.g., the Institute of Public Administration and the Institute of Comparative Law, which has several Centres), so the new identity system had to work on many levels for a variety of entities.

What personality and brand attributes were you asked to convey?

The client wished to be distinctive and to convey a sense of calmness.

Who was the target audience?

The target audiences were professors and students, as well as other educational institutions of law and science.

Talk about the collaborative working process between you and your clients.

When they were at their old location, I was not able to convince the client to develop a new logo. The law and higher education are slow-changing, conservative fields. After several years, when renovation was completed and the faculty had moved to the new building, our first project was to produce a brochure about the renovation, the architecture, and the story of the many years it took to move from the central university building to their own separate one. The brochure was finished in December 2001. Since that time I have also designed some materials for their New Year celebrations. Over time, the client's trust has grown. When the faculty's new secretary general came with the request for a publishing department identity, I proposed the name "Littera Scripta Manet," and designed the logo, both of which were well received by the client.

The logo for the *Pravna fakulteta* utilizes the concept of balance, historically symbolic of justice. The "f" suggests a scale that weighs the "P" (pravo, Slovenian for law) and the "I" (iuridica, Latin for law). The stationery system, below, conveys conservative elegance.

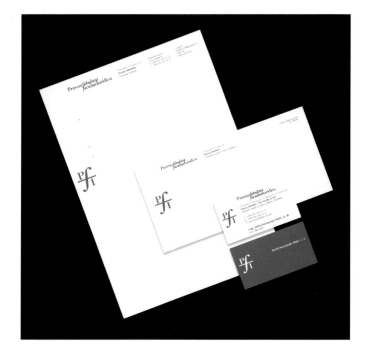

Why did you make the aesthetic choices you made?

Balance is a very old symbol for the law, especially for the courts. Truth, an essential component of the law, is typically in dynamic balance between two opposing sides—the plaintiff and the defendant. For the faculty, I developed a symbol that plays on the concept of balance, with the center of the "f" acting as the pivot point between the "P" (pravo is the Slovenian word for law) and the "I" (iuridica is the Latin word for law). I love to work in classical proportions to create a timeless quality, but I also think that a logo should be dynamic, a little bit witty, and ingenious. I chose the color blue because it represents wisdom.

What applications did you design using the logo? In what media?

The corporate identity has thirty-two elements, such as memorandum, invoices, envelopes, business cards, etc. I only design elements for print applications, another agency creates web pages, which also use a new identity system.

Why did the client choose you to design this logo?

We were chosen for several reasons—first, our studio's architect, Andrej Mlakar, has experience in renovation projects and was involved in the new building, and second because our promotional brochure gave the client trust in KROG's work.

—Edi Berk

Landor Associates	Executive Creative Director: Margaret Youngblood	Art Directors: Margaret Youngblood, Eric Scott; Designer: Kisitina Wong, Cameron Imani (Enviromental Graphics); Production: Tom Venegas, Wayne De Jager; Consultants: Liz Magnusson, Russ Meyer; Project Manager: Bill Larsen, Stephen Lapaz (Identity System)

H&R BLOCK®

H&R Block, traditionally known as a reliable, approachable tax expert, was revitalizing its organization with a new vision to expand well beyond this role. Through acquisitions and new business developments, H&R Block had developed a portfolio of diversified product and service offerings designed to meet all the financial needs of current, as well as prospective, clients. From home mortgages to financial planning and investing, H&R Block's vision was to become an approachable provider of financial services to Main Street America and beyond.

The H&R Block corporate identity needed to be revitalized to express the new vision for the company. They asked Landor Associates to develop a new brand identity that would expand the perception of the H&R brand beyond its historical roots in tax preparation. Since H&R Block has more than 10,000 retail offices, one of the key applications for the new identity system would be signage and interiors. The new identity elements needed to be interchangeable in order to have stature, as well as bold promotional attitude, in both the retail environment and on corporate materials.

Originally, H&R Block was known as middle America's tax preparator, but the new identity helps expand the perception of H&R Block as a financial services company for both middle- and high-income individuals alike.

Landor developed a new corporate identity system, anchored by the green block. The block, an obvious graphic representation of the company's name, expresses the solid relationship between H&R Block and its customers. Overall, the contemporary yet flexible identity system communicates a dynamic, new and expanded H&R Block— emotionally engaged with its financial services clients, and able to communicate different key messages to its expanding audience.

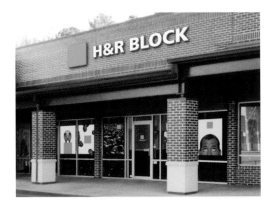

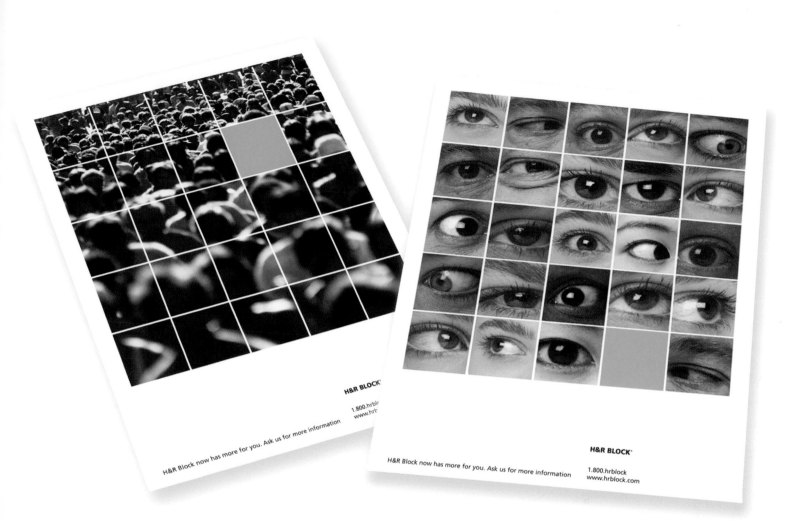

H&R BLOCK

1.800.hrblock
www.hrblock.com

H&R Block now has more for you. Ask us for more information

The H&R Block identity, seen left in building signage, and above in the company's sales brochure, features a green block symbol, which is an obvious graphic representation on the company's name, as well as an expression of the solid relationship between this financial services company and its customers. The green square is often used as a super graphic and a freestanding element as long as H&R Block is clearly identified with the primary signature, seen upper left, somewhere else in the application. The logo is used in a variety of media, including environmental, web, print, broadcast, and identity systems and was designed to be flexible enough to work well in all of these.

JAL

Landor, Tokyo worked with Japan Airlines to create a new identity when Japan Airlines and Japan Air System merged to become JAL. The resulting JAL brand mark needed to express a fresh business philosophy and strategy, while being flexible enough to apply at every touchpoint that travelers, airline employees, and travel advisors have exposure to the brand.

Landor was presented with the challenge of developing a global design worthy of representing JAL's position as Japan's leading airline in the twenty-first century. JAL strove to improve their brand value with their primary target audience: the passenger. Landor, an acknowledged expert in branding as well as airline identity projects, had designed the previous JAL logo fourteen years ago. Clearly, JAL had confidence in the firm.

The project was started in April 2002, and is scheduled to be finished in April 2004, when the integration and rollout process will be complete. The development of the new JAL mark took approximately three months. Several other related projects, such as implementing the logo on numerous and varied applications, is an ongoing task. Airline identity programs are, of course, large undertakings. In JAL's case, Landor designed approximately 300,000 items, including aircraft graphics, ticket counter signage, tickets, amenity packages, uniforms, and so forth.

In terms of the aesthetics and concept of the new logo, Landor designed "The Arc" symbol that reaches dynamically toward the sky and represents the sun. The arc was derived from the motif of a rising sun, one of the best known icons of Japan.

Japan Airlines' new JAL brand mark, as seen on the aircraft, right, features a graphic element that designers at Landor's Toyko office call "The Arc." In its dynamic rise toward the sky, the arc symbol also represents the sun, one of the best known icons of Japan.

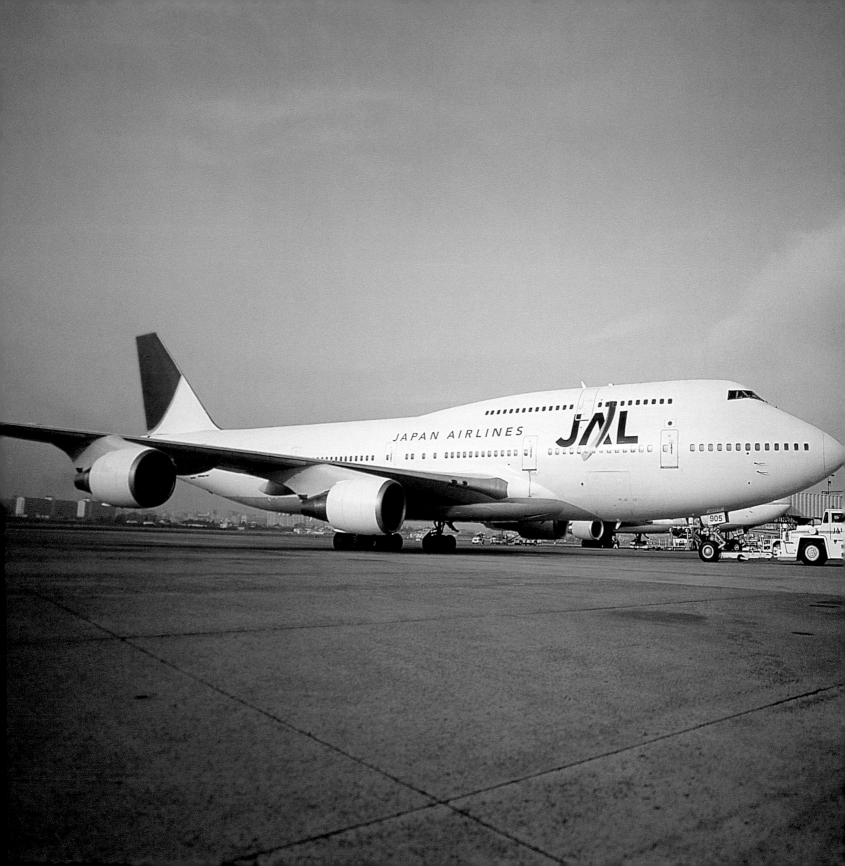

Liska + Associates, Inc.	Creative Director: Steve Liska	Art Director: Stev Liska
		Designer: Kim Fry
		Photography: Todd Rosenberg, Cheryl Mann

**HUBBARD
STREET**
DANCE
CHICAGO

Since 1977, Hubbard Street Dance Chicago (HSDC) has earned the reputation as one of the most innovative contemporary American dance troupes. It is known throughout the U.S. and the world for its passionate and eclectic approach to performance. HSDC has grown to include a second company, Hubbard Street 2, as well as the Lou Conte Dance School, a division that runs dance-based education and community programs. The company now brings challenging work from both American and international choreographers to audiences worldwide.

The client's most urgent goal was to create materials for HSDC's twenty-fifth anniversary Spring 2003 Engagement that would help increase ticket sales. But before designers Liska + Associates could produce appropriate materials, they needed to redefine the company brand. This would involve designing an updated identity and crafting a brand strategy that the company could grow with.

HSDC began with choreographer Lou Conte and four dancers who performed for senior citizens. Gradually it evolved into an

internationally known troupe featuring Broadway-inspired American dance. In recent years, however, HSDC had shifted its focus from performing purely American dance to performing new work from international choreographers. When Jim Vincent became artistic director, his experience and professional relationships ensured that the company would continue to pursue a global artistic vision.

The Hubbard Street Dance Company logo, designed by Liska + Associates, uses an icon formed by the juxtaposition of a bold typographic "H" intersecting with a fluid "S," all contained within a formal square, as seen right, in a poster for the group.

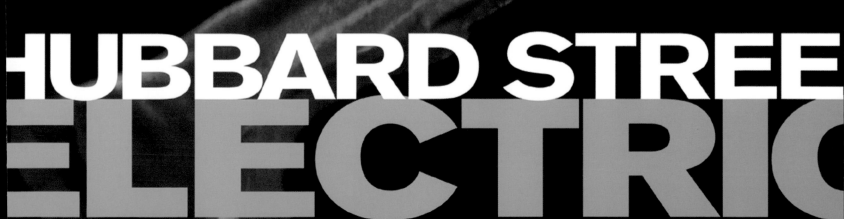

HUBBARD STREET
DANCE
CHICAGO

JIM VINCENT,
ARTISTIC DIRECTOR

HUBBARD STREE

ELECTRIC

While HSDC was changing, however, its brand did not—consequently, it no longer represented the company. Part of the challenge was to design a brand that did. In addition, Liska + Associates had to address issues of awareness to achieve the client's goal of attracting new audiences, sponsors, and donors. Although many people were familiar with the Hubbard Street name, quite a few did not know what type of dance the company now featured, or what to expect from a performance. Ironically, the company was better known outside of its hometown, as it spends only a few weeks performing in Chicago and the remainder of the year traveling around the globe. The twenty-fifth anniversary Spring Engagement debuted with a three-week dance series in Chicago, which gave the designers the opportunity to rebuild interest and awareness in local audiences, and to communicate what Hubbard Street embodies today.

Liska + Associates' final challenge, once the rebranding project was completed, was to make sure that all the twenty-fifth anniversary program materials were available to the various promoters around the world who bring Hubbard Street to their cities. In the past, promoters had created their own marketing materials, which were inconsistent with the Hubbard Street brand and contributed to the public's confusion. An easy-to-use, cost-effective program for distributing HSDC marketing materials anywhere in the world needed to be developed.

The target audience for the redesign were the HSDC insiders—dance aficionados, cultural tourists, dance and arts media people, badge-value people (those who attend the most popular arts performances to maintain their image and social status). Of course, it was also important to attract new audience members—people either unaware of the company or who don't typically attend dance performances.

The first step in Liska + Associates' strategy was defining what makes the brand. Since it was critical to define the Hubbard Street Dance Chicago brand before expressing it through new materials, the designers started a dialog with key people at the dance company to establish its attributes, personality, and key points of difference. They discussed what was different about the HSDC of today versus what it had been in the past. Working with this information, the core audience was defined. Market research data that the company had gathered from audience members was also analyzed. With this information came an understanding of what Hubbard Street embodies today.

Although a key difference is that Hubbard Street was now performing pieces from choreographers around the world, it was determined that the troupe's most consistent characteristic has always been its imaginative and bold approach. It became clear that the HSDC brand essence is defined by its artistic style, not by its repertoire, which is constantly changing. Above all, Liska +

Associates remained focused on how they could help achieve Hubbard Street's goal of selling more tickets than ever to its twenty-fifth anniversary Spring Engagement.

Once Hubbard Street's personality was defined, the second step was to begin developing HSDC's new visual branding. This involved creating logos for each of the troupe's divisions: Hubbard Street 2 and the Lou Conte Dance School.

The new identity reflects the company's artistic vision, as it juxtaposes formal elements with fluid, changing ones. Each of the four divisions has a logo that clearly links it to the equity of the Hubbard Street name so that people will recognize that all the divisions are connected. Liska + Associates also developed all aspects of the brand, from its color palettes, imagery, and fonts, to a tagline that emphasized HSDC's longevity and personality.

To communicate what the Hubbard Street Dance Chicago brand represents Liska + Associates made design choices that would capture the energy of an HSDC performance, project boldness (the company's most distinguishing characteristic), visually connect the four divisions under the HSDC umbrella, show the range of dance genres that HSDC performs, avoid dance clichés in the treatment of HSDC images and their art direction, and ultimately, compel people to want to attend a performance.

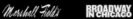

25 YEARS

HUBBARD STREET
DANCE CHICAGO

JIM VINCENT,
ARTISTIC DIRECTOR

HUBBARD STREET
25 YEARS

25 Years of Bold Moves in Chicago.

March 25–April 13
Ford Center for the Performing Arts, Oriental Theatre

3 breathtaking premieres
3 enthralling programs
3 electrifying weeks of Hubbard Street old and new!

Program information: **hubbardstreetdance.com**

TARGET   Marshall Field's   BROADWAY IN CHICAGO   FORD CENTER FOR THE PERFORMING ARTS • O·R·I·E·N·T·A·L •

Photo: Todd Rosenberg. Design: Liska + Associates

Liska + Associates designed ads that project
Hubbard Street's boldness as a company
by using dynamic images of dancers, vivid
colors and strong, bold typography. The ads
were the first item released to the public
to introduce the twenty-fifth anniversary
Spring Engagement, and were key to ticket
sales. Photo: Todd Rosenberg

The third step was forming a long-term brand strategy. To succeed in building ticket sales for Hubbard Street, the new brand needed to appeal to a broad range of people. Once they attend, people generally react to a Hubbard Street performance with an overwhelmingly enthusiastic response that often transforms them into long-term fans. So the company's brand materials were infused with the same excitement and energy as a HSDC performance. Each piece became an opportunity to give potential audience members a better idea of what a performance is like and to break down their preconceptions about dance.

Rather than choosing cold, impersonal images, the designers promoted an empathy with dancers who appear very human. Clichéd dance images were avoided. Instead, Liska + Associates sought individual ones that fit the personality of the troupe. The Hubbard Street materials project elements of anticipation and suspended movement to intrigue people on an emotional level while capturing their attention. The HSDC identity system uses drama to present the company's performances as events not to be missed, emphasizing their boldness and excitement through color, type, and imagery.

The fourth step was developing the twenty-fifth anniversary materials. With this new brand strategy as a foundation, the designers used the identity system to create both the twenty-fifth anniversary Spring Engagement materials and general brand materials for the dance company and its various divisions. Liska + Associates designed applications for a comprehensive range of media: ads, direct mail pieces, brochures, posters, signage, banners, a website, and a television commercial.

The final step in the collaboration between Liska + Associates and their client was to leave instructions for others who will continue to produce brand materials, either internally at HSDC or through external vendors. Liska + Associates developed a solution that would also support promoters around the world with consistently branded marketing materials that could be used to advertise a twenty-fifth anniversary Hubbard Street performance in their cities. An online brand manual now contains all the brand standards, including everything from a general definition of the brand's personality and attributes to specifications for its color palette and typography. It also includes approved art files that users can download

to create Hubbard Street materials, as well as detailed instructions for reproducing brand elements such as ads. This interactive, password protected manual is accessible from anywhere through the Internet and costs nothing to distribute.

Hubbard Street Dance Chicago not only met their goal for increased ticket sales during their twenty-fifth anniversary Spring Engagement, they exceeded them. At a time when arts organizations around the country were forced to adapt to the challenges of a slow economy, the new communication program succeeded in helping Hubbard Street expand interest and draw new audiences to see the dance company in action. The Hubbard Street Dance Chicago rebranding program also attracted attention from the local business media, including columnist Lewis Lazare at the *Chicago Sun-Times*.

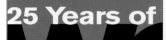

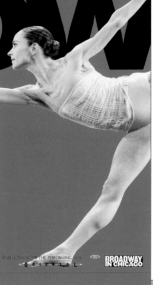

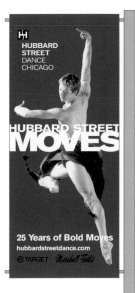

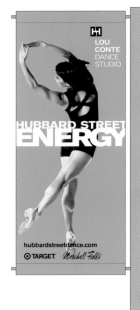

Banners on streetlight poles outside the Chicago theater where Hubbard Street performs built awareness about the company and encouraged people to find out more about attending a performance by visiting the HSDC website. These banners also connected Hubbard Street's various divisions by picturing each logo.

PHILHARMONIE ESSEN

Who is the client? What do they do?
Our client was the Philharmonie Essen, the institution which
manages the Philharmonic Orchestra of Essen, Germany, as well
as its concert hall.

What problem were you asked to solve?
Essen, one of the biggest towns in Germany, is located in the highly
populated and industrialized area along the river Ruhr. There is a
vibrant cultural scene with numerous internationally acclaimed music
and art festivals. Formerly under joint administration with Essen's
theater and ballet, the Philharmonie Essen was now to be established
as an autonomous institution. The Philharmonie Essen aims to play
a major part in the development and cultivation of the city's cultural
scene, and to extend its already excellent reputation, both nationally
and internationally. A strong corporate identity was needed to
communicate the new independent status, as well as to deliver a
lasting visual framework to represent the client.

Who was the target audience?
We were designing primarily for an educated audience.

What was the creative time frame?
It took about three months.

What applications did you design for this logo? In what media?
Mostly we developed all kinds of print material—stationery, business
cards, advertisements, programs, brochures—but we did some work
for use on the Internet as well.

Why did the client choose you to design this logo?
Our presentations, coupled with our conceptual approach, convinced
the client of Manx's ability to cope with the challenge of developing
a successful and strong corporate identity for a renowned cultural
institution.

Why did you make the aesthetic choices you made?
The whole design is based upon a handwritten typeface, exclusively
designed for the Philharmonie Essen. This was done to reflect the
one-of-a-kindness of a great concert or performance captured in the
uniqueness of handwriting. A number of meta-signs were derived
from this typeface, including the logo.

—Iris Thieme

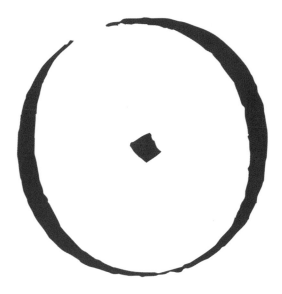

PHILHARMONIE
ESSEN

Manx designed the elegant identity for
the Philharmonie Essen Orchestra of Essen,
Germany, based on a handwritten version
of a classic serif typeface.

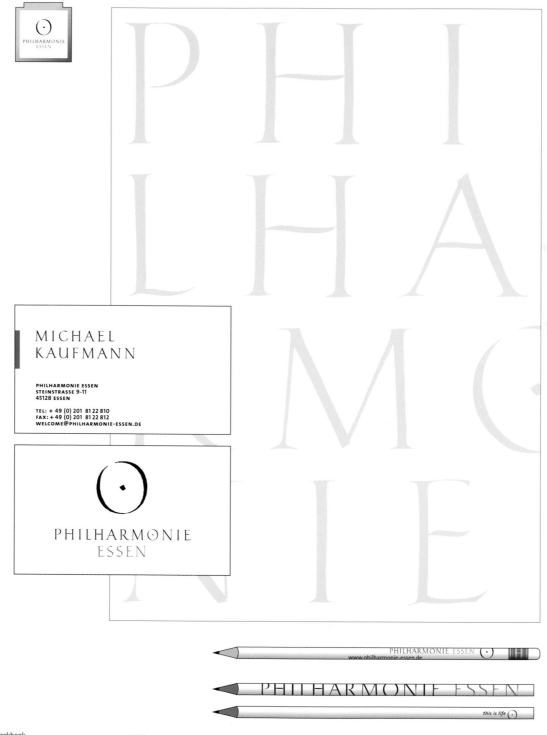

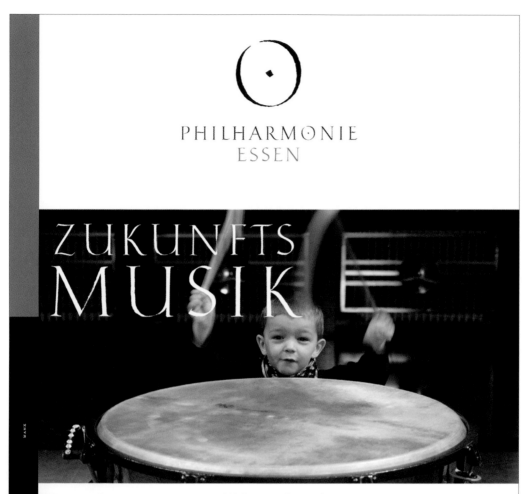

NOCH IST ES ZUKUNFTSMUSIK, ABER AB JUNI 2004* WIRD DIE THEATER & PHILHARMONIE ESSEN UM EINE WEITERE SPARTE UND SPIELSTÄTTE REICHER: NEBEN DEM ERFOLGREICHEN AALTO-THEATER MIT OPER, ORCHESTER UND BALLETT UND DEM SCHAUSPIEL IM GRILLO-THEATER WERDEN IN DER PHILHARMONIE ESSEN REGIONALE, NATIONALE UND INTERNATIONALE KÜNSTLER DAFÜR SORGEN, DASS ESSEN NOCH BESSER KLINGT!

*ERÖFFNUNG DER PHILHARMONIE ESSEN

FREUEN SIE SICH MIT UNS AUF DIE PHILHARMONISCHE ZUKUNFT! MELDEN SIE SICH BEI UNS, UND WIR INFORMIEREN SIE GERNE ÜBER DIE WEITERE PLANUNG DER PHILHARMONIE ESSEN. **WWW.PHILHARMONIE-ESSEN.DE**

this is life

The stationery system, opposite, and print advertisement, left, both make use of the Philharmonie Essen icon, which features a handwritten, unconnected circle surrounding a central dot, visually expressing the experience of a performance by this renowned cultural institution.

VENDARIA
moving pictures. moving products.

Vendaria, an Internet company whose technology and services enable manufacturers to showcase their product to online shoppers, entered the market just as e-commerce began to lose its initial luster. The startup company needed to be positioned as exceptionally tech-savvy, professional, and stable.

Methodologie coined the name Vendaria to emphasize the two major aspects of their core business: selling products (vend) and making them sing (aria). The tagline—moving pictures, moving products—captures these related aspects. The signature is a strong reflection of the brand platform, the free-form "V" symbol lends movement and emotional energy, which complements the stable, confident logo of the company name presented in all-caps.

A clean, sophisticated website and business-paper system express the company's credibility. Shades of gray and red evoke a highly professional image, while subtle touches of design originality capture Vendaria's innovative offerings.

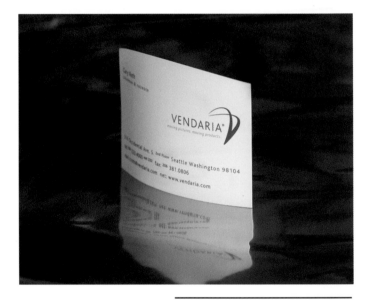

The Vendaria logo expresses the energy and movement of the client's Internet retailing services. The business card, above, and web page, right, speak to a balance of credibility and innovation.

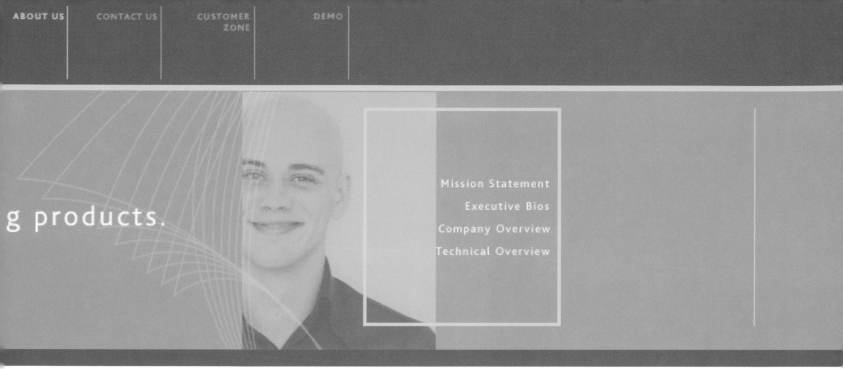

ABOUT US   CONTACT US   CUSTOMER ZONE   DEMO

g products.

Mission Statement
Executive Bios
Company Overview
Technical Overview

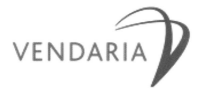

VENDARIA

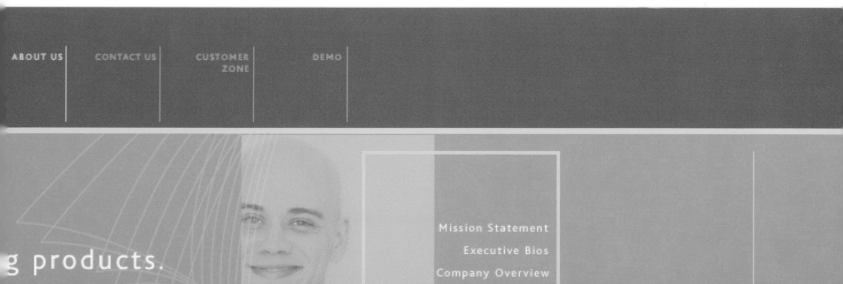

ABOUT US   CONTACT US   CUSTOMER ZONE   DEMO

g products.

Mission Statement
Executive Bios
Company Overview
Technical Overview

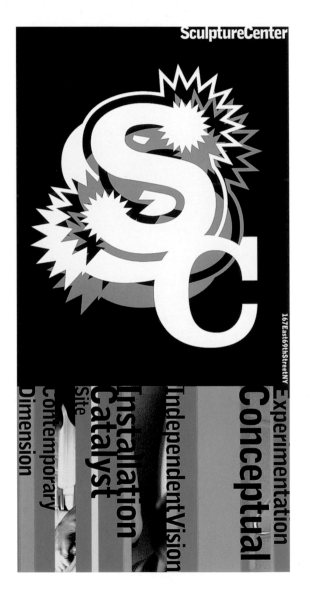

SculptureCenter is a New York–based, not-for-profit gallery space showcasing new and upcoming artists. When SculptureCenter made the shift in their programming from traditional three-dimensional sculpture to art that *insinuates* volume and dimension, Morla Design was called upon to create an identity system that would raise awareness of the center's new purpose.

Morla Design's solution, as applied to posters, announcements, press kits, and invitations uses a mixture of typographic variations of the "SC" monogram throughout the system to reinforce SculptureCenter's identity and appeal to a younger, downtown audience. A simple yet aggressive color palette of silver, black, and day-glo colors add bold elegance, while straightforward layouts provide easy updates for future rollout.

The poster, left, and stationery systems, right, for SculptureCenter, an artists' gallery space in New York, boldly feature a logo created by Morla Design. Insinuating volume and dimension, the logo uses an aggressive color palette of silver, black, and day-glo colors to add a strong progressive elegance.

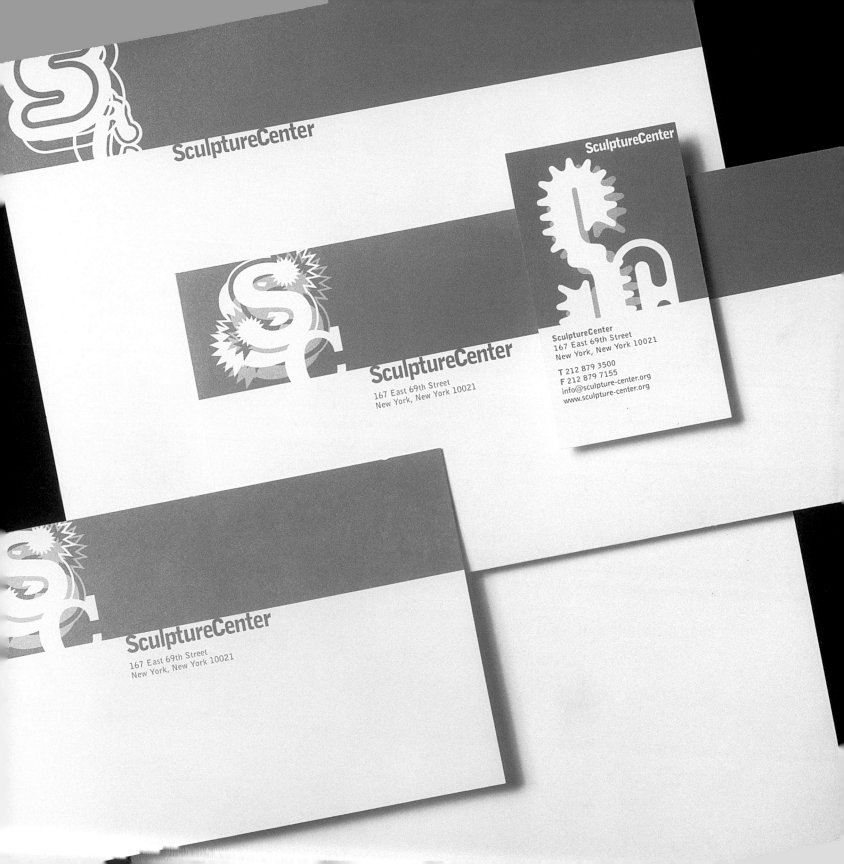

SculptureCenter

SculptureCenter
167 East 69th Street
New York, New York 10021

SculptureCenter
167 East 69th Street
New York, New York 10021

T 212 879 3500
F 212 879 7155
info@sculpture-center.org
www.sculpture-center.org

SculptureCenter
167 East 69th Street
New York, New York 10021

Ogilvy & Mather/ Brand Integration Group New York/Los Angeles	Executive Creative Director: Brain Collins; Managing Director/Brand Strategy: Judd Harner; Senior Brand Strategist: Laurie Cohen	Design Director: Thomas Vasquez; Designer: Jason Ring (Identity System); Designers: Edward Chiquitucto, Jason Ring (Packaging System); Creative Director: Michael Ian Kaye; Senior Designer: Alan Dye; Designers: Bill Darling, Sooyhyen Park (CeBit Booth)

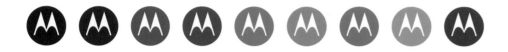

Motorola, a global technology leader and one of the world's largest manufacturers of cell phones, hired Ogilvy & Mather in late 2000 to revitalize their 72-year-old brand. Although Motorola had literally invented the mobile phone in 1983, it was beginning to lose market share.

When Motorola introduced a line of cutting-edge phones, Ogilvy & Mather seized that opportunity to recast the brand's image by positioning it at the intersection of fashion and advanced technology. The brand name "Moto," an abbreviation of Motorola, was adopted globally as a key part of the brand's new identity and communication platform.

In 2001, Motorola was hunting for a firm to redesign its famous logo when it talked to Ogilvy's Brand Integration Group (BIG). Brian Collins, executive creative director of BIG, lobbied Motorola to retain their classic "em-signia" mark and make it more contemporary with fresh meaning. Motorola hired BIG to create a new identity and global packaging system based on this direction. The project had to be completed within one year.

BIG worked closely with its agency partners to drive the new identity system throughout the advertising campaign, which included print, TV, outdoor, direct response, interactive, and retail communications. The launch of Moto dovetailed with the emerging consumer trend to view cell phones as an expression of personal style. The bold graphics and iconic, high-fashion photography in the advertising resonated with the very consumers Motorola needed to attract. By the end of 2002, Motorola had overtaken Nokia as the number one cell-phone manufacturer in North America.

As part of the Moto launch, BIG developed the design system for a 32,000-square-foot retail/trade show environment called MotoWorld for CeBit, the world's leading telecommunications trade show, held in Hanover, Germany. MotoWorld simultaneously brings the flexible, larger-than-life design platform of the new identity system to life and showcases Motorola products, accessories, and services. From 2002 to 2003, more than one million people have visited the exhibit and experienced Motorola's blend of leading-edge technology and style.

The redesigned Motorola identity system retains the classic "em-sigia" mark, while repositioning it as the leading U.S. mobile phone manufacturing company, at the intersection of fashion and advanced technology.

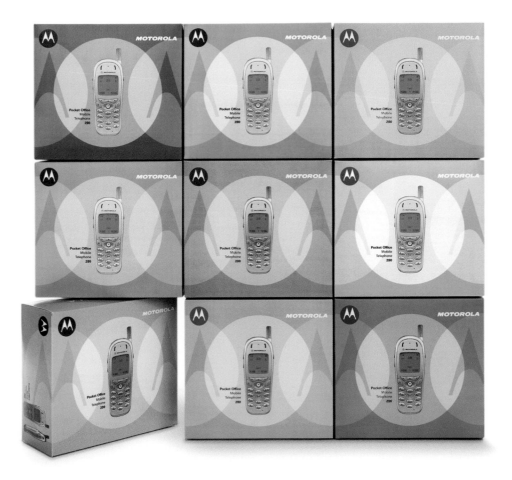

The product packaging, above, is an important part of the Motorola "Moto" re-brand, and features both the logotype and symbol, as well as bold graphics to attract youthful consumers.

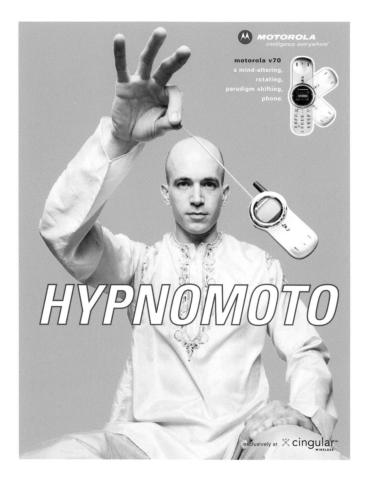

As part of the Moto launch, BIG developed the design system for a retail/trade show environment called "MotoWorld," pictured right, as well as print advertisements, seen above. Both applications have a larger-than-life quality with a prominent use of high-fashion style photography.

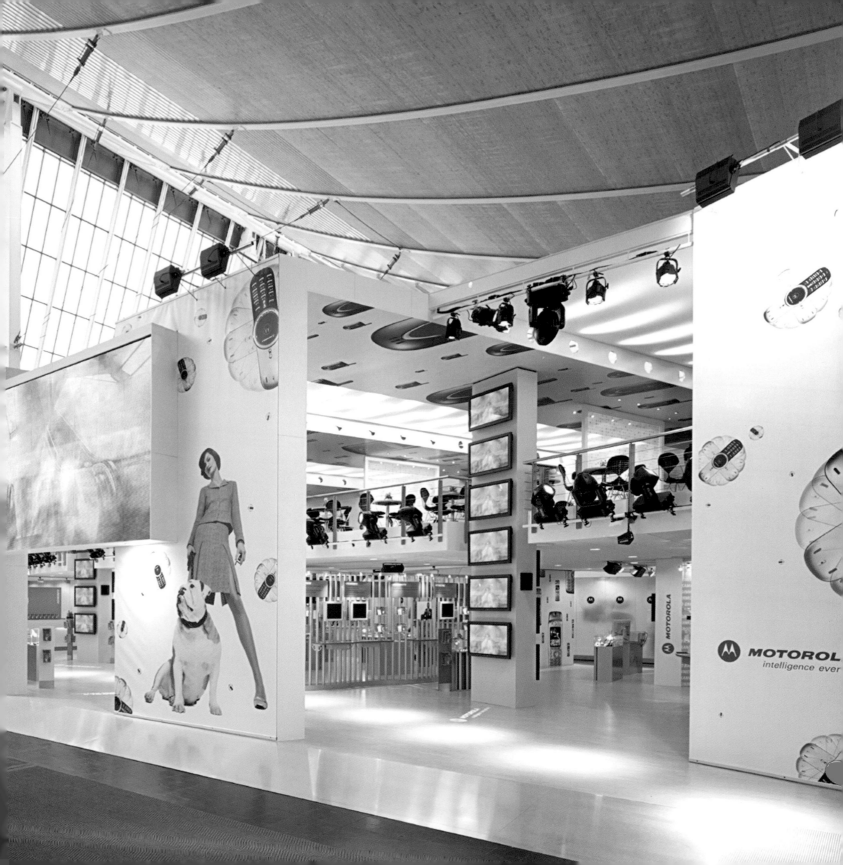

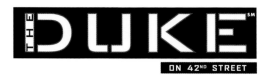

The New 42nd Street Studios is a new building on 42nd Street, located between Broadway and Eighth Avenue in New York, developed by New 42nd Street and designed by Charles Platt of Platt Byard Dovell. The building houses ten floors of rehearsal space for performing-arts groups, as well as the 199-seat Duke Theater on the second floor.

Paula Scher and her team at Pentagram saw the building as a factory for performers. The branding is influenced by de Stijl (an art movement characteized by the use of rectangular shapes and primary colors, as exemplified in the work of Piet Mondrian) and Dutch modernist typefaces. So Pentagram created an identity system that relies heavily on large words set in varied fonts. The logo is an example of the abstract geometric style that alludes to the mathematical order and harmony so prized by de Stijl.

The Pentagram team was broken into two segments: the graphic designers who worked on the identity and the print applications, and the environmental designers who determined ways to integrate and implement the identity within the architecture. According to creative director, Paula Scher, "the project phases were: 1) the big idea, 2) demonstration of the big idea in a variety of situations, 3) shop drawings, and 4) installation. The finished signage installation was almost a direct translation of our initial idea and drawings." The designers created environmental graphics and wayfinding signage for the building based on the new identity, which respects the architecture, activity, and spirit of the place. The environmental graphics are the primary application of the new identity. Throughout the building, graphics perform in the space—oversized words fill narrow hallways, pointing visitors to different floors and rooms. The floor-based system of wayfinding was inspired by the tape marks put down on stages to indicate performers' positioning. The directional words are inlaid on the floor in durable laser-cut vinyl and

The New 42nd Street Studios is a ten-floor performing-arts rehearsal space in New York City. Pentagram's identity system, as seen in the exterior marquee sign, right, for the studios was influenced by de Stijl and Dutch modernist graphics.

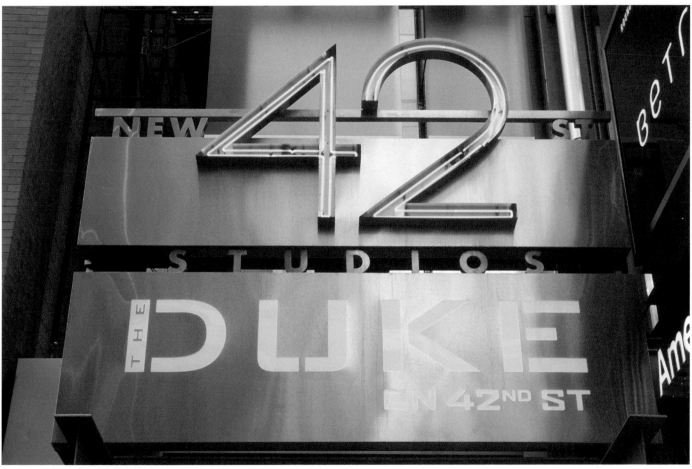

Photographer: Peter Mauss/Esto

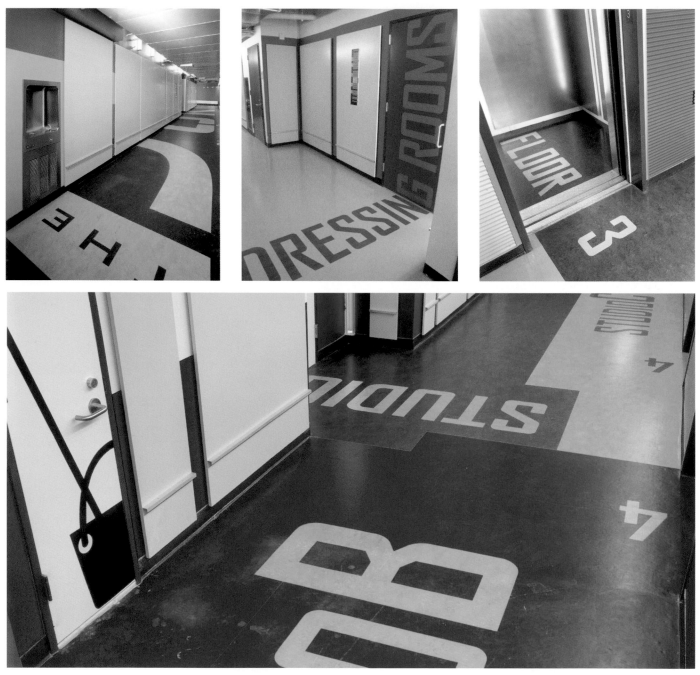

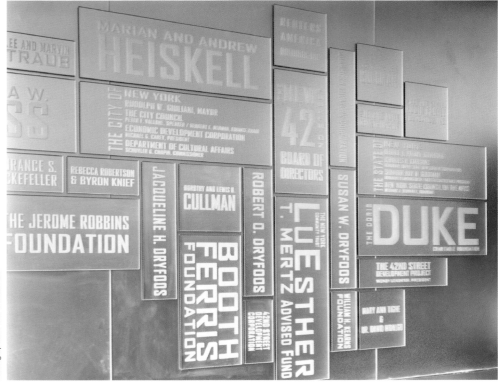

Photographer: Peter Mauss/Esto

continue up the walls when necessary. In the elevators the word "floor" appears inside the car, with the corresponding number positioned at the opening on each level. Applications of typography on the building directory (and in etched mirrored glass on the donor wall) are more traditionally placed but still reflect the frenzy of live performance and the jumble of signage in nearby Times Square.

Pentagram had an existing relationship with the architect of the New 42nd Street Studios, Charles Platt. Scher says, " We had a great relationship, and I love Charles's work. On this project he was very open to having the building graphics collaborate with the architecture." The collaboration was a success. Identity graphics, a distillation of 42nd Street's pulsating neighborhood, make the street and building look good. Since completing the 42nd Street project, Pentagram has since designed a new identity and website for the architects Platt Byard Dovell.

museumofse**x**

The Museum of Sex is dedicated to preserving and presenting the history and cultural significance of human sexuality. Pentagram's logotype for the museum is simple: the words are presented in a single line of delicate, sans serif typography, culminating in an extra-bold "x" at the end of the word "sex." An "x" has been the traditional rating of movies with strong sexual content, and the designation has become more broadly associated with any "forbidden" material. Emphasizing the "x" creates a point of distinction for the logo and also provides a design element that can be used elsewhere on its own (in tickets, signage, etc.). The graphic program is intended to communicate the message that the museum is serious, but not boring; candid, but not prurient. The identity is accessible and does not try to be too clever about referencing the subject matter, which should speak for itself.

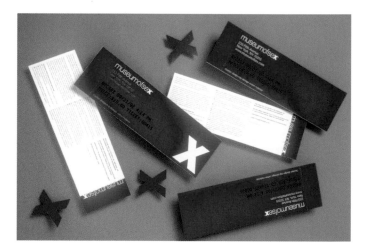

Emphasizing the "x" with extra-bold letterforms at the end of a delicate line of typography is an effective logo for New York's Museum of Sex. The "x" also works alone as an icon to symbolize forbidden and erotic material, as seen above and right, in the entrance tickets and stickers for the museum.

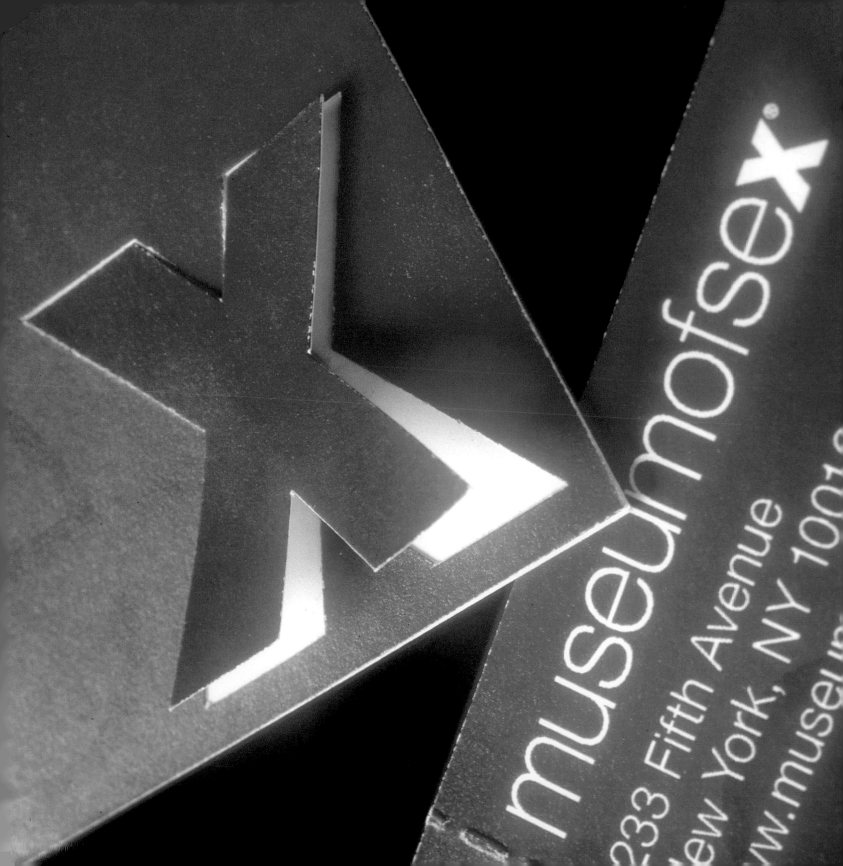

museumofsex
233 Fifth Avenue
New York, NY 1001
w.museum

Design Within Reach (DWR) is a contemporary furniture catalog retailer for a design-sensitive public. Much of modern furniture is manufactured by international furniture companies, and many purveyors of these products are unable to get the stock to the customer in a timely and affordable manner. DWR is a breakthrough retailer because they warehouse the stock, and can get products quickly and reasonably to the buyer. It is truly "design within reach" as the name promises.

Pentagram's creative director Kit Hinrichs had worked with DWR founder Rob Forbes, when Forbes was at The Nature Company, another catalog retailer. When Forbes decided to start his own catalog retail business, Design Within Reach, he looked to Hinrichs and the Pentagram team, who worked and partnered with him right from the beginning to help shape the brand. Forbes had little money, but he had a good idea. Since Hinrichs and Forbes had a history of working together in the past, there was a lot of trust, and, very importantly, they share a common design aesthetic. Pentagram truly helped to incubate Design Within Reach.

Pentagram was challenged to visualize the DWR concept by designing the company's first catalog. The logo came out of the development of the catalog. The name itself clarified the concept, and represented the idea of the design-based business, so the logo is representative of the look of the furniture as well as the client's business idea. The brand attributes are: simplicity, modernism, and clarity. Also the logo needed to express a professional, architectural quality—to feel a bit "inside" to designers.

It's a simple, straightforward logo, with the name set in Futura, a great turn-of-the-century typeface that is modern and geometric. Pentagram felt that it conveyed modernism, and represented the furniture well. The designers chose red because it is a great accent color. Hinrichs liked the clean simplicity of a primary color and the fact that after yellow, red is the most attention-getting color for humans. Also, red worked well in conjunction with the natural materials used in the DWR products.

From the beginning, DWR was targeted to a niche market of people in the design profession. The preferred customers are people who appreciate design, and will purchase furniture through a catalog (about 90% of DWR's business is catalog sales). DWR started out with a list of 100,000 names; they now run millions of catalogs every season. According to Hinrichs, "Rob Forbes's catalog reaches more designers than any other design publication."

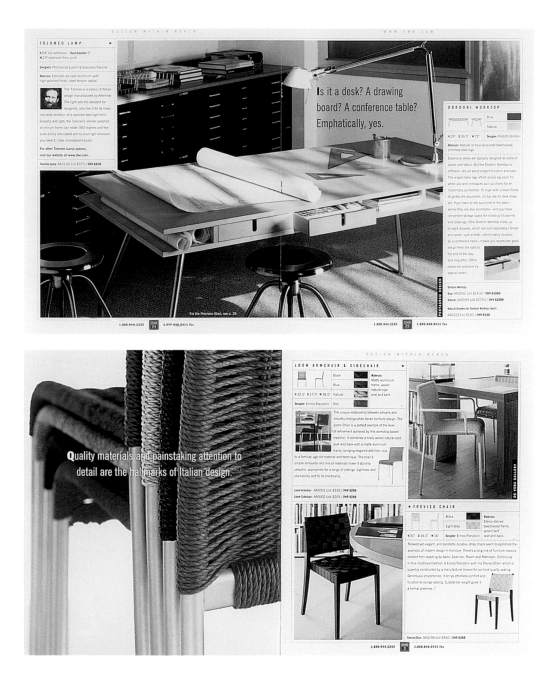

Spreads from the Design Within Reach catalog, left, as well as the logo itself, represent the clean modern lines of the furniture that the company sells. Simple typography, classic geometry, and an accent of red are at the heart of the logo, conveying a sense of modern "design."

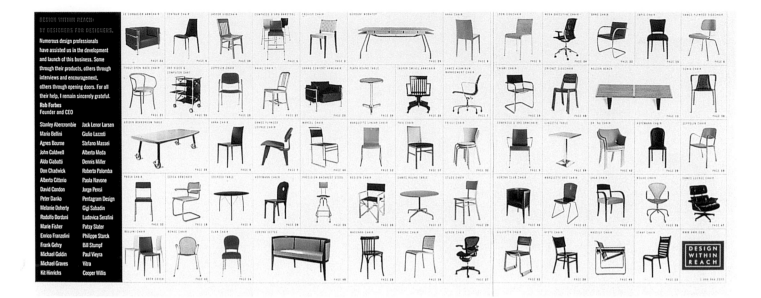

The creative time frame for the logo was a couple of weeks in development, however there were about six months of research and development on the branding and catalog prior to logo design. The total time for development of the logo and first catalog was about six to eight months. Pentagram is now in their fourth year of working with Design Within Reach.

Pentagram developed the DWR catalog, which is now designed and produced by an internal team at DWR, as well as the DWR website, and some retail environmental graphics. They also participated in the design of some experimental work and created a calendar for DWR that is available for purchase through the catalog. Currently, Hinrichs is developing the new DWR Profile Catalog and Pentagram partner, Rob Bruner, is designing some tables that DWR will retail.

In response to DWR's success, Kit Hinrichs says, "It's great to see a place in the retail environment for this company. People were starved for good design. Design Within Reach has an economical point of view, they made sure that design is not just for rich people." Pentagram believed in their client, and played an integral part in the development of the company.

High style without high prices, literally, "design within reach" is the goal of this furniture retailer. Pentagram was challenged to present these ideas in graphic terms as seen in the DWR launch poster, above.

Catalog covers feature the Design Within Reach logo, which uses the Futura typeface contained with a rule and a red box, as seen at right.

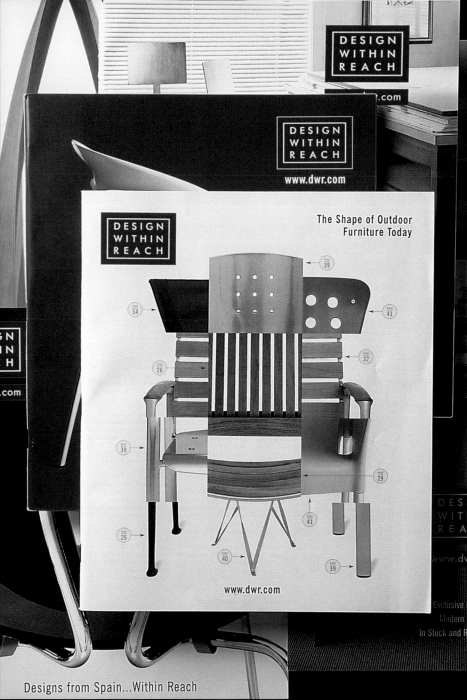

| Pentagram Design, Limited | Art Director: David Hillman | Designers: David Hillman, Deborah Osborne
Photography: Nick Turner |

THE WING | 寰宇堂

Cathay Pacific Airlines required an identity for their new first-class and business-class lounges, restaurants, bars, and spas at Chep Lap Kok, the new international airport in Hong Kong, designed by Foster and Partners. The project required the generation of lounge names, as well as the development of related visual identities and a functional, clear, and appropriate signage system.

The objective was to create an overall visual attitude communicating a sense of sophistication and elegance—an oasis for the stressed or exhausted traveler. It was also important for the names, identities, and graphic language to complement the minimalist lounge interiors, designed by architect John Pawson. Pentagram named the first-class and business-class lounges "The Wing," and created a horizontal, bilingual logotype that is appealing and legible to both local and global travelers. Bars and lounge areas within The Wing were individually named in order to differentiate one from the other, and included "The Haven," "The Long Bar," and "The Runway Bar."

The logotypes were combined with a sophisticated graphic language. A number of cool, serene images were commissioned for printed collateral, with a simple palette of fresh, aquatic colors. The business-class area of The Wing features a range of atmospheric soft-focus photographs, while the first-class area displays a series of sharper black-and-white images. These visual devices were just as important as the logotype in defining the spirit of the identity.

Creative director David Hillman and his team at the London office of Pentagram had a very close working relationship with project architect John Pawson to ensure that the identity and visual elements were complementary to the interiors. The project was completed in approximately three months, and was launched in the summer of 1999.

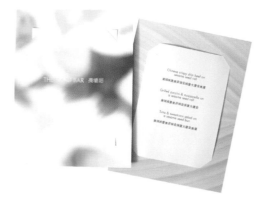

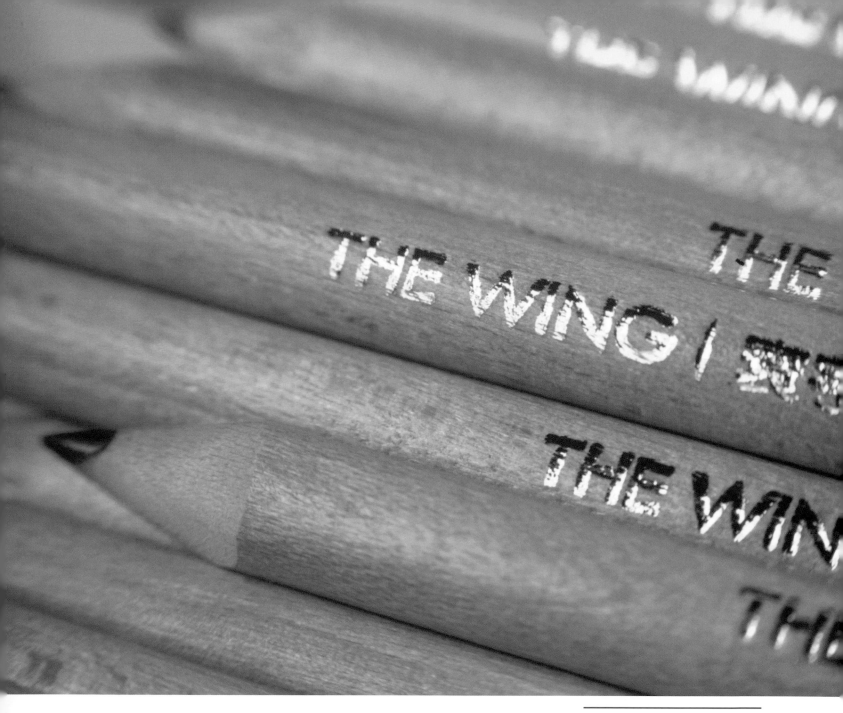

The Wing logo, which communicates a sense of sophistication and elegance, was applied to a variety of objects, including pencils, above, used in the lounge to create brand continuity.

Pentagram designed print applications including menus, corporate (and passenger) stationery, and bar accessories such as napkins, coasters, and sugar sachets. The design program also included a signage system with a series of brushed, acid-etched, stainless-steel plates, in-filled with cool gray. In addition, the client asked Pentagram to select the crockery, cutlery, and other accoutrements for all lounge areas, bars, and restaurants to maintain a strong and consistent visual language.

Cathay Pacific chose to work with Pentagram because the firm had created many effective and appropriate logos in the past for a number of Hong Kong–based and other far-eastern clients. Pentagram had also worked with one of the clients in Hong Kong on another project, who recommended Pentagram for the Cathay Pacific job.

Aesthetically, the identity reflects the need to present The Wing (and other areas) as an oasis for exhausted travelers, and to complement the sophistication and elegance of the lounges themselves. It was also integral for the solution to be legible to travelers from around the world, and to reflect the brand values of Cathay Pacific without conflicting with their core identity.

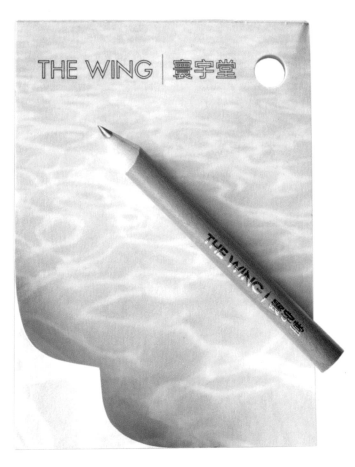

The Wing notepad, above, and the stationery system, opposite, reflect the fresh aquatic color palette, and atmospheric soft-focus photographs used by Pentagram to convey a sense of serenity for weary travelers at Hong Kong's Chep Lap Kok International Airport.

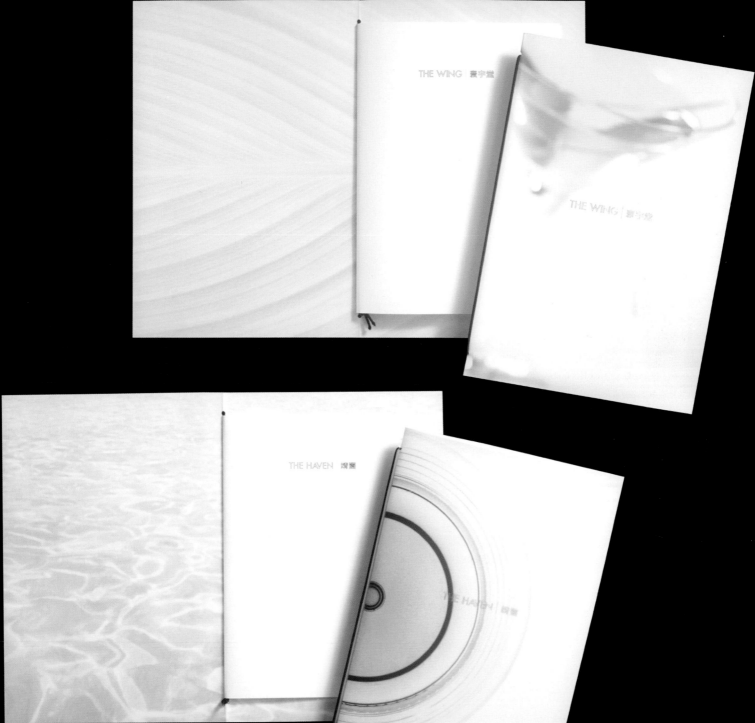

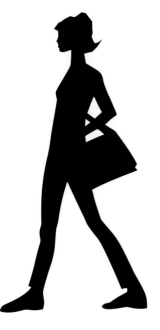

Alex Goes is an up-market women's sportswear line launched by Quiksilver. Ph.D was involved in all aspects of the development of this clothing line from the beginning. They developed the name and identity, worked on product development, and the art direction and advertising.

Targeted for smart, hip, active women, Alex Goes is a flexible identity. There is no single logo for Alex. A lone green dot—a Go Light— appears on the exterior of the garments, whereas one of thirty different custom-woven labels adorns the inside of each piece. The project was essentially an exercise in nonbranding to establish a brand. Ph.D tries to be smart, and reflect the intelligence of their clients in the work they produce, and Alex Goes is a great example of this philosophy.

In addition to the identity, Ph.D designed a full range of applications, including stationery, advertising, print collateral, clothing labels, hangtags, and promotional items.

alex goes

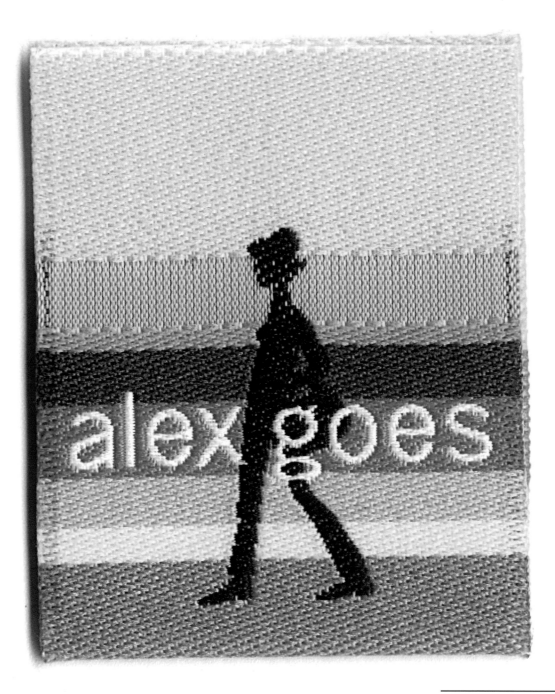

One of the thirty different custom-woven labels for Quicksilver's Alex Goes brand of women's sportswear features one of the many logos created for the company.

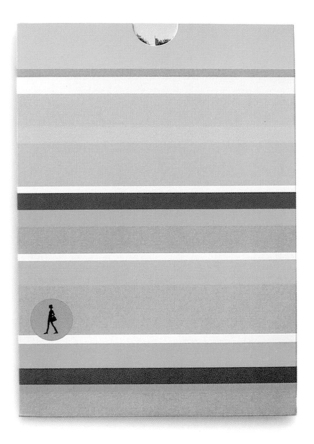

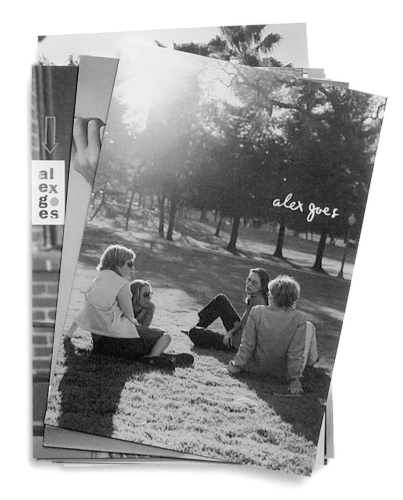

Promotional sales brochures for Alex Goes
fit inside a slipcase with finger tab.
These pieces reflect the hip, active
women who are the brand's customers.

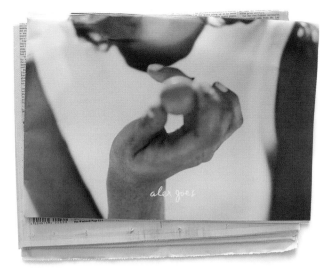

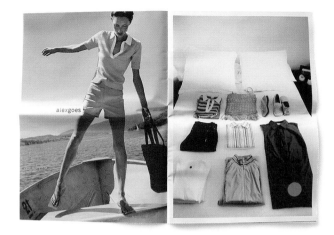

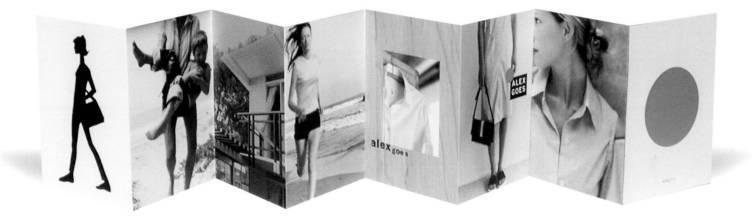

Ph.D creative director Clive Piercy calls their work for Alex Goes "an exercise in un-branding." They developed a variety of logos, not just one, for their client. These logos were used very discreetly because the designers believe that the target audience for this product line is sophisticated and weary of being advertised to. The promotional pieces above illustrate the Alex Goes logo in use both in the collateral and on the products themselves.

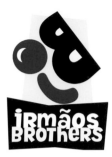

Who is the client? What do they do?

The Irmãos Brothers is a clown group that has gone through different members, sizes, and styles since 1993, but have always worn the "Blues Brothers" style of sunglasses and the red clown nose. The Brothers produce theater, live performances, magic and humor variety shows, and act in commercials, TV shows, and stunts.

What problem were you asked to solve?

In the two opportunities we had to design the Irmãos Brothers logo, 1996 and 2002, we were asked to design the sunglasses and a red-nose clown face for each member of the group. In 1996, the original quartet of guys had become a trio of two guys and one girl, each with a characteristic feature (personality and face). It was also important to maintain an emphasis on the group's name, which was inspired by the Blues Brothers movie. Because the first logo had been around for a few years, we didn't want to lose its main characteristic, which was the faces of the performers.

In 2002, the group became a real company, with a different number of "Brothers" depending on the gig. A television commercial would require two or three Brothers with greater acting skills, while an intermission show at a beach soccer game, for instance, would call for up to nine acrobat Brothers. Therefore, we decided to create a logo that would symbolize a "universal Brother," rather than portraying a specific number of Brothers. The logo can also be read as the groups initials, "iB." The typography was slightly redesigned (more chubby), in keeping with the dancing letters mood, and applied to a stylized bow-tie over a colored background shape.

The evolution of the logo for the clown troupe, The Irmãos Brothers, can be seen at right. All the logos feature a version of a clown face. As the group evolved from the original four members, to three clowns, to an ensemble group of variable size the logo had to change. Their most recent incarnation is represented by the most abstract logo.

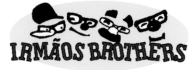

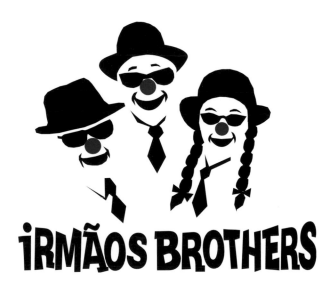

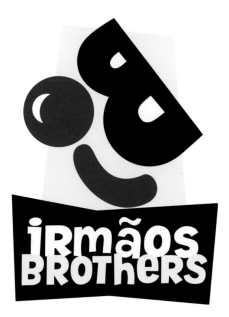

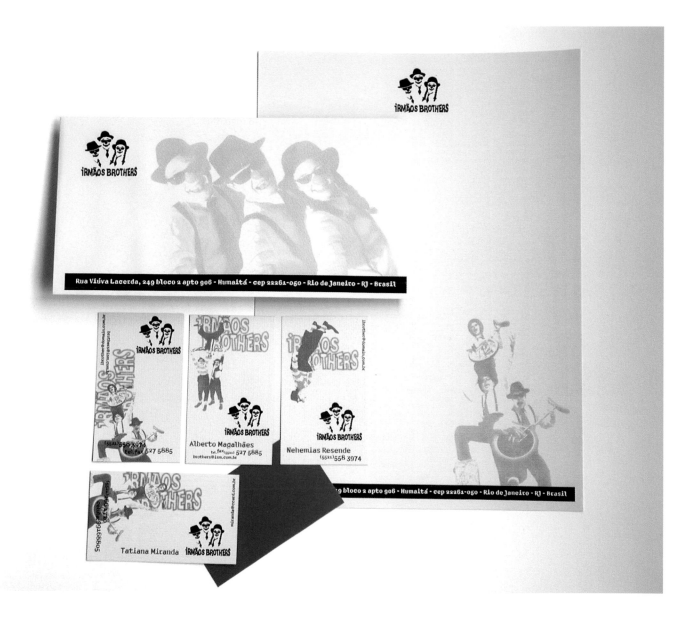

What personality and brand attributes were you asked to convey?

Circus clown fun, but with a modern approach.

Who was the target audience?

Kids (ages five to twelve) needed to be able to relate to the group's red-nose clown style, but adults (parents and clients) needed to feel that the Brothers were reliable and meant business.

Talk about the collaborative working process between you and your client.

They are great to work with. The 1996 logo and stationery were very well-received by the two remaining Brothers from the original team, Nehemias Rezende and Alberto Magalhães. Although they were really eager to abandon the original logo, since it didn't represent the actual crew anymore, they were still kind of attached to the idea of having their faces on it. After the 1996 logo helped them to acquire national recognition and some really nice work opportunities, they've trusted our suggestions and given us complete freedom. In the 2001 redesign, they were once again surprised by the "one face to represent many" concept. We feel that we always give them a bit more than they expect, and it is always a pleasure to work with creative, good-humored clients who respect the work you do.

What was the creative time frame?

Two to three weeks, from the phone ringing with the project to "We love it, here's the check!"

What applications did you design for this logo? In what media?

For the 1996 logo, the low budget years, we created one-color stationery and two-color business cards, as well as postcards, posters, flyers, show tickets, silk-screened T-shirts, etc. From 2001 on: four-color stationery, posters, invitations, announcements, banners, postcards for three different shows, logos, newspaper ads, silk-screened T-shirts, set decorations, and a Brothers unicase font.

Why did the client choose you to design this logo?

The writer of the Irmãos Brothers' 1996 show "Olimpíadas Brothers" ("The Brothers Olympics") knew Porto+Martinez's Marcelo Martinez (who is also an award-winning cartoonist) from the years when both were contributors to the Brazilian edition of *MAD* magazine.

—Bruno Porto

The 1996 version (2nd) of the Irmãos Brothers identity system helped the clowns acquire national attention. The system features both the character-driven logo and actual photographs of the entertainers.

A. ashford.com

Ashford.com, the largest luxury retailer online, sells exclusively high-end items such as watches, jewelry, diamonds, other accessories, and gifts. Ashford.com had been the first company to sell expensive watches online, but with the addition of a visionary new CEO, the company believed that it could be a bigger enterprise, and emerge as an exclusive high-end retailer. Rigsby Design was asked to create the main corporate identity to support that growth and the consequent repositioning of their client in the marketplace.

Rigsby started the identity project with a month of market research. They looked at how people buy, especially online, and what the value of Ashford.com might be to customers versus a "bricks and mortar" store. The question came down to "Why would someone buy a $30,000 watch online?" The client had retained the consulting firm Rosetta, which had done a lot of consumer, e-commerce, and general Internet research. When Rigsby reviewed and evaluated this research, the identity solution became apparent. The designers then synthesized the information to develop appropriate business, marketing, and identity strategies.

Typically, Rigsby Design does extensive research on their larger projects so that background data informs their design. This was the case with the Ashford.com identity, where the logo answered the design criteria. The identity system was strategic—everything the designers and client thought it should be. It was also unique in relation to Ashford.com's competitors— it definitely stood out.

Rigsby Design defined the personality and brand attributes as: sophisticated, upscale, luxury. They created an identity system that is classically elegant and appeals to both male and female customers. Asford.com's core target customers are wealthy, busy, time-restricted people from twenty to thirty years of age. The identity project took almost two years in total to implement.

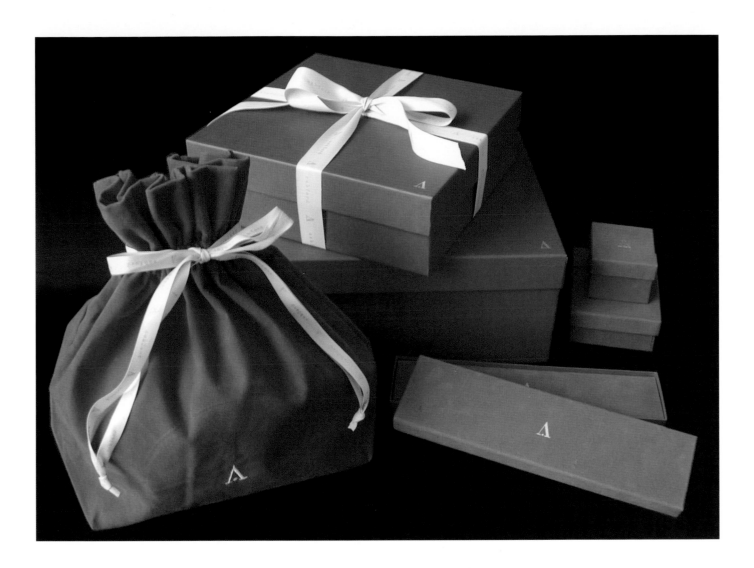

Rigsby Design worked with Ashford.com, a luxury goods retailer, to create a sophisticated, upscale identity system. The designers carried the branding through the packaging, seen above.

Besides the logo, Rigsby designed packaging, the annual report, various corporate communications, and the website. Because of the designer's extensive involvement with the client, everything spoke with one cohesive voice. Although Ashford.com has recently been bought out, they are still adhering to the templates developed by Rigsby Design.

Rigsby came to the project with a strong background in identity programs. Personality-wise the firm was a good fit with the new CEO/director of marketing Kenneth (Kenny) Kurtzman. Kurtzman gave the designers a good deal of license to form recommendations. It was a highly collaborative, great working relationship with a lot of trust and respect on both sides. In the case of Ashford.com, dealing directly with the CEO made all the difference in the success of the identity design.

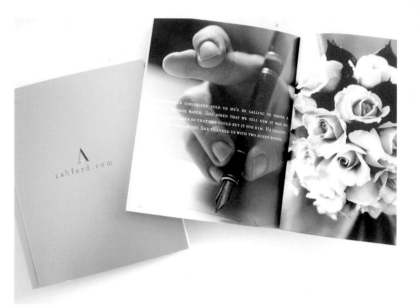

The Ashford.com print materials, at right, use the simple logo as a focal point on covers.

The stationery system, opposite, features classic typography, rich stock, and quality printing to reflect the upscale merchandise sold by Ashford.com.

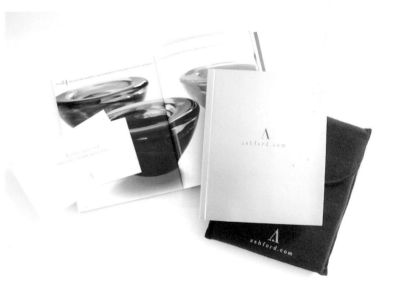

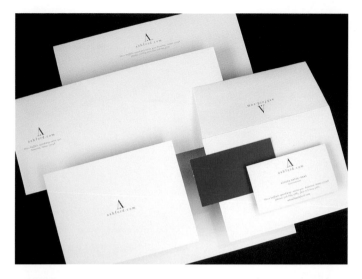

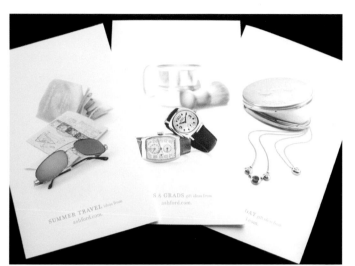

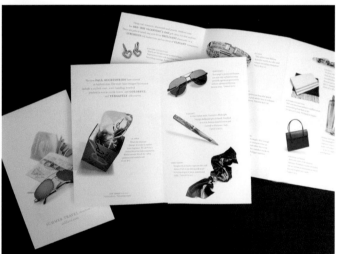

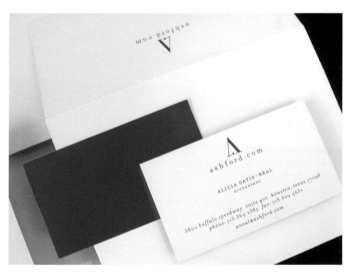

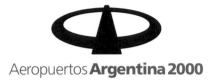

Aeropuertos **Argentina 2000**

Who is the client? What do they do?

Aerorpuertos Argentina 2000 is the Argentinean consortium that manages thirty-three airports throughout the country, including Ezeiza International Airport, Bariloche International Airport, and Cordoba International Airport.

What problem were you asked to solve?

Argentinian airports had a high level of visual pollution and traffic flow through the airports was chaotic—these had a direct impact on service and on the passengers.

What personality and brand attributes were you asked to convey?

It was necessary to create a corporate image for the company, as well as to provide the airport system with visual coherence. The logotype we developed refers to the world as a runway.

Who was the target audience?

The target audience was mainly international and domestic passengers. This category also included couriers, airport employees, and service providers working in the airports.

Talk about the collaborative working process between you and your client.

An extensive series of meetings, with a lot of content and feedback, occurred during the whole creative process between our company and the client. Every single point of view was taken into account when designing the identity. Emphasis was placed mainly on passengers' needs, however, employees' issues and concerns also impacted our work.

What was the time frame?

It took three years of creation and implementation. Implementation was done on a daily basis, at all airport locations, all over the country.

What applications did you design for this logo? In what media?

Applications included: airplane interiors and exteriors, indoor and outdoor design of offices, security system elements, signage, check-in counter graphics, totems, airway vehicles, luggage tags, boarding passes, catering elements, stationery, television commercials, and magazine and newspaper advertisements.

Why did you make the aesthetic choices you made?

The logotype is a combination of the world and a runway. The color palette provides a kind of solidness and calmness. This was contrasted with the yellow, which enhances security and generated the brand's presence through the repetition of reference icons throughout the airports.

—Guillermo Stein

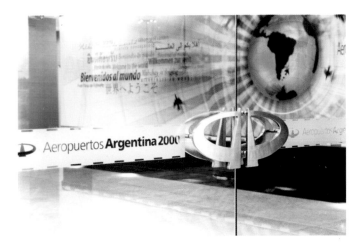

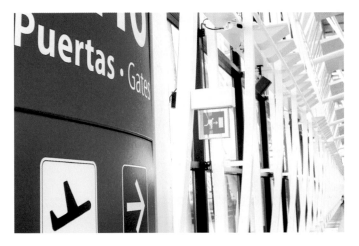

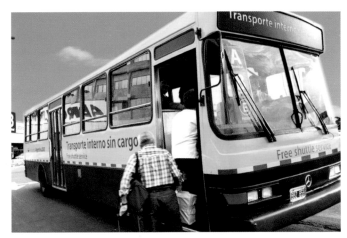

Steinbranding's logo for Aeropuertos
Argentina, an Argentine airport management
company, evokes the world of aviation.
A combination of a globe and an airplane
runway, it also suggests the letter "A."
Pictured above are a variety of logo
applications in use at airports.

sichtbar

Sichtbar Augenoptik is an exclusive optician in the midtown area of Stuttgart, Germany. The focus of the boutique is excellent individual service and an outstanding range of products. They offer only high-quality glasses by select designers, as well as other choice optical products with well-known labels.

Angela and Hans Schneider, the owners of Sichtbar, asked Stilradar to redesign their entire communication concept because the logo and corporate identity system no longer reflected the client's philosophy. The client wished to use the circle of the existing logo in the new design. A key problem was the integration of this circle with a typographic wordmark.

Stilradar had to come up with a logo that was unique and fresh, though it did not require a long duration of validity. The target audience was design-oriented consumers. In addition, existing clients, familiar with the old logo, needed to be able to recognize and accept the new one.

The collaborative process between Stilradar and their client was very good. The conceptual ideas, the style of typography, the circle signet, and the arrangement of a set of pictogram icons were accepted by the client very quickly. Defining the color palette, however, took much longer. The old identity color was blue. The designers suggested that keeping this color would be a good idea, but the client wanted something different. A wide range of colors were recommended by the designers; Sichtbar opted for a deep purple for the logo and a smooth green as an accent. When the stationery was being printed, though, the client stopped the run and decided to return to the original blue color. Nevertheless, the designers found their client to be very relaxed and open-minded. One of Stilradar's first clients, they remain among their favorites.

sichtbar

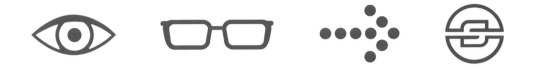

GERBERSTRASSE   17
7   0   1   7   8
S T U T T G A R T
T   E   L   E   F   O   N
0711 . 607 98 81
T   E   L   E   F   A   X
0711 . 607 98 82

The logo is designed in one color for easy and effective use in all medias. It was applied to a variety of pieces, including graphics used in the shop, and for mailings and stationery. There was no exact deadline for launching the new corporate identity, but from the first briefing to the printed result, it took nearly two months.

When Stilradar asked the client why they were chosen for the project, Sichtbar replied that they wanted a small graphic design agency that could provide intensive support. Furthermore, they loved the designers' work and the creative potential for collaboration. Sichtbar also realized that the designers understood their philosophy and the new direction they wanted to go with the company.

In the briefing the designers were asked to integrate the circle into the new identity. Their initial thought was to separate the circle from the Sichtbar name. The circle signet is a stylized "eye," which also suggests an "s." So, the icon is a symbiosis of "eye" (optician) and "s" (Sichtbar). The first step was to develop a typeface for "Sichtbar" that was modern but not too trendy. It was for this reason that the seraphs were integrated into the typeface. Next, Stilradar tried to combine the typeface and the signet. However, they noticed that the equal combination of signet and typeface was not harmonic. This led to the next step, which was to find a solution using both elements in a balanced way. The concept was to develop a story around the "s" signet. Toward that end, three more icons were developed that tell the story—if you have any problems with your eyes, then you might need glasses, therefore go to Sichtbar. It is a playful and unusual identity incorporating several logo icons. Continuing in this metaphorical style, the Sichtbar address graphic was designed to resemble a vision test.

The address graphic element designed as part of the Sichtbar identity, above left, resembles an eye examination chart.

Sichtbar, an optic boutique, needed a unique identity system that reflected high quality and high style. The company challenged Stilradar to integrate the circle symbol of the existing logo with the new icon's signet "s."

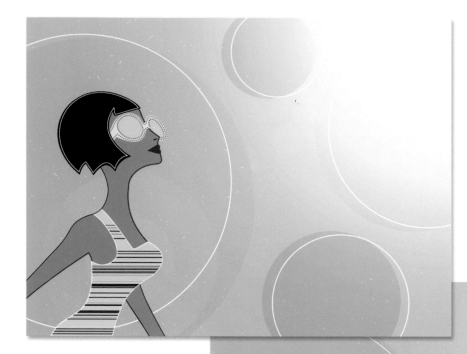

Trends der Mailänder Messe.

Geniessen Sie die ersten Sonnenstrahlen
mit einer neuen Sonnenbrille. Lassen Sie
sich beraten – in der sichtbar.

sichtbar

Gerberstraße 17 | 70178 Stuttgart | 0711. 607 98 81

A series of direct mail promotions
incorporate stylish illustrations reminiscent
of old travel postcards were created as a
fresh way to appeal to Sichtbar's design-
oriented customers. Milan (above), Paris,
and the Strand (opposite) are a few of the
luxe destinations featured in the promos.

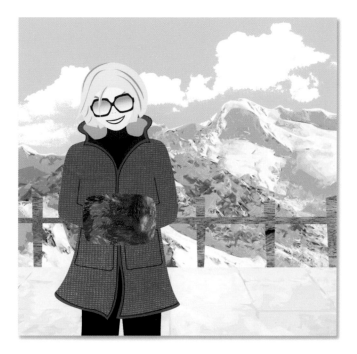

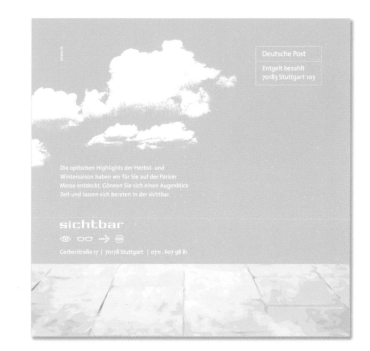

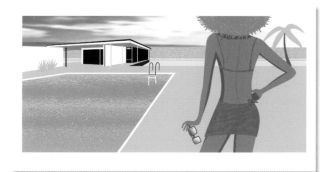

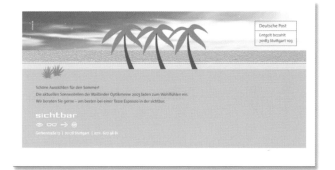

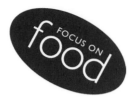

Who is the client? What do they do?

The Design Dimension Educational Trust is a charity that leads a wide range of cultural education projects. It is renowned for its innovative work with young people and teachers. Focus on Food is a food-education program led and managed by The Design Dimension Educational Trust that supports the teaching of cooking in school curricula. Food education forms only part of the UK's primary and secondary school design and technology curriculum. At the core of Design Dimension's work is teaching young people and their teachers about design and how to use it to benefit education.

What problem were you asked to solve?

We were asked to create a symbol that communicates the ethos of what Focus on Food is, and what its aims are for its target audience, which is primary and secondary school teachers and children.

What personality and brand attributes were you asked to convey?

We were asked to convey the concepts of fresh, educational, and fun to both teachers and children. The logo needed to be an instantly recognizable symbol that would become synonymous with excellence in food teaching.

Who was the target audience?

Primarily the audience was children four to nineteen years of age. Secondarily, we were targeting teachers, from their initial teacher training through their continuing professional development.

Talk about the collaborative working process between you and your client.

The client is a very design-aware organization. Focus on Food is an RSA (Royal Society of Arts) program. The RSA is a charity that encourages sustainable economic development and the release of human potential. The initial design concept meetings went extremely well. Subsequently, a strong bond and common understanding of the theme developed. It steered the identity and formed the basis of a mutually productive working relationship that exists to this day.

What was the time frame?

The initial time frame was one month to get the identity and supporting materials (such as stationery) produced. The quarterly educational magazine, which is approximately sixty-four pages long, is geared toward students and teachers and usually takes between two and three months to produce an issue from design to production.

What applications did you design for this logo? In what media?

Applications range from stationery, printed literature, stickers, aprons, a website, carrier bags, posters, brochures, magazines, a video, and the Cooking Bus. There are many more, but this is the main remit of materials I have produced. We are currently aiming to produce a range of kitchen items: crockery, magnets, tea towels, and aprons.

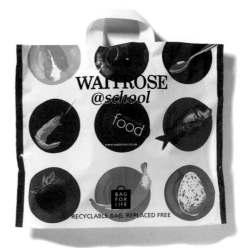

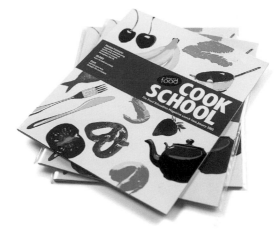

Why did the client choose you to design this logo?

Evidence of previous design work, instant empathy with client, excellent communication and understanding of Focus on Food's aims and its clientele, and the way in which the elements of the education program fit together.

Why did you make the aesthetic choices you made?

It says bright, fresh, modern, but timeless. Fun, with an educational message. Our goal was to appeal to a broad audience, from young children to adults, so a strong visual link to fruit labeling, as seen on individual pieces of fruit for sale in shops and supermarkets, seemed appropriate. Linking a familiar labeling system to an educational identity gave the Focus on Food logo a cheery familiarity and a positive association.

Is there anything else you'd like to add?

The response from the clients' key audiences—teachers, children/students, and decision makers—has been extremely positive. The identity has tremendous visual appeal, is easily recognizable, and the client is convinced that the identity has helped Focus on Food become the leading support for food education in the country.

—Zoë Scutts

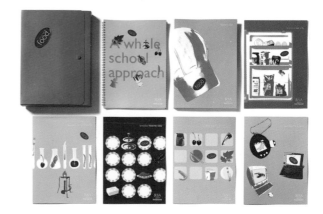

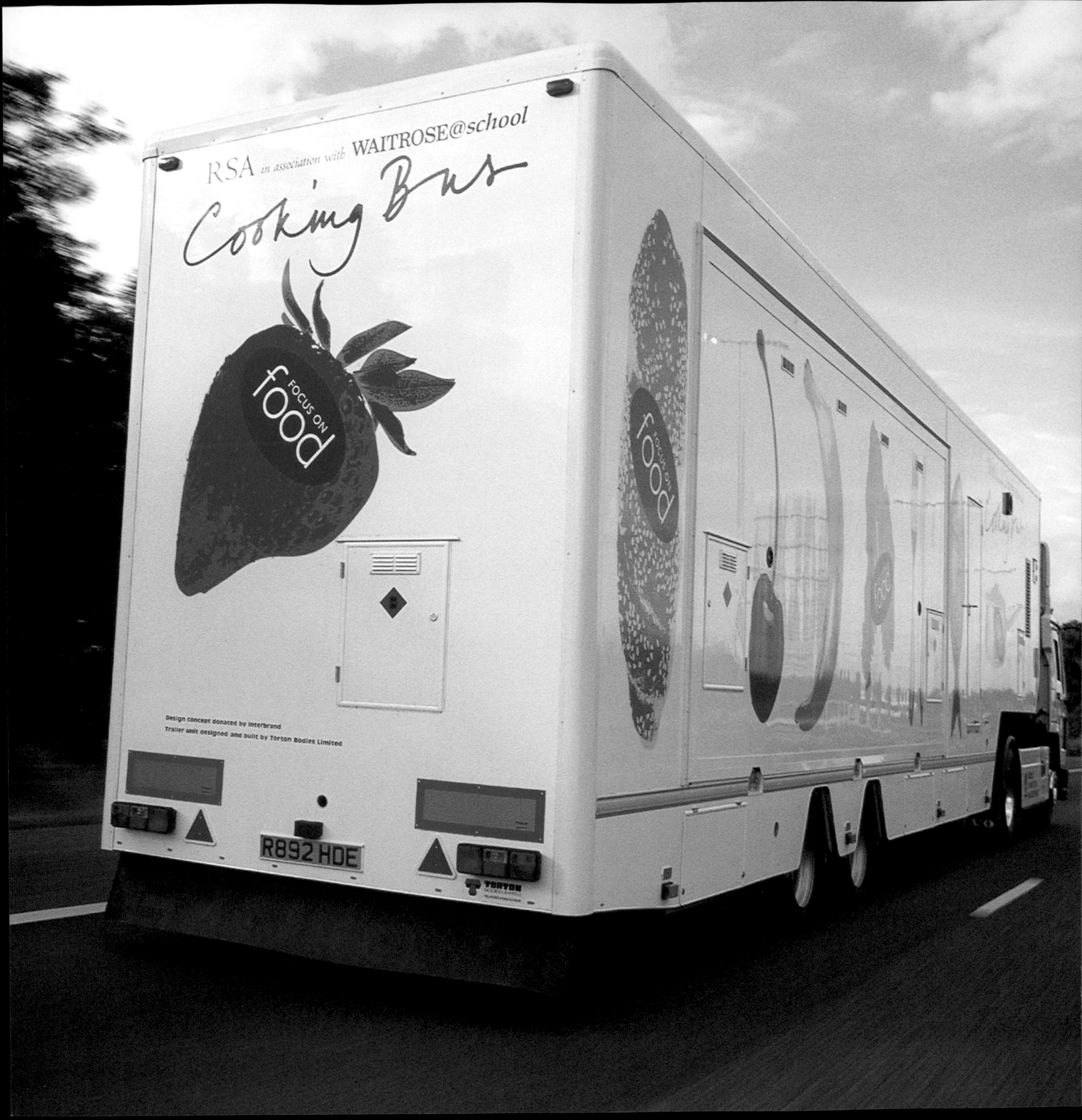
RSA in association with WAITROSE@school
Cooking Bus
FOCUS ON
food
Design concept donated by Interbrand
Trailer unit designed and built by Torton Bodies Limited
R892 HDE
TORTON

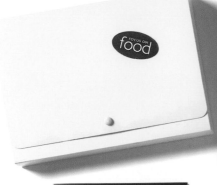
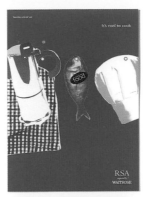
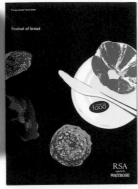
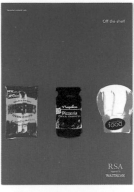
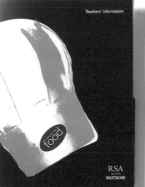
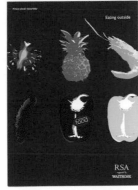
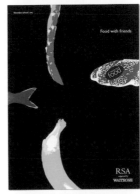
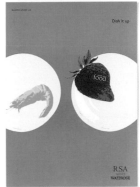
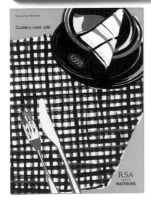
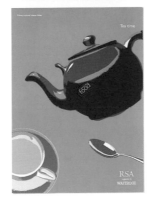
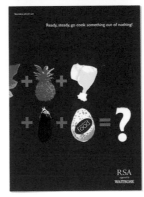
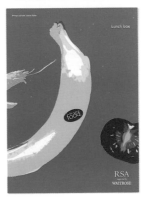

The Cooking Bus, left, is a mobile classroom that trains secondary school children to prepare food.

The Focus on Food logo, seen above in a series of brochures, suggests product code stickers frequently seen on individual pieces of fruit for sale in supermarkets. Designers at Untitled, kept the typography simple and bold for easy recognition.

✕ cingular

Cingular
A name that stands alone.

When BellSouth and SBC Communications merged their eleven existing wireless properties in 2000, the result wasn't just the second-largest wireless company in the U.S. It was also the nation's most relevant wireless brand.

This was no accident. Early on, BellSouth and SBC asked VSA to develop their new company's brand, from strategy to name to visual identity. To make the company stand out in an overcrowded, communication-saturated marketplace, VSA positioned the company as the "refreshing alternative" in the wireless industry. They focused on technology as an enabler of human communications—as a single source for interaction and individualized services, as a channel for personal expression, and as a means for individual achievement. No matter what form technology may take, Cingular promised to make it understandable, usable, and valuable in your life.

This brand positioning led VSA and its client to the Cingular name. In a nationwide marketplace where its peers' names bring to mind "The Phone Company," Cingular offered simplicity that was differentiating. The graphic identity of the new company followed the same logic, capturing the essence of the company through its human form and feel—simple, playful, enabling—and lending itself to a powerful retail presence.

Today, the Cingular name and identity are everywhere. Built on more than pervasiveness, the value of the brand is its relevant, resonant message in a consumer-unfriendly marketplace.

The identity for Cingular, the second-largest wireless company in the U.S., reflects the brand positioning of technology as an enabler of human communication. The figurative icon, opposite, captures the essence of the company in a simple, playful graphic form.

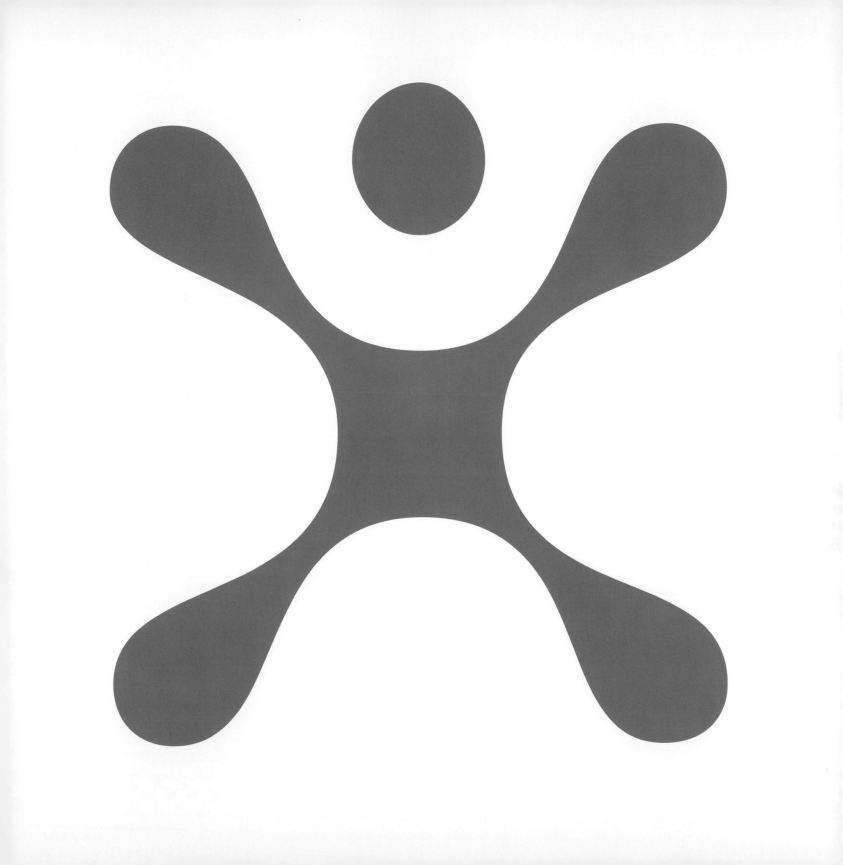

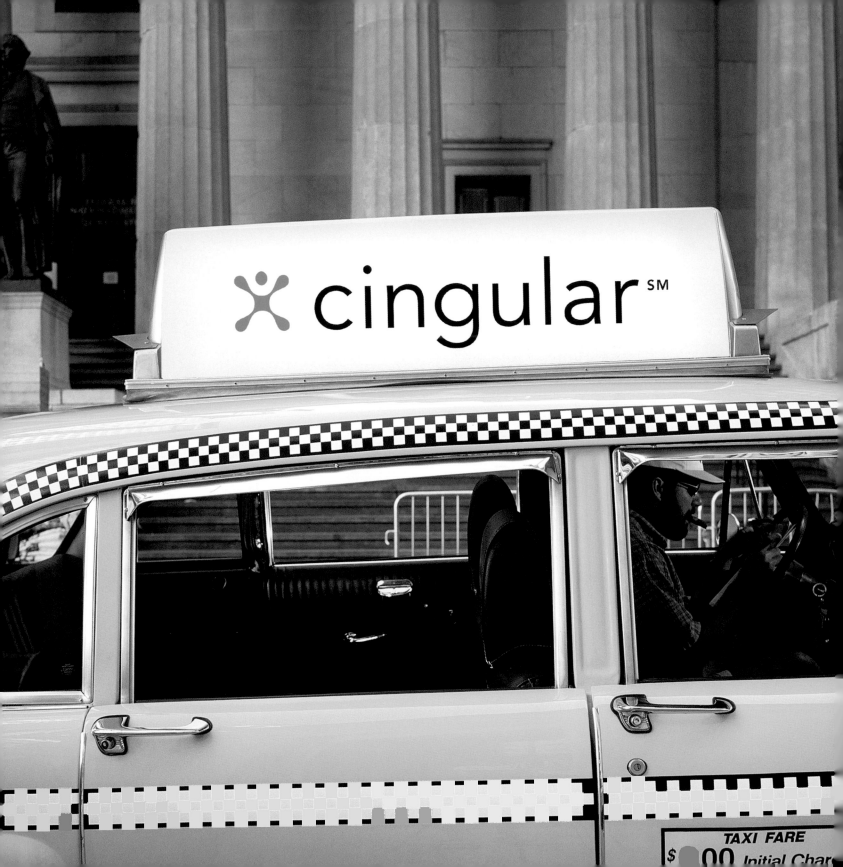

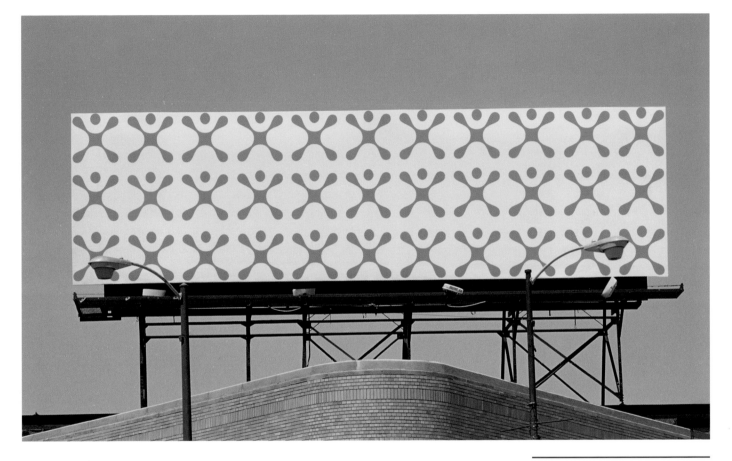

The strength of the Cingular logo is apparent in the advertisement on the taxi top, left, and on the billboard ad, above, as it cuts through the clutter of messages in the urban environment.

John Bielenberg
Founder, Project M, The Bielenberg
Institute at the Edge of the Earth
Co-Founder: C2

Creative Director: John Bielenberg

Designers: John Bielenberg,
Chuck Denison
Photography: Victor John Penner

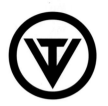

Who is the client? What business/service/product do they provide?
Virtual Telemetrix, Inc. (VT) is a forward-thinking, risk-taking, global enterprise offering best-of-breed solutions to empower mission-critical synergies.

What problem were you asked to solve? Why make a logo?
VT asked us to design a symbol to be embossed on the urinal cakes in the executive bathroom. Lucky for us, we were able to expand that small assignment into a global branding initiative.

What personality, culture, brand attributes, were you asked to convey?
VT wanted to borrow the accumulated power and equity associated with fascist iconography throughout world history. Their motto was "a huge %&#*! Company needs a huge %&#*! "brand."

Who was the target audience your were designing for?
Primarily small, medium, and large.

Talk about the collaborative working process between you & your client.
It was very strange. We never actually talked to, or met, the actual "client." Very unusual.

What was the time frame? How long did it take to create this.
I think it took about forty minutes to design the symbol but we were able to stretch the retainer for two years. We refer to this as a "total cash extraction solution."

What applications did you design for this logo? In what media?
All media! From patterns sewn into sock fabric to vapor trails from the VT Gulfstream jet.

Why did the client choose you to design this logo?
We spent six months on the urinal cake RFP and honestly I think it just wore them down.

Why did you make the aesthetic choices you made? Ultimately, why does this logo look like it does?
I like the international paper logo a lot, so I just turned it upside down and adapted it into a VT.

Anything else you'd like to add?
You should see the VT fountain. It's really neat.

—John Bielenberg

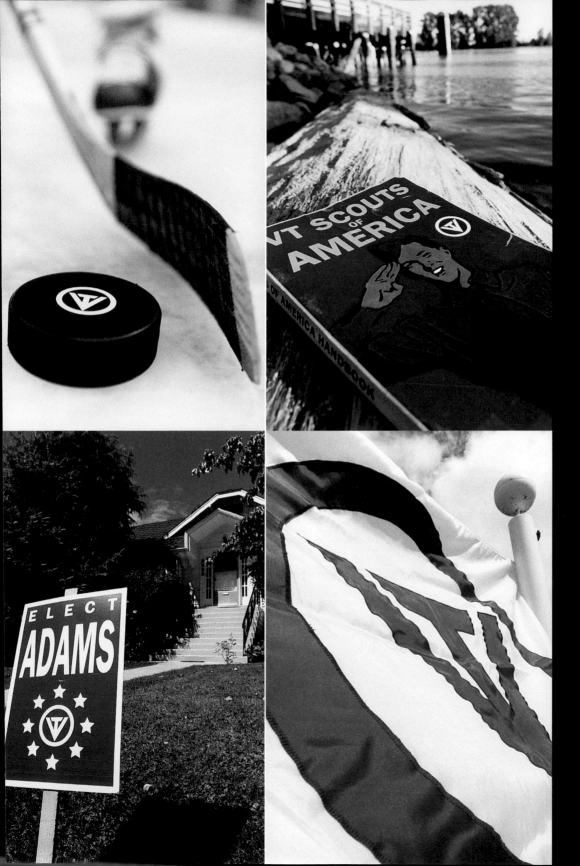

The idea of identity changes as our culture shifts. Virtual Telemetrix is a fictional corporation created by John Bielenberg. The visuals, copy, and tone force the viewer to question credibility and content. Once it becomes clear that the information presented is fiction, the viewer then will apply the same filter to actual companies. The VT presentation is more than a parody of "market-ese" and corporate vernacular, it is a concise point of view on contemporary corporate message and identity.

Designe® Logo Gallery

A selection of our contributor's company logos.

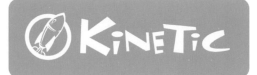

1

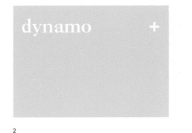

2

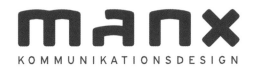

KOMMUNIKATIONSDESIGN

3

Pentagram

4

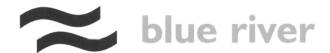

blue river

5

THE OFFICE OF CLEMENT MOK

6

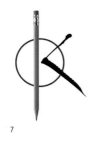

7

8

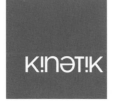

9

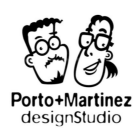

Porto+Martinez
designStudio

10

AdamsMorioka

11

Liska+Associates

12

the johnson banks logo

13

Atelier Works

14

Chermayeff & Geismar Inc.

15

CONCRETE
DESIGN COMMUNICATIONS INC.

16

Frankfurt Balkind

17

S A M A T A M A S O N

18

13. Johnson Banks
15. Chermayeff & Geismar Inc.
17. Frankfurt Balkind

14. Atelier Works
16. Concrete Design Communications Inc.
18. SamataMason

Lost Logos

A selection of logos that are no longer in use.

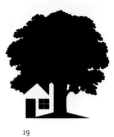

19

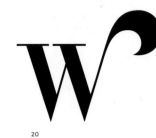

20

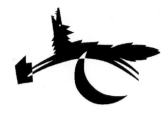

21

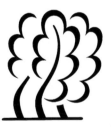

22

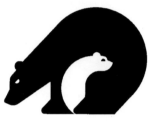

23

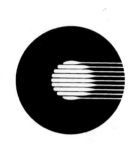

24

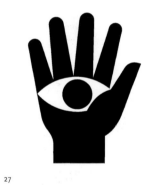

25

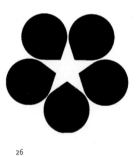

26

27

19. Hillman- Cedric Linsey
22. Hillman- Scottish Trade Center
25. Hillman- Golden Grove

20. Hillman- Wave Development
23. Michael Vanderbyl-
California Conservation Center
26. Michael Vanderbyl- U.S. Air Force Arts

21. Michael Vanderbyl- Coyote Books
24. Michael Vanderbyl- Court & Chain
27. Michael Vanderbyl- On Command

TORONTO
2008

28

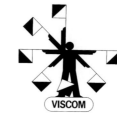

29

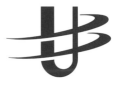

30

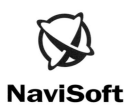

NaviSoft

31

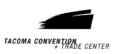

32

UB Networks

33

TACOMA CONVENTION
+ TRADE CENTER

34

35

scient

36

---

28. **Concrete-** Toronto Olympics
31. **Clement Mok-** NaviSoft
34. **Methodologie-**
    Tacoma Convention Trade Center

29. **Michael Vanderbyl-** Kalelekai
32. **Michael Vanderbyl-** Makani Kai
35. **Michael Vanderbyl-** Kona Coast

30. **Hillman-** Viscom
33. **Clement Mok-** UB Networks
36. **Clement Mok-** Scient

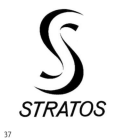

STRATOS

37

THE ELLIOTT

38

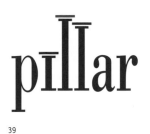

p**i**llar

39

SMITH & HAWKEN

40

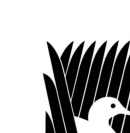

41

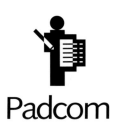

42

43

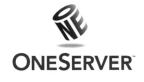

OneServer™

44

Padcom

45

---

37. **Hillman-**Stratos
40. **Michael Vanderbyl-** Smith & Hawken
43. **Michael Vanderbyl-** D'ICILA Cosmetics

38. **Methodologie-** The Elliott
41. **Clement Mok-** Netpulse
44. **Clement Mok-** One Server

39. **Clement Mok-** Pillar
42. **Michael Vanderbyl-** Canyon Lakes
45. **Clement Mok-** Padcom

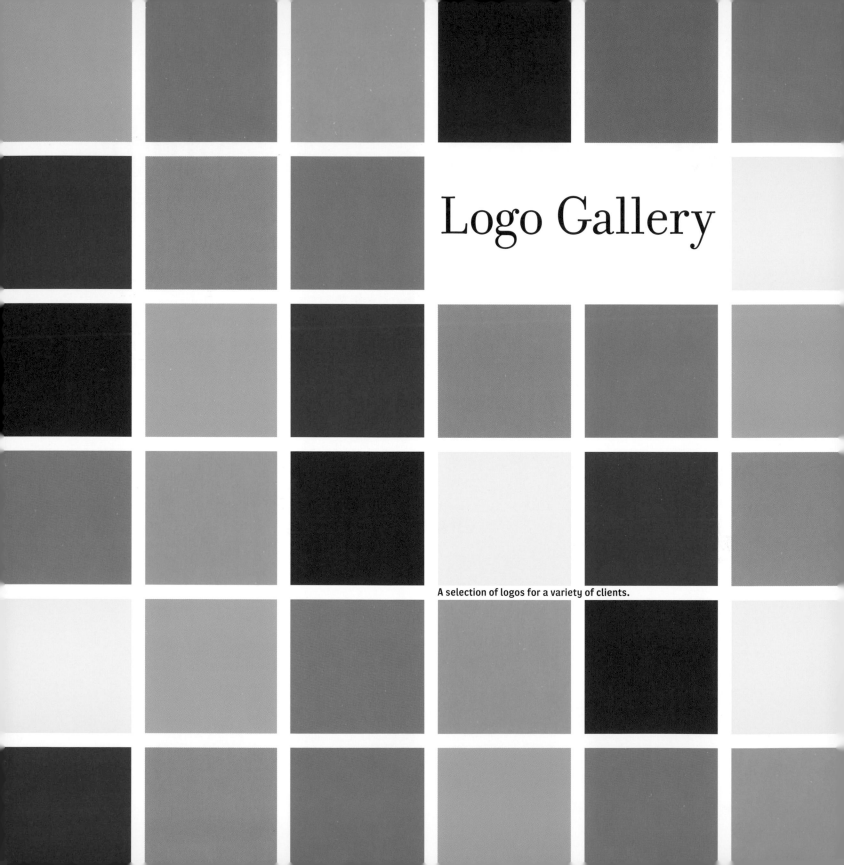

Logo Gallery

A selection of logos for a variety of clients.

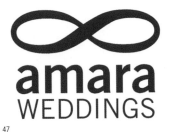

Jetmagic.

Fly a different way

46

amara
WEDDINGS

47

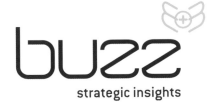

buzz

strategic insights

48

URBANGOODS.com

49

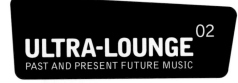

ULTRA-LOUNGE 02
PAST AND PRESENT FUTURE MUSIC

50

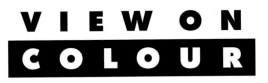

VIEW ON
COLOUR

51

---

46. **Dynamo-** Jet Magic
48. **CPd-** Buzz
50. **Dynamo-** Ultra-Lounge

47. **Kinetic Singapore-** Amara Weddings
49. **AdamsMorioka, Inc.-** Urban Goods
51. **Anthon Beeke-** View on Colour

UN
studio
FOLD

52

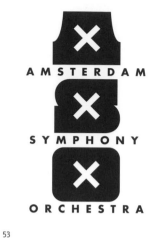

AMSTERDAM

SYMPHONY

ORCHESTRA

53

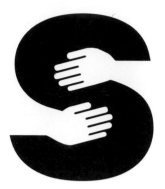

54

PATHE!

55

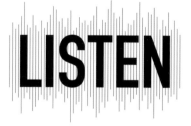

56

SEKONDA

57

52. **Anthon Beeke-** UNstudio
55. **Landor San Francisco-** Pathe

53. **Anthon Beeke-**
Amsterdam Symphony Orchestra
56. **Kinetik-**Listen

54. **Atelier Works-** Stockwell
57. **Hillman-** Sekonda

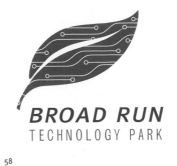

BROAD RUN
TECHNOLOGY PARK

58

swi•m

59

fizz

60

61

KEHO

62

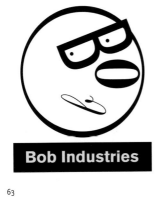

Bob Industries

63

58. Kinetik- Broad Run
61. Tom & John Design- N

59. Volker Dürre- Swim
62. Volker Dürre- Keho

60. Lippa Pierce- Fizz
63. AdamsMorioka, Inc.- Bob Industries

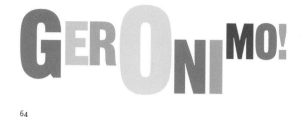

64

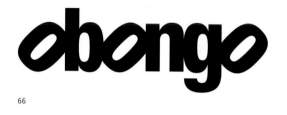

66

eProsper

65

NEDERLAND

67

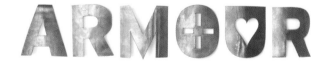

68

ARMOUR

69

---

64. Lippa Pierce- Geronimo
66. Hillman- Obongo
68. Volker Dürre- Sound Space Design

65. Tom & John Design- eProsper
67. Anthon Beeke- Nederland
69. Anthon Beeke- Armour

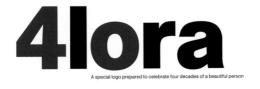

A special logo prepared to celebrate four decades of a beautiful person

70

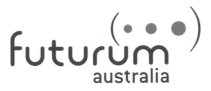

71

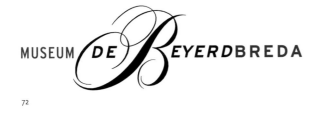

72

First & 42nd.

73

ez'ech

74

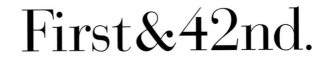

75

DESIGNER DIRECTORY

AdamsMorioka,Inc.
8484 Wilshire Boulevard
Suite 600
Beverly Hills, CA 91604
Telephone: 323.966.5990
Fax: 323.966.5994
Contact: Noreen Morioka
noreen@adamsmorioka.com
www.adamsmorioka.com

Atelier Works
The Old Piano Factory
5 Charlton Kings Road
London NW5 2SB
Telephone: +44 (0)20.7284.2215
Fax: +44 (0)20.7284.2242
Contact: Ian Chilvers
ian@atelierworks.co.uk
www.atelierworks.co.uk

Studio Anthan Beeke
Keizersgracht 451
1017 DK Amsterdam
The Netherlands
Telephone: 31 20 4194419
Fax: 31 20 4194626
Contact: Sacha Happée
studio@beeke.nl

blue river
The Foundry,
Forth Banks
Newcastle Upon Tyne
NE1 3PA, UK
Telephone: +44 (0)191 2610000
Fax: : +44 (0)191 2610010
Contact: Simon Douglas
design@blueriver.co.uk
www.blueriver.co.uk

C2: A Creative Capital Network
25 Congress Street
Belfast, ME 04915
Telephone: 207. 338. 0101
Contact: John Bielenberg
email: john@c2llc.com
www.c2llc.com

Cahan & Associates
171 Second Street, 5th Floor
San Francisco, CA 94105
Telephone: 415.621.0915
Fax: 415.621.7642
info@cahanassociates.com
www.cahanassociates.com

Carter Wong Tomlin
29 Brook Mews North
London, W2 3BW, UK
Telephone: 020.7569.0000
Fax: 020.7569.0001
Contact: Philip Carter
p.carter@carterwongtomlin.com
www.carterwongtomlin.com

Chermayeff & Geismar, Inc.
15 East 26th Street, 12th Floor
New York, NY 10010
Telephone: 212.532.4499
Fax: 212.889.6515
Contact: Steff Geissbuhler
info@cgnyc.com
www.cgnyc.com

**Concrete Design
Communications, Inc.**
2 Silver Avenue, Main Floor
Toronto, ON M6R 3A2
Canada
Telephone: 416.534.9960
Fax:416.534.2184
Contact: Diti Katona and John Pylpczak
mail@concrete.ca
 www.concrete.ca

CPd
2nd Floor, 333 Flinders Lane
Melbourne Vic 3000 Australia
Telephone: 61 3 9620 5911
Fax: 61 3 9620 5922
Contact: Dianne O'Hehir
d.oherir@cpdtotal.com.au
www.cpdtotal.com.au

CPd
100 Harris Street, Pyrmont
New South Wales 2009, Australia
Telephone: 61 2 9692 0088
Fax: 61 2 9592 0910
Contact: Inga Lidums
I.Lidums@cpdtotal.com.au
www.cpdtotal.com.au

Crosby Associates
203 N Wabash Avenue, Suite 200
Chicago, IL 60601
Telephone: 312.346.2900
Fax: 312.346.6818
Contact: Kerry Hackett
kerry@crosbyassociates.com
www. crosbyassociates.com

Doyle Partners
1123 Broadway, Suite 600
New York, NY 10010
Telephone: 212.463.8787
Fax: 212.633.2916
Contact: Stephen Doyle
doyle@doylepartners.com
www. doylepartners.com

Volker Durre
2931 Fairmount Avenue
La Crescenta, CA 912143
Telephone: 310.699.0564
Contact: Volker Durre
v.durre@verizon.net

Dynamo
5 Upper Ormond Quay
Dublin 7, Ireland
Telephone: 353 1 8729244
Fax: 353 1 8729224
Contact: Damian Cranney / Brian Nolan
info@dynamo.ie
www.dynamo.ie

Format Design
Grosse Brunnen Str. 63a
Hamburg, Germany
Telephone: 040 32086910
Fax: 040 32086905
Contact: Knut Ettling
ettling@format-hh.com
www.formatdesign.net

Frankfurt Balkind
345 Hudson Street, 12th Floor
New York, NY 10014
Telephone: 212.515.7703
Fax: 212.830.7600
Contact: Kent Hunter
khunter@hhny.com
www.frankfurtbalkind.com

Johnson Banks
Crescent Works
Crescent Lane
Clapham London
sw4 9rw, UK
Telephone: 44 (0)20 7587 6400
Fax: 44 (0)20 7587 6411
Contact: Michael Johnson
Michael@johnsonbanks.co.uk
www.johnsonbanks.co.uk

Kinetic Singapore
2 Leng Kee Road
Thye Hong Centre
#04-03A Singapore 159086
Telephone: 65. 63795320
Fax: 65.64725440
Contact: Roy Poh
roy@kinetic.com.sg

KINETIK
1436 U Street, NW, Suite 404
Washington, D.C. 20009
Telephone: 202.797.0605
Fax: 202.387.2848
Contact: Jeff Fabian
kinetik@kinetikcom.com
www.kinetikcom.com

Kontrapunkt
Knezova 30
1000 Ljubljana, Slovenia
Telephone: +386.15756606
Fax: +386.15195072
Contact: Eduard Cehovin
eduard.cehovin@siol.net
www.cehovin.com

KROG
Krakovski nasip 22
1000 Ljubljana, Slovenia
Telephone: 386 41 780 880
Fax: 386 1 4265 761
Contact: Edi Berk
edi.berk@krog.si

**Landor Associates
International Limited**
Sogo Hirakawacho Building, 6th Floor
1-4-12 Hirakawacho, Chiyoda-ku
Tokyo 102-0093 Japan
Telephone: 81-3-3263-2291
Fax: 81-3-3263-2292
Contact: Tsutomu Egawa
tsutomu_egawa @jp.landor.com

Lippa Pearce Design
358a Richmond Road, Twickenham
London, TWI 2DU, UK
Telephone: 020 8744 2100
Fax: 020 8744 2770
Contact: Design Directors: Domenic Lippa
/ Harry Pearce
Contact: PR/Media: Abigail Silvestré
mail@lippapearce.com
www.lippapearce.com

Liska + Associates
515 North State Street
 23rd Floor
Chicago, IL 60610-4322
Telephone: 312.644.4400
Fax: 312.644.9650
Contact: Steve Liska
steve@liska.com
www.liska.com

Manx Kommunikations Design
Hammer Str 156
45257 Essen
Germany
Telephone: 49 (201)84 83 011
Fax: 49 (201)84 83 020
Contact: Iris Thieme
thieme@manx.de
www.manx.de

Methodologie, Inc.
808 Howell Street, Suite 600
Seattle, WA 98101
Telephone: 206.623.1044
Fax: 206.625.0154
Contact: John Carroll
info@methodologie.com
www.methodologie.com

Mevis & Van Deursen
Gelderseuade 101
1011 EM Amsterdam
The Netherlands
Telephone: 31-20-6236093
Fax: 31-20-4272640
Contact: Armand Mevis,
Linda Van Deursen
mevd@xs4all.nl

The Office of Clement Mok
Telephone: 415.782.6055
Contact: Clement Mok
infor@cmcd.com
www.cmcd.com

Morla Design
463 Bryant Street
San Francisco, CA 94107
Telephone: 415.543.6548
Fax: 415.543.7214
Contact: Jennifer Morla
info@morladesign.com
www.morladesign.com

Ogilvy & Mather/
Brand Integration Group
309 W. 49th Street
New York, NY 10019
Telephone: 212.237.4354
Fax: 212.237.4106
Contact: Brian Collins
Brian.Collins@ogilvy.com

Pentagram
204 Fifth Avenue
New York, NY 10010
Telephone: 212.683.7000
Fax: 212.532.0181
Contact: Michael Bierut, Paula Scher
info@pentagram.com
www.pentagram.com

Pentagram
387 Tehama Street
San Francisco, CA 94103
Telephone: 415.896.0499
Fax: 415.896.0555
info@pentagram.com
www.pentagram.com

Pentagram Design Ltd.
11 Needham Road
London
W11 2RP, UK
Telephone: +44 (0)20 7229 3477
Fax: +44 (0)20. 7727 9932
Contact: Steven Bateman
email@pentagram.co.uk
www.pentagram.com

Ph.D
1524a Cloverfield Boulevard
Santa Monica, CA 90404
Telephone: 310.829.0900
Contact: Michael Hodgson
mick@phdla.com
www.phdla.com

Porto + Martinez designStudio
Rua Capistrano de Abreu 44/101
Humaita 22271-000 Rio de Janeiro, RJ
Brasil
Telephone: 55.21.2539.3146
Fax: 55.21.2539.3146
Contact: Bruno Porto
design@portomartinez.com

R+MAG Graphic Design
Via del Pescatore 3
80053 Castellammare di Stabia (Napoli)
Italy
Telephone: 00 39 081 870 5053
Fax: 00 39 081 870 5053
Contact: Raffaele Fontenella
info@remag.it

Rigsby Design
2309 University Boulevard
Houston, TX 77005
Telephone: 713.660.6057
Fax: 713.660.8514
Contact: Lana Rigsby
rigsby@rigsbydesign.com
www.rigsbydesign.com

Sagmeister, Inc
222 West 14th Street
New York, NY 10011
Telephone: 212.647.1789
Fax: 212.647.1788
Contact: Stefan Sagmeister
stefan@sagmeister.com

SamataMason
101 S. First Street
Dundee, IL 60118
Telephone: 847.428.8600
Fax: 847.428.6564
Contact: Greg Samata
greg@samatamason.com
Contact: Dave Mason
dave@samatamason.com
www.samatamason.com

Segura Inc.
1110 North Milwaukee Avenue
Chicago, IL 60622-4017
Telephone: 773.862.5667
Fax: 773.862.1214
Contact: Carlos Segura
carlos@segura-inc.com
www.segura-inc.com

Steinbranding
El Salvador 5675
(C141BQE) Buenos Aires
Telephone: (5411)4011 5555
Fax: (5411)4776 5706
Contact: Angie Panelo
prensa@steinbranding.com
www.steinbranding.com

Stilradar
Schwabstr.10a
70197 Stuttgart / Germany
Telephone: 0711/887 55 20
Fax: 0711/882 23 44
Contact: Raphael Pohland, Simone Winter
info@stilradar.de
www.stilradar.de

Stone Yamashita Partners
355 Bryant Street, Suite 408
San Francisco, CA 94107
Telephone: 415.536.6600
Fax: 415.536.6601
Contact: Susan Schuman
susan@stoneyamasita.com
www.stoneyamasita.com

Tenazas Design
1403 Shotwell Street
San Francisco, CA 94110
Telephone: 415.970.2390
Fax: 415.970.2399
Contact: Lucille Tenazas
pet@tenazasdesign.com
www. tenazasdesign.com

Tom and John: A Design Collaborative
1475 Fourteenth Street
San Francisco, CA 94103
Telephone: 415.621.6800
Contact: John or Tom
info@tom-john.com
www.tom-john.com

Untitled
Radar Studio
Coldblow Lane
Thurnham.
Maidstone
Kent
ME14 3LR, UK
Telephone: 01622 737722
Fax: 0162 738644
Contact: Zoe Scutts
zoe@untitled.co.uk

Vanderbyl Design
171 Second Street
San Francisco, CA 94105
Telephone: 415.543.8447
Fax: 415.543.9058
Contact: Michael Vanderbyl
michael@vanderbyldesign.com
www.vanderbyldesign.com

VSA Partners
1347 S. State Street
Chicago, IL 60605
Telephone: 312.895. 5090
Fax: 312. 895.5720
Contact: Dana Arnett
vsa@vsapartners.com
www.vsapartners.com

BIBLIOGRAPHY

Birren, Faber, Editor. *The Elements of Color: A Treatise on the Color System of Johannes Itten*. New York: Van Nostrand Reinhold, 1970.

Blackwell, Lewis, and David Carson. *The End of Print: The Grafik Design of David Carson*. San Francisco: Chronicle, 2000.

Chermayeff, Ivan, Tom Geismar, and Steff Geissbuhler. *TM: Trademarks Designed by Chermayeff & Geismar*. New York: Princeton Architectural Press, 2000.

Dondis, Donis A. *A Primer of Visual Literacy*. Cambridge, MA: MIT Press, 1973.

Fella, Edward. *Edward Fella: Letters on America*. New York: Princeton Architectural Press, 2000.

Gardner, Bill, and Catharine Fishel. *LogoLounge: 2,000 International Identities by Leading Designers*. Gloucester, MA: Rockport Publishers, 2003.

Friedman, Mildred, Editor. *Graphic Design in America: A Visual Language History*. New York: Abrams, 1989.

Hall, Peter, and Michael Bierut, Editors. *Tibor Kalman, Perverse Optimist*. New York: Princeton Architectural Press, 1998.

Heller, Steven. *Paul Rand*. London: Phaidon Press, 1999.

Hess, Dick, and Marion Muller. *Dorfsman & CBS*. New York: American Showcase, 1987.

Jacobson, Egbert, Editor. *Trademark Design*. Chicago: Paul Theobald, 1952.

Jaspert, W. Pincus, W. Turner Berry, and A. F. Johnson. *The Encyclopaedia of Type Faces*. London: Blandford Press, 1953.

Johnson, Michael. *Problem Solved: A Primer in Design and Communication*. London: Phaidon Press, 2002.

Kirkham, Pat. *Charles and Ray Eames: Designers of the Twentieth Century*. Cambridge, MA: MIT Press, 1995.

Meggs, Philip B. *A History of Graphic Design (Third Edition)*. New York: Wiley, 1998.

Meggs, Philip B. *Type and Image: The Language of Graphic Design*. New York: Wiley, 1992.

Moss, Marie Y. *Hello Kitty® Hello Everything!: 25 Years of Fun*. New York: Abrams, 2001.

Müller-Brockmann, J. *The Graphic Artist and His Design Problems*. New York: Hastings House, 1961.

Neuhart, John, Marilyn Neuhart, and Ray Eames. *Eames Design: The Work of the Office of Charles and Ray Eames*. New York: Abrams, 1989.

Pentagram. *Pentagram Book Five*. New York: Monacelli Press, 1999.

Rosen, Ben. *The Corporate Search for Visual Identity*. New York: Van Nostrand Reinhold, 1970.

Tuckerman, Nancy, and Nancy Dunnan. *The Amy Vanderbilt Complete Book of Etiquette*. New York: Doubleday, 1995.

Wheeler, Alina. Designing Brand Identity: *A Complete Guide to Creating, Building, and Maintaining Strong Brands*. New York: Wiley, 2003.

Young, Doyald. *Logotypes & Letterforms: Handlettered Logotypes and Typographic Considerations*. New York: Design Press, 1993.